365-DAY DEVOTIONAL

BELIEVE

WHAT I BELIEVE. WHO I AM BECOMING.

RANDY AND
ROZANNE FRAZEE

ZONDERVAN

Believe 365-Day Devotional
Copyright © 2015 Randy and Rozanne Frazee

Requests for information should be addressed to:

Zondervan, Grand Rapids, Michigan 49530

ISBN 978-0-310-36133-6

Cover design: Extra Credit Projects

Printed in the United States of America

15 16 17 18 19 20 21 /RRD/ 22 21 20 19 18 17 16 15 14 13 12 11 10 9 8 7 6 5 4 3 2 1

To Max and Denalyn Lucado . . .
your devotion to Jesus and your desire
to become more like him inspires us.

The devotional you hold in your hand has a simple but profound framework. It is designed to help you *think* more like Jesus, *act* more like Jesus, and *be* more like Jesus. As you embark on this journey through the thirty key ideas of the Bible, it is our conviction that a person who knows what they believe and why, and who practices that faith in concert with the indwelling presence of God, will most definitely be on their way to becoming more like Jesus. It is not only our conviction; it is our prayer for you.

BELIEFS

God

Personal God

Salvation

The Bible

Identity in Christ

Church

Humanity

Compassion

Stewardship

Eternity

PRACTICES

Worship

Prayer

Bible Study

Single-Mindedness

Total Surrender

Biblical Community

Spiritual Gifts

Offering My Time

Giving My Resources

Sharing My Faith

VIRTUES

Love

Joy

Peace

Self-Control

Hope

Patience

Kindness/Goodness

Faithfulness

Gentleness

Humility

INTRODUCTION:
THE JOURNEY OF "BELIEVE"

"If you can do anything, take pity on us and help us."

"'If you can'?" said Jesus. "Everything is possible for one who believes."

Immediately the boy's father exclaimed, "I do believe; help me overcome my unbelief!"

MARK 9:22–24

Jesus declares with authority, "Everything is possible for one who believes." Truly believing the key ideas of the God found in the Bible is a powerful proposition, isn't it? Throughout the teaching of Jesus, and the whole Bible for that matter, we are encouraged to believe not just in our heads but also in our hearts. We are invited to believe these powerful truths not only as the right answers but also as a way of life. When we do, everything is possible.

The journey of *belief* actually begins with the confession of *unbelief*. As you turn the page and peer into the key beliefs, practices, and virtues of the Christian faith, turn to God with a willingness to be honest with him. Like the man in Mark 9, tell him where you are in the form of a prayer request: "I do believe some things, Lord, but would you help me overcome what I am struggling to believe?" If you do, he will.

Then, watch out, because everything is possible for the one who believes.

PART 1: THINK

What Do I Believe?

THE TEN KEYS OF "THINK"

God

Personal God

Salvation

The Bible

Identity in Christ

Church

Humanity

Compassion

Stewardship

Eternity

LEARNING TO THINK LIKE JESUS

Do not conform to the pattern of this world, but be transformed by the renewing of your mind. Then you will be able to test and approve what God's will is.

ROMANS 12:2

Can you remember the first time you donned a pair of polarized sunglasses? If you're like me, you took them off and put them back on several times because you couldn't believe the difference they made in what you saw. Cutting down on glare gives objects clarity and makes colors more vivid.

As Christians, what we believe—or the internal lens of our mind—impacts how we live and who we become. For example: If you view God as personal and involved in your daily life, you will experience more joy. If you see people as God sees them (belief in humanity), you will become gentler toward others. If you believe that everything you are and own belong to God (belief in stewardship), you will more naturally offer your time and resources to help others.

Jesus desires to give us new internal lenses by transforming our minds. He does this as we firmly establish ourselves in what we believe.

You have begun a journey of renewing your mind. As you meditate on what you believe, you will adopt a worldview that profoundly reduces glare and reveals clarity about how you should act to become more like Jesus. Soon others will notice the vivid difference. Hopefully you will too!

DAY 3

GOD

May the grace of the Lord Jesus Christ, and the love of God, and the fellowship of the Holy Spirit be with you all.

2 CORINTHIANS 13:14

When you face a mirror, your reflection appears. It can be a lonely experience that can send you straight to the gym to shed extra pounds or to your makeup bag to cover blemishes. Your flaws glare at you. Stepping in front of the mirror of life, you may have a similar experience. You notice your weaknesses and think, *I can't.*

You were created in God's image to live in community—you were never meant to do life alone. God is a community of Father, Son, and Holy Spirit. They move and breathe together. You cannot know the love of the Father without experiencing the grace of Jesus and the fellowship of his Spirit. Jesus said, "Anyone who has seen me has seen the Father" (John 14:9). As it is with the nature of God, so it is with the nature of humanity.

When you live in community, your strengths come together with others' and your weaknesses are shored up. That united group of people reflects God's perfect image.

Step in front of life's mirror alone, and a human reflection appears. Step in front of the mirror surrounded by your community, and God appears.

> **"I BELIEVE THE GOD OF THE BIBLE IS THE ONLY TRUE GOD—FATHER, SON, AND HOLY SPIRIT."**

PERSONAL GOD

I lift up my eyes to the mountains—where does my help come from? My help comes from the LORD, the Maker of heaven and earth.

PSALM 121:1–2

Are you in a valley right now, facing a mountain you didn't expect? Maybe that mountain seems so overwhelming you can't imagine being on top, let alone getting to the other side. Is God really with you? Does he care about your struggle?

Imagine taking a deep breath and stepping back so that you can see not just the mountain you are facing but the entire range of mountains. The psalmist prompts you then to look even higher than the massif to the one who created it. You will find your help there.

This psalmist later reminds you in verse 5, "The LORD watches over you." He is the "shade at your right hand." He's as close as your shadow. Like your shadow, he will be with you every step of the way. He doesn't want you to take even one step alone.

Can't even muster the strength to look up? Your loving heavenly Father is close enough to place his strong hands under your chin and help you lift your eyes to him. *Value!*

> **"I BELIEVE GOD IS INVOLVED IN AND CARES ABOUT MY DAILY LIFE."**

SALVATION

It is by grace you have been saved, through faith—and this is not from yourselves, it is the gift of God—not by works, so that no one can boast.

EPHESIANS 2:8–9

Vincent Ardolino watched the Twin Towers explode from his little tugboat in New York Harbor on 9/11. Minutes later, as the towers fell, people swarmed the pier, desperate to vacate the island. Roads, subways, trains, bridges—everything was shut down. The only escape? The water. Many of them leaped in, fearing for their lives.

Vincent urgently turned the prow of his boat toward the island as his wife exclaimed, "What if there's another attack?!" His response was, "If I only rescue one person, that's one less person who will suffer and die." Joined by every boat on the water, Vincent became involved in the greatest sea evacuation since World War II, when 339,000 soldiers were rescued over the span of nine days in Dunkirk. On 9/11, 500,000 civilians were rescued in less than nine hours through the grace gift of these captains. Each person jumping into a boat accepted the gracious gift of a rescue, putting their faith in the boat and its captain.

Jesus offers you the only boat leaving the island of death. You need only jump in with faith and trust him, the Captain.

"I BELIEVE A PERSON COMES INTO A RIGHT RELATIONSHIP WITH GOD BY GOD'S GRACE THROUGH FAITH IN JESUS CHRIST."

All Scripture is God-breathed and is useful for teaching, rebuking, correcting and training in righteousness, so that the servant of God may be thoroughly equipped for every good work.

2 TIMOTHY 3:16–17

Remember the first time you walked outside in the winter as a child and saw your breath? Perhaps you leaned too close to a window and saw moisture appear as you exhaled. The oxygen we breathe in becomes carbon dioxide in our lungs. These gases are both invisible, but as we exhale, the carbon dioxide mixes with water vapor, and because cold air has less water vapor than the warm air from our lungs, it produces fog.

But what happens when God exhales? The word for "God-breathed" in 2 Timothy is *theopneustos*, and it gives us a clue. *Theo* means "God"; *pneustos* means "spirit" or "breath." The first time we see God exhaling is in Genesis when he is breathing life into the nostrils of Adam. In 2 Timothy we again see him breathing out, but instead of fog, God's spirit or breath becomes words on the tips of men's pens. Those words bring life to all who study them.

Next time you see your breath on a cold day, remember God exhaled and created words for us to live by. We call it the Bible.

> **"I BELIEVE THE BIBLE IS THE WORD OF GOD AND HAS THE RIGHT TO COMMAND MY BELIEF AND ACTION."**

IDENTITY IN CHRIST

To all who did receive him, to those who believed in his name, he gave the right to become children of God.

JOHN 1:12

The words "It's a boy!" at the birth of our second child brought Rozanne and me tremendous joy. We already had a girl; now we had a boy. Life was perfect—until we noticed that our baby boy was missing his left hand and forearm. Immediately questions flashed through our minds. *Sports? How would the kindergarteners treat him? Where would his wedding ring go? Never mind marriage; what girl would love him with so many men out there with two hands?* And the most alarming question: *Would we love him?* Nurses swaddled our little David and laid him in our arms. And in that moment our greatest fear evaporated. We loved him; there was nothing he had to do to earn our love. He was our son.

Our actions make us feel that God could never love us. The truth is, he loves us not because of what we've done, but because of what he has done. He loves us because of who we are—his children.

Today David is a successful attorney and has a beautiful wife who loves him dearly. He played sports better than most kids with two hands! While that brings us great joy, it isn't why we love him. We love him because he's our son.

God feels the same about you!

> **"I BELIEVE I AM SIGNIFICANT BECAUSE OF MY POSITION AS A CHILD OF GOD."**

CHURCH

Speaking the truth in love, we will grow to become in every respect the mature body of him who is the head, that is, Christ.

EPHESIANS 4:15

What mother tells her child to chew a pill that is meant to be swallowed? Most likely the child would promptly spit out the pill because of its bitter taste. A thoughtful mother smashes the pill and smothers it in applesauce so the pill goes down easier. Wisdom tells her that if her child spits it out, the healing benefit will be lost.

God calls us to challenge each other to spiritual growth, but if the challenge comes without love, it's the same as chewing a pill that's meant to be swallowed. As a wise believer, you should surround yourself with a few trusted friends who, beyond the shadow of a doubt, love you while your spiritual temperature is normal. Whenever you begin to experience a rise in your spiritual temperature, you can give them permission to challenge you in love.

We all falter from time to time. By preemptively choosing loving believers to monitor your spiritual temperature, you ensure that the truth you have to swallow will be given to you in love. You will also be able to follow their example if and when you need to give the pill of tough love to someone else.

> "I BELIEVE THE CHURCH IS GOD'S PRIMARY WAY TO ACCOMPLISH HIS PURPOSES ON EARTH."

DAY 9

HUMANITY

For God so loved the world that he gave his one and only Son, that whoever believes in him shall not perish but have eternal life.

JOHN 3:16

Most Americans claim they are Christian. They aren't Muslim, Jewish, or Hindu; they were raised in church or attend church, and they try to live by the golden rule.

Nicodemus was no different. He was one of the spiritual leaders—in our world, he'd be teaching the adult Sunday school class and serving on the elder board. Nicodemus had memorized all the laws and tried to live out each one. Secretly approaching Jesus, he was sure Jesus would assure him he had done everything needed to gain a relationship with God. After all, he had been working for this his whole life. And that is when Jesus said the words above, from the most famous verse in the Bible. They were spoken not to a person outside the church, but to one of its leaders.

Many people attempt to live good lives, working hard to make sure they secure an eternal relationship with their Creator. Like Nicodemus, however, they have missed the one thing they need to gain access to a true relationship with God. God wants nothing more than to be in relationship with you, but unless you accept the free gift of his Son, you cannot enter into it.

> "I BELIEVE ALL PEOPLE ARE LOVED BY GOD AND NEED JESUS CHRIST AS THEIR SAVIOR."

COMPASSION

Defend the weak and the fatherless; uphold the cause of the poor and the oppressed. Rescue the weak and the needy; deliver them from the hand of the wicked.

PSALM 82:3–4

Freddy was a classmate of mine in junior high school. He had a condition referred to (at the time) as "water on the brain." The excess fluid around his skull created an oversize and awkward head for Freddy. Junior high school is an awful place to be different. Immature people create the worst possible names for our apparent weaknesses. Freddy was called Watermelon Head.

One day between classes in a hallway filled with people, a group of boys started picking on Freddy. They called him names and shoved him around. This was the same year I became a Christian. Something was stirring in me, something that wasn't there before—or perhaps I should say *Someone*.

I felt compelled to go and stand between Freddy and the bullies. But in the end, I did nothing. Forty years later I still think about this incident. As a new, immature Christian, I failed Freddy, and he took the abuse with no advocate. I am so sorry, Freddy. With God's forgiveness granted, I wake up each day praying for the courage to "defend," to "uphold the cause," and to "rescue" the Freddys God puts in my life.

> "I BELIEVE GOD CALLS ALL CHRISTIANS TO SHOW COMPASSION TO PEOPLE IN NEED."

DAY 11

STEWARDSHIP

Offer hospitality to one another without grumbling.

1 PETER 4:9

Every house hunter or renovator on HGTV at some point during the show exclaims something like, "Now I can see myself entertaining here!" Or, "This backyard would be great for having friends over for barbecuing," or, "This kitchen will be awesome for hosting!" Apparently everyone wants to entertain, but they're just one major move or remodel away from actually pulling it off.

In Scripture, hospitality appears in the form of a command, not a suggestion. "Do not forget to show hospitality" (Hebrews 13:2). "Share with the Lord's people who are in need. Practice hospitality" (Romans 12:13). Whether we live in an apartment or house, a mansion or cottage, whether it needs to be remodeled or is brand-new, our homes are gifts from God, and he expects us to share them willingly and cheerfully with others.

Your home belongs to him as much as your heart does. When you see yourself as the manager of your home instead of the owner, the doors of your home will open much more easily.

Jesus doesn't want you to wait until your house is perfect before you open it up and share it with others.

> **"I BELIEVE EVERYTHING I AM AND EVERYTHING I OWN BELONG TO GOD."**

ETERNITY

*"Do not let your hearts be troubled. You believe in God;
believe also in me. My Father's house has many rooms;
if that were not so, would I have told you that I am going
there to prepare a place for you?"*

JOHN 14:1–2

After twenty-two years of living in Texas, we were moving. Leaving behind our life troubled our hearts. Our new bungalow in Chicago needed some work before we moved in, so Randy headed north, determined to prepare the house for our family. As he left, I wanted to go with him, but it was more strategic for me to stay behind and finish handling all the details to ensure a smooth transition. My husband would be back to take us home, to the place he was preparing for our family.

When Jesus told his disciples he was leaving, they desperately wanted to go too. But strategically he needed to leave them behind to share the gospel with others to build his kingdom. So he taught them how their hearts could be comforted while he was gone: by believing his promise to return.

Is your heart troubled by your circumstances? Comfort yourself with Jesus' promise to return and to take all of us who believe in him home, to the place he has prepared for us.

> **"I BELIEVE THERE IS A HEAVEN AND A HELL AND THAT JESUS WILL RETURN TO JUDGE ALL PEOPLE AND TO ESTABLISH HIS ETERNAL KINGDOM."**

GOD

The heavens declare the glory of God; the skies proclaim the work of his hands. . . . Their voice goes out into all the earth, their words to the ends of the world.

PSALM 19:1, 4

Galaxies upon galaxies stretch out in the heavens for distances beyond human imagination. Unseen by the naked eye, electrons spin around a nucleus. Seasons come and go in a set pattern, and puppies, kittens, and infants are born. The water cycle keeps the earth alive, and the circulatory system—heart, veins, vessels, capillaries—helps keep a person alive.

God has revealed himself—and continues to reveal himself—throughout his creation, at both macro and micro levels. Consider the vastness of the ocean and the details of an infant's hand. Picture the rolling hills of the plains, and imagine the fragile, intricate art of a snowflake.

God reveals himself so clearly throughout his creation that at the end of the day, no one will have an excuse for not putting their trust in him. As the apostle Paul said, "Since the creation of the world God's invisible qualities—his eternal power and divine nature—have been clearly seen, being understood from what has been made, so that people are without excuse" (Romans 1:20).

> **"I BELIEVE THE GOD OF THE BIBLE IS THE ONLY TRUE GOD—FATHER, SON, AND HOLY SPIRIT."**

PERSONAL GOD

You have searched me, LORD, and you know me. You know when I sit and when I rise; you perceive my thoughts from afar. You discern my going out and my lying down; you are familiar with all my ways. Before a word is on my tongue you, LORD, know it completely.

PSALM 139:1–4

Who is the person closest to you? Is it your mom or dad, your child, a sister or brother, your spouse or best friend? Now think—as close as you are, do you truly know everything about them?

When you are not with them, can you tell if they are sitting or standing? Can you discern their thoughts from afar? Are you able to declare everything they are about to say before the words leave their mouth? All this is impossible even with someone we consider to be our soul mate.

Your God knows all these things about you. He watches your every movement every moment of every day. He knows if you are sitting or standing, coming or going. He knows your every thought before you speak a word.

What are you doing right now? Is there something in your heart you want to say to God at this very moment? He already knows your thoughts, but tell him anyway. He loves to hear from you!

"I BELIEVE GOD IS INVOLVED IN AND CARES ABOUT MY DAILY LIFE."

SALVATION

Surely he took up our pain and bore our suffering, yet we considered him punished by God, stricken by him, and afflicted.

It was not fair.

Jesus, the wise but enigmatic Rabbi, had not broken any laws. Jesus, who was falsely accused and then condemned by a kangaroo court in full violation of Jewish law, should not have been rushed to the cross. He had done nothing wrong. It was not fair!

He who had healed and fed, who had freed and forgiven, was nevertheless "despised and rejected by mankind . . . and we held him in low esteem" (v. 3). No angels intervened as Jesus was "led like a lamb to the slaughter" (v. 7)—and the sins he died for were ours! It's not fair.

But it was God's good plan. We have broken plenty of his laws. We are guilty of iniquity after iniquity—disobedience and delinquency. That cross should have been ours. But Jesus was pierced. Not us. Jesus was crushed. Not us.

It's not fair . . .

It's grace.

> **"I BELIEVE A PERSON COMES INTO A RIGHT RELATIONSHIP WITH GOD BY GOD'S GRACE THROUGH FAITH IN JESUS CHRIST."**

"As the heavens are higher than the earth, so are my ways higher than your ways and my thoughts than your thoughts."

ISAIAH 55:9

D raw a circle to represent all possible knowledge. Now mark in that circle the amount of knowledge you think you have gained at this point of your life.

Most people put a dot somewhere in the circle. An occasional college student has filled in part of the circle! Seeing that empty circle helps us remember that a tremendous amount of knowledge exists that we haven't mastered—and will never master.

Even though science has made great strides, it still cannot come close to filling the circle. Only God has all knowledge.

God's Word reminds us that we will never understand everything there is to know. His ways are immeasurably higher than ours. The finite brain of even the most brilliant human being is nothing compared to the infinite intelligence of God.

The realization that we will never understand everything might be terrifying except that God's Word also reassures us of his infinite love for us, his children. He reveals to us only what we need to know, so trust his infinite wisdom.

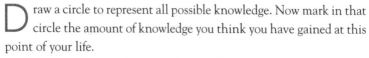

"I BELIEVE THE BIBLE IS THE WORD OF GOD AND HAS THE RIGHT TO COMMAND MY BELIEF AND ACTION."

IDENTITY IN CHRIST

"Holy Father, protect them by the power of your name, the name you gave me."

JOHN 17:11

The sentry at the marine corps base stopped the car. The driver was a teenager, but the identifying tags on the front bumper indicated that this car belonged to a two-star general. What was going on?

The sentry asked to see the driver's ID. The picture matched the driver, and his last name matched the name of the base's two-star commanding general. The boy's appearance had prompted questions; his name had immediately prompted respect, an apology, a very sharp salute, and, yes, entry onto the base.

A name can definitely impact how we're treated. Sometimes a name can open doors, command respect, prompt special treatment, and carry with it unique privileges. A name can, however, also invite scorn, discrimination, and cruelty.

Our identity as believers—as children of God—may cause us to experience scorn, discrimination, and even cruelty in this world. So Jesus asked God to protect us. At the same time, being a child of God will mean forgiveness, the indwelling of the Holy Spirit, and, yes, entrance into the new kingdom to spend eternity with God. What an amazing privilege to find your identity in the name "child of God"!

> **"I BELIEVE I AM SIGNIFICANT BECAUSE OF MY POSITION AS A CHILD OF GOD."**

*In Christ we, though many, form one body, and each
member belongs to all the others.*

ROMANS 12:5

Sally Jones, a first-grade Sunday school teacher, demonstrated to her
class the children's poem "Here's the church; here's the steeple;
open the doors and see all the people." Then she said, "Now do it with
me," forgetting that David, one of the little boys in the class, had been
born without a left hand.

As she began to lead the class in the exercise, she remembered
David, but before she had a chance to retract her words, Wyatt, the
boy sitting next to David, reached over with his left hand, placed it in
David's right hand, and said, "Here, David, let's do it together." Putting
their hands together, they created the church.

What a beautiful picture of how God designed his church to work.
He never meant us to live or serve alone. Instead, he gave us to each
other as gifts. We need each other for encouragement, support, extra
hands, and care.

Never again should "Here's the church; here's the steeple" be done
alone.

> **"I BELIEVE THE CHURCH IS GOD'S PRIMARY WAY
> TO ACCOMPLISH HIS PURPOSES ON EARTH."**

HUMANITY

> *"Whoever hears my word and believes him who sent me has eternal life and will not be judged but has crossed over from death to life."*

JOHN 5:24

Each of the gospel writers had a particular focus, and John's was Jesus' offer of forgiveness and hope of restoration to God for eternity for everyone. He frequently used the words *all* and *whoever*:

- "To all who . . . believed in his name, he gave the right to become children of God" (1:12).
- "Whoever believes in the Son has eternal life" (3:36).
- "Jesus said, . . . 'I, when I am lifted up from the earth, will draw all people to myself'" (12:30, 32).

You are included in the "all" and the "whoever" because God extends his offer of love to people throughout all time, to people around the world. And God wants you to share his love with the "whoevers" you know. To whom will you extend God's love today? "All"? "Whoever"? Yep, everyone is loved by God!

> **"I BELIEVE ALL PEOPLE ARE LOVED BY GOD AND NEED JESUS CHRIST AS THEIR SAVIOR."**

COMPASSION

Endow the king with your justice, O God, the royal son with your righteousness. May he judge your people in righteousness, your afflicted ones with justice.

PSALM 72:1–2

Have you noticed that compassion doesn't come naturally? We are self-centered beings who can be oblivious to other people's needs and hurts. If we do notice their pain and suffering, we are probably too busy or stingy or self-absorbed to make any effort to come alongside them in a practical way.

Thankfully, the Holy Spirit can change our hearts and make us more like Christ, more compassionate in thought, word, and deed. And, thankfully, as the psalmist stated, we can pray for God's transforming power to make others—and us—more compassionate people.

In Psalm 72, the psalmist was praying for the king to be compassionate as he ruled. In verse 4, the psalmist's request was more specific: "May [the king] defend the afflicted among the people and save the children of the needy." Note that the psalmist took his petition to the source of all compassion, the great and eternal King, the all-compassionate God himself.

Follow the psalmist's example and ask God to make his people's hearts more compassionate—starting with yours.

> **"I BELIEVE GOD CALLS ALL CHRISTIANS TO SHOW COMPASSION TO PEOPLE IN NEED."**

STEWARDSHIP

The earth is the LORD'S, and everything in it, the world, and all who live in it; for he founded it on the seas and established it on the waters.

PSALM 24:1–2

Yesterday as I stood in the checkout line at the grocery store, I realized I forgot my reusable bags. I'm embarrassed to admit I didn't take time to get out of line to get them from my trunk. I was in a hurry. The sad truth is I forget them often.

Today I read that the Pacific Ocean continues to be a dumping ground for plastics, sewage, chemical waste, radioactive waste, and other toxins.[1]

A poll suggests atheists and agnostics are far ahead of Christians in championing environmental preservation.[2] We Christians may have different solutions to the problem, but ignoring the charge we have been given by God is wrong.

The earth belongs to the Designer, Creator, and Sustainer of life, and he has entrusted this planet to our care (Genesis 2:15). As Christians we should be leading this effort. We can begin by each doing our part—me first.

Tomorrow I commit to go back out to my car and get my bags, even if I'm in a hurry. What will you be doing?

> **"I BELIEVE EVERYTHING I AM AND EVERYTHING I OWN BELONG TO GOD."**

The Lord himself will come down from heaven, with a loud command, . . . and the dead in Christ will rise first. After that, we who are still alive and are left will be caught up together with them in the clouds to meet the Lord in the air.

1 THESSALONIANS 4:16–17

After three literal run-ins with deer on the highway, Donna decided she'd had enough. She called the local radio station and pleaded with the hosts to help her pressure the Department of Highway Safety to move the Deer Crossing signs to low-traffic areas—for the deer's safety. She sincerely believed that if the signs were moved, the deer would follow. Try as they might, the patient radio hosts were unable to help Donna understand those signs were intended for human drivers, *not* deer.

Do you plead with God to remove wars, hatred, and violence from this world? Do you beg him to relieve hard circumstances or heal you or someone you love? Your patient heavenly Father wants to change your perspective. The ills of this world are merely signs that this is not your home. Imperfections in this life should make you long for the future kingdom he is preparing for you. The signs may not be moving, but you will be when Jesus returns.

"I BELIEVE THERE IS A HEAVEN AND A HELL AND THAT JESUS WILL RETURN TO JUDGE ALL PEOPLE AND TO ESTABLISH HIS ETERNAL KINGDOM."

DAY 23

GOD

"You will seek me and find me when you seek me with all your heart. I will be found by you."

JEREMIAH 29:13–14

A recent study revealed that 94 percent of all adopted children want to know something about their biological parents, even if it is only which parent they resemble the most. There is a mysteriously strong bond between children and their parents that cannot be erased, even by years of separation. It causes grown men and women to go to great lengths to find their birth parents.[3]

Sin separated us from our heavenly Father, but he created us with a supernatural bond and a desire to seek him, much like adopted children pursue their biological parents. He not only wants you to meet him; he also desires a deep, intimate relationship with you.

Even when adopted children give much time, energy, and heart to locating their biological parents, they may or may not be successful. God calls you to pursue him with your whole heart, and if you do, he promises you will find him.

> **"I BELIEVE THE GOD OF THE BIBLE IS THE ONLY TRUE GOD—FATHER, SON, AND HOLY SPIRIT."**

PERSONAL GOD

[Sarai] said to Abram, "The LORD has kept me from having children. Go, sleep with my slave; perhaps I can build a family through her."

Abram agreed. . . . He slept with Hagar, and she conceived.

GENESIS 16:2, 4

The God of the Bible is all-powerful, all-knowing, and eternal. But is he good? Does he love us and have a plan for us? Clearly Abram and Sarai questioned his faithfulness, or they would not have tried to fulfill his plan in their own way and in their own time.

Think back over your life. Have you ever grabbed the reins from God? How do you know you can really trust God with every aspect of your life? Consider what you know of biblical history. Talk to people who have been walking with Jesus for years and ask their opinion. Read the biographies of people who followed the Lord and consider those testimonies. Reflect on ways God has answered your prayers. Ask God to help you see evidence of his provision for you and his presence with you.

And then look again at Genesis 16. Does the almighty God need your help to fulfill his promises to you? Granted, he may need your cooperation, but he doesn't need your intervention—and his Spirit will help you discern which is which.

> **"I BELIEVE GOD IS INVOLVED IN AND CARES ABOUT MY DAILY LIFE."**

SALVATION

*Light has come into the world, but people loved darkness
instead of light because their deeds were evil.*

JOHN 3:19

Pick up a stone lying along a forest path and watch the bugs underneath scurry away. Turn on the kitchen light and see the cockroaches flee to safety. It's hardly a complimentary comparison, but we are a lot like those bugs. We enjoy our sin in the dark, wallowing in the muck of life and gorging to our heart's content on the world's pleasures.

If we're honest, we'll admit that one of the reasons we turn away from our relationship with a holy God and his commands is because we often actually like our sin. The outburst of anger or the juicy bit of gossip spoken out of envy can be very satisfying. The aftermath, not so much. Falling into step with the world's values can bring acceptance and pleasures that are enticing, but in the end those earthly rewards leave us empty and distant from God.

Jesus came to dispel the darkness and bring the light of his goodness and love so you can enjoy those things that bring lasting and heavenly rewards. May this eternal incentive cause you to leave the darkness and head toward the light of Christ.

"I BELIEVE A PERSON COMES INTO A RIGHT RELATIONSHIP WITH GOD BY GOD'S GRACE THROUGH FAITH IN JESUS CHRIST."

THE BIBLE

"I am the light of the world. Whoever follows me will never walk in darkness, but will have the light of life."

JOHN 8:12

Imagine all the people in the world traveling in little boats, each making their own way through the vast ocean, the stars overhead blocked out by clouds and only a small light at the bow of each vessel to guide the way. Sound futile? Sound hopeless? Sound dangerous? Sound familiar? It should, because this is how many people live their lives.

Far too many of us go through life this way, without a North Star to direct us. Just glance at the evening news or look at the lives of the people you know, and you'll see that without truth, confusion reigns.

Wouldn't it be helpful to have a North Star to guide your way through the confusing and often dark and dangerous sea of life? God knows that without him, we drift alone, lost, unprotected, into treacherous waters. He gave us a North Star, the Bible, to provide the light we need to lead us where he wants us to go. His Word is the star that will lead you to True North. Follow it! You can depend on it!

> **"I BELIEVE THE BIBLE IS THE WORD OF GOD AND HAS THE RIGHT TO COMMAND MY BELIEF AND ACTION."**

IDENTITY IN CHRIST

If we are children, then we are heirs—heirs of God and co-heirs with Christ, if indeed we share in his sufferings in order that we may also share in his glory.

ROMANS 8:17

The Waltons . . . The Du Ponts . . . These are some of the wealthiest families in the world, and their descendants will be heirs to immense fortunes. But according to the Bible, those who are "heirs of God," people who have named Jesus their Savior and been adopted into God's family, will receive the most valuable fortune. They are co-heirs with Christ.

Preacher J. C. Ryle considered this glorious inheritance of God's children the only inheritance worth having because, unlike earthly inheritances, it won't disappoint; it will last for eternity; and it is within our reach the way riches and renown may not be.[4]

Unfortunately, Scripture says we will also share in Jesus' sufferings. If your circumstances are difficult, remember that Jesus knew suffering far more intense than what we will experience. Paul knew true sufferings, too, but in light of the hope he had, he wrote, "I consider that our present sufferings are not worth comparing with the glory that will be revealed in us" (v. 18). That can be your hope too.

> **"I BELIEVE I AM SIGNIFICANT BECAUSE OF MY POSITION AS A CHILD OF GOD."**

CHURCH

A great persecution broke out against the church in
Jerusalem, and all except the apostles were scattered.

ACTS 8:1

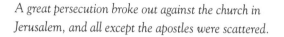

Some Iraqi Christians, living as close as nine miles from Islamic State–controlled areas, did not hesitate to celebrate Holy Week 2015. As one believer said, "Easter gives us new hope."[5] Not long afterward, thirty Christians were killed by Islamic State terrorists, who made a video of the horror. Around the world, people who saw the images knew that these people died for their faith in Jesus.[6]

"Great persecution" of God's church happens today just as it did in first-century Jerusalem, and God continues to use it to accomplish his purposes. He strengthens individual believers; they cling to him when evil robs them of home and family. He strengthens the body; when one believer's faith weakens, another's faith can buoy him up. God also spreads the truth about his Son, Jesus; rather than squelch it, persecution tends to cause Christianity to spread like a virus as it did with the early church.

Open Doors USA offers this perspective on persecution and preaching: "Pray that through this disruptive time the seeds of the gospel will be scattered, and pray that they will land in ready-made soil of those who don't know Jesus yet."[7]

> "I BELIEVE THE CHURCH IS GOD'S PRIMARY WAY TO ACCOMPLISH HIS PURPOSES ON EARTH."

HUMANITY

In Christ Jesus you are all children of God through faith, for all of you who were baptized into Christ have clothed yourselves with Christ. There is neither Jew nor Gentile, neither slave nor free, nor is there male and female, for you are all one in Christ Jesus.

GALATIANS 3:26–28

Six-year-old Ava was sent to clean her room. A few minutes later she asked her mom if she could go play with friends. Her mother asked, "Did you straighten your room?" "Yes, I did, Mom." Out to play she went.

Later, Mom walked into Ava's room and found all the stuffed animals on the floor instead of on the bed. Sighing agitatedly, Mom started to pick up the toys and put them on Ava's bed. But her sigh turned to a chuckle as she realized her daughter had carefully organized the animals. The bears were together, her dolphin and mermaid were together, the dogs were all together, and so were the cats. She had straightened her room! Mom realized she had judged her daughter's efforts based on her own expectations.

Do you judge others as though the way you think is the only right way? Remembering we're all created differently but loved equally by God helps you become more patient and understanding of others.

> **"I BELIEVE ALL PEOPLE ARE LOVED BY GOD AND NEED JESUS CHRIST AS THEIR SAVIOR."**

COMPASSION

A man with leprosy came to him and begged him on his knees, "If you are willing, you can make me clean."

Jesus . . . reached out his hand and touched the man. "I am willing," he said. "Be clean!"

MARK 1:40–41

Compassion literally means "to suffer with."[8] Jesus is God's compassion, who came to ease our suffering and repair the brokenness of our human condition. Jesus, full of compassion, reached out to touch and heal the leprous man. Jesus, moved with compassion, has reached out to touch and heal our diseased hearts.

God in Christ chose to suffer *with us* as a man for thirty-three years and to ultimately suffer *for us* on the cross to reconcile us with himself. Because God is compassionate, he did not merely mourn our sad condition from afar. He entered into this world and laid his hands on those who needed healing and who suffered so that we could spend eternity with him. God's act of compassion to us is the Man, Jesus.

If you find yourself running low on compassion, remember that Christ Jesus was moved with compassion to reach out to you and meet your greatest need: reconciliation with God. This will enable you to reach out to those around you, enter into their suffering, and demonstrate his love by being the healing and compassionate hand that meets their needs.

"I BELIEVE GOD CALLS ALL CHRISTIANS TO SHOW COMPASSION TO PEOPLE IN NEED."

DAY 31

STEWARDSHIP

"Well done, good and faithful servant! You have been faithful with a few things. . . . Come and share your master's happiness!"

MATTHEW 25:21

When you were little, your parents might have given you a small allowance to save and spend so you could begin to learn how to manage money and be responsible with your choices. The older you got and the more responsible you were, the more allowance you were given and the more opportunities you had to work to earn more.

The Bible says that the better stewards we are of God's blessings, the more he will entrust to us. The more we love and serve him, the more people he will put in our lives to love and the more opportunities we will have to serve in his name.

God wants us to see ourselves not as owners but as managers of our lives and all the blessings he bestows. God ultimately owns the resources, but we are charged with caring for them and investing them in ways that yield results for the kingdom of God.

God has entrusted you with resources and skills. He doesn't want these blessings to sit idle. Take the blessings he has given you and use them for his glory so that one day you will hear, "Well done, good and faithful servant!"

> **"I BELIEVE EVERYTHING I AM AND EVERYTHING I OWN BELONG TO GOD."**

> *"Where, O death, is your victory? Where, O death, is your sting?"*
>
> **1 CORINTHIANS 15:55**

Search "Why do people fear death?" on the Internet, and over 354 million results appear. The first responses are "There is nothing beyond" and "Fear of no after life [sic]. Who you are or were is lost forever . . . Oblivion . . . All good deeds for nothing."[9]

If you ask, "Why don't Christians fear death?" over 153 million results appear. The first website listed is Bible.org, referencing the disciples coming to understand that Jesus' death and resurrection "is God's way to heaven" and "the means by which we can live forever with Christ."[10]

And what a life that will be! In *The Great Divorce*, C. S. Lewis put it this way: "All loneliness, angers, hatreds, envies, and itchings that [our earthly life] contains, if rolled into one single experience and put into the scale against the least moment of the joy that is felt by the least in Heaven, would have no weight that could be registered at all."[11]

You don't need to fear death if you come to understand Jesus' death and resurrection. Instead, you can live in joyful anticipation of eternal life with Jesus.

> **"I BELIEVE THERE IS A HEAVEN AND A HELL AND THAT JESUS WILL RETURN TO JUDGE ALL PEOPLE AND TO ESTABLISH HIS ETERNAL KINGDOM."**

GOD

> *"You are a king, then!" said Pilate.*
>
> *Jesus answered, "You say that I am a king. In fact, the reason I was born and came into the world is to testify to the truth. Everyone on the side of truth listens to me."*
>
> *"What is truth?" retorted Pilate.*

JOHN 18:37–38

What is truth?" This is the question for the ages. The implications of how we answer cannot be understated.

If there is no such thing as truth, there is no such thing as right. If there is no such thing as right, there is no such thing as wrong. If there is no such thing as wrong, then anything goes. If there is no absolute truth from God about God and humanity, then we can all choose our own personal version of truth—Billy Graham's or Hugh Hefner's, Hitler's or Mother Teresa's. History has recorded the devastating consequences of choosing individualized versions of the truth.

God has given you answers to your most important questions about truth, and his wisdom and knowledge can be found in the Bible. God's ultimate answer came in the form of a man. Truth came into the world to testify to God's truth. His name is Jesus.

John 14:6 contains Jesus' answer: "I am the way and the truth and the life." What would be your answer?

> **"I BELIEVE THE GOD OF THE BIBLE IS THE ONLY TRUE GOD—FATHER, SON, AND HOLY SPIRIT."**

PERSONAL GOD

The angel of God called to Hagar . . . , "What is the matter, Hagar? Do not be afraid; God has heard the boy crying as he lies there."

GENESIS 21:17

Think about the tears you've shed alone. Is any experience lonelier? Moments like those can fuel hopelessness and despair. Questions like "Does *anyone* care?" and "Where is God?" can pierce your soul.

Be encouraged by how Hagar and Ishmael experienced the Almighty's love. Sent away from Abraham's house and into the desert by jealous Sarah, they ran out of water, and at that point Ishmael cried and, at a distance, Hagar did too.

Notice the beauty and comfort of the angel's words: "God has heard the boy crying." God heard Ishmael and Hagar when they cried. God has heard you cry, and he will continue to hear you and comfort you. What amazing love!

You can never run beyond the reach of God. You can never cry so silently that he misses your pain—or too loudly that he finds it off-putting. Your heartache expressed through your tears is an invitation for the Lord to draw near to you with a heart of compassion and a love that acts.

"I BELIEVE GOD IS INVOLVED IN AND CARES ABOUT MY DAILY LIFE."

SALVATION

She will give birth to a son, and you are to give him the name Jesus, because he will save his people from their sins.

MATTHEW 1:21

During World War I, the *London Times* asked G. K. Chesterton, along with other great thinkers of the day, "What is wrong with the world?" Chesterton's succinct reply was "Dear Sirs, I am."[12]

Chesterton understood something many of us don't. When faced with adversity or problems, we naturally look outward for blame instead of inward. We try to change the world around us when what needs to change is our hearts.

God gave the Israelites the Law, which was impossible to follow perfectly, to reveal the internal human problem—sin. The Law was God's X-ray to expose the true corrupt nature of their souls so that they could see it, confess it, and call out to God to save them. Nothing and no one else but God had the power to truly transform.

God sent Jesus to the cross so that he could replace your sin with his righteousness, your selfishness with his love. Only Jesus can save you from who you are without him. Turning our hearts over to him is the only thing that will truly change the world. Have you let him change you?

> "I BELIEVE A PERSON COMES INTO A RIGHT RELATIONSHIP WITH GOD BY GOD'S GRACE THROUGH FAITH IN JESUS CHRIST."

THE BIBLE

Beginning with Moses and all the Prophets, he explained to them what was said in all the Scriptures concerning himself.

LUKE 24:27

Looks like an intense conversation!" said the Man as he caught up to the two travelers.

"Haven't you heard Jesus of Nazareth was crucified? And we'd had such hope that he was going to redeem Israel," one of them answered.

His companion added, "Some women went to his tomb this morning. It was empty. Some angels told them Jesus was alive."

With a half smile, the Man started at the beginning and shared with them what the Old Testament scriptures said about the Messiah and how this Jesus had fulfilled them all. He challenged them about how slow they were to believe all that the prophets had foretold.

The travelers shared dinner with Jesus, who suddenly "disappeared from their sight" (v. 31). Imagine their surprise when they finally recognized who he was and were left wondering why they hadn't sooner. We're left wishing we could have such an encounter!

The good news is, we can. Jesus told his followers his Spirit would "teach you all things and will remind you of everything I have said" (John 14:26). As you open God's Word, ask him for wisdom and guidance.

> "I BELIEVE THE BIBLE IS THE WORD OF GOD AND HAS THE RIGHT TO COMMAND MY BELIEF AND ACTION."

IDENTITY IN CHRIST

The LORD will watch over your coming and going both now and forevermore.

PSALM 121:8

Does God really watch over us this closely? Why would he? Most of my days would make an insomniac fall asleep. I love my routine and to-do lists, but how could this be a good use of the divine Creator's time?

The answer is stamped on almost every page of Scripture. He loves and cares deeply for us. Easy to understand; hard to grasp.

Right now I'm in a hospital room. My grandson was born yesterday. As he lies in his crib, I hover over him, mesmerized by his every move—every twitch of his eye, every move to the right or to the left. A yawn is big news. The smirk on his face evoked by gas sure looks like a genuine smile to me. To anyone else, this would seem like a colossal waste of time. Not for me. I love my grandson.

Oh! This is how God feels about me, but with so much more depth and perfection.

My grandson is clueless of my intense love for him. Just like we are clueless of God's love for us as we wander through life unaware he's intrigued with our every move. Only as you come to terms with this reality and soak it in will you begin to live the life God intends for you!

> **"I BELIEVE I AM SIGNIFICANT BECAUSE OF MY POSITION AS A CHILD OF GOD."**

I consider my life worth nothing to me; my only aim is to finish the race and complete the task the Lord Jesus has given me—the task of testifying to the good news of God's grace.

ACTS 20:24

If you've played the game *Would You Rather?* you know that people's answers can reveal much about them.

Would you rather speak in front of five thousand people for thirty minutes or be without your cell phone for three days? Would you rather win a Grammy or an Olympic Gold Medal? Would you rather be happy and poor or sad and rich?

If we asked the apostle Paul if he would rather serve the Lord or [anything else], he would undoubtedly say, "Serve the Lord." Not one to make statements lightly, he declared, "I consider my life worth nothing to me." He would rather testify "to the good news of God's grace" than be occupied with any other task the world offers.

God's church needs leaders who are passionate and committed to serving the Lord, but it also needs servants in the pews who are passionate and committed to the specific tasks God has assigned them. Every believer is a minister of the good news, like Paul.

Ask God to fuel your passion for his purposes on earth.

"I BELIEVE THE CHURCH IS GOD'S PRIMARY WAY TO ACCOMPLISH HIS PURPOSES ON EARTH."

DAY 39

HUMANITY

The LORD said to [Hosea], "Go, marry a promiscuous woman and have children with her, for like an adulterous wife this land is guilty of unfaithfulness to the LORD."

HOSEA 1:2

When someone is in love, no demonstration of that love is too extreme. A room full of roses. Written declarations of love. The heroic sacrifice. Consider one way God demonstrated his love for Israel despite their unfaithfulness to him.

Wanting his wayward people to realize what they were doing and how much he loved them, God asked his prophet Hosea to marry an immoral woman named Gomer. Hosea would play the part of God; Gomer, the part of Israel.

Hosea provided Gomer with a wonderful life of love and provision. But she chose to spurn Hosea's love, leave him, and return to her immoral lifestyle. Evidently she became a slave, and God told Hosea to track down his wife, purchase her, take her back into his home, and love her. What Hosea did for Gomer, God did for the people of Israel.

What God did for Israel, he did for all humanity when he sent his Son to die on the cross. We were all enslaved to sin, Jesus paid the price with his life in order to purchase us back, and God welcomed us once again into his warm embrace. What wondrous love!

> **"I BELIEVE ALL PEOPLE ARE LOVED BY GOD AND NEED JESUS CHRIST AS THEIR SAVIOR."**

COMPASSION

Naomi said, . . . "[Boaz] has not stopped showing his kindness to the living and the dead. . . . That man is our close relative; he is one of our guardian-redeemers."

RUTH 2:20

Ruth lost the only man she ever loved. She'd had no children. Her dreams were shattered. The only thing she had left was a compassionate woman, Naomi, who hadn't treated her like a daughter-in-law but rather like a daughter-in-love. Now Naomi was leaving too! Ruth couldn't bear it. So she decided not to say good-bye but to pack her bags and go with her. Now Ruth would compassionately help Naomi start a new life in a strange land. That's when she met Boaz.

Boaz had heard of Ruth's kindness to his relative Naomi, so when he noticed her in his field, he invited her to continue to glean there and even instructed his men to leave some stalks of grain behind for her.

Ruth was in need. Boaz extended compassion to her, and later in Ruth 4, he took her as his wife and became her guardian-redeemer.

Jesus is our guardian-redeemer. His compassion redeems us for all eternity.

Compassion begets compassion. Who needs a touch of compassion from you today? Find a way to show others the compassion Jesus has shown you.

> "I BELIEVE GOD CALLS ALL CHRISTIANS TO SHOW COMPASSION TO PEOPLE IN NEED."

STEWARDSHIP

"No one can serve two masters. . . . You will be devoted to the one and despise the other. You cannot serve both God and money."

LUKE 16:13

What has mastery over us?

A review of the recent websites we've visited indicates what fills our mind. A glance at the calendar shows what dominates our time. And a look at the check register reveals what we invest our money in. Jesus warned us that money can rival God's place of supremacy in our lives, and one of Jesus' disciples added that "the love of money is a root of all kinds of evil" (1 Timothy 6:10).

If our inventory of where our money flows doesn't show godly priorities, one of two things is true: either we don't really believe that everything we own comes from God, or we know it does but have never truly adopted it in our hearts as a way of life.

Read Luke 16:1–15 and you'll see that we are encouraged to be shrewd with our resources like the servant in the story. Yet unlike the servant, whose goal was to save his job, we shouldn't use our resources selfishly; we should use God's resources to help others.

God wants us to creatively find ways to bless others with what he has blessed us with so he can be our only master.

> **"I BELIEVE EVERYTHING I AM AND EVERYTHING I OWN BELONG TO GOD."**

ETERNITY

> As [Elijah and Elisha] were walking along and talking together, suddenly a chariot of fire and horses of fire appeared and separated the two of them, and Elijah went up to heaven in a whirlwind.
>
> 2 KINGS 2:11

Can you imagine being at this remarkable event? Or how about seeing Enoch disappear when God took him to heaven, or the resurrected Son of God ascend into the sky? What amazing demonstrations of God's power! What compelling evidence that life on this planet is not all there is, that more awaits us.

Modern science cannot explain these supernatural events. And we can't go back in time to witness Elijah, Enoch, or Jesus being taken to heaven in bodily form. But consider Martin Luther's observation: "Our Lord has written the promise of resurrection, not in books alone but in every leaf of springtime." Scripture tells us that he has also set eternity in our hearts (Ecclesiastes 3:11). We're made to hope for it.

Life is more joyful when you live with a sense of his presence with you. Life is more hopeful when you are aware of God's promise of resurrection. The God who loves you has the whole world in his hands and will take you to be with him because of the scars they bear.

"I BELIEVE THERE IS A HEAVEN AND A HELL AND THAT JESUS WILL RETURN TO JUDGE ALL PEOPLE AND TO ESTABLISH HIS ETERNAL KINGDOM."

DAY 43

GOD

Choose for yourselves this day whom you will serve. . . . As for me and my household, we will serve the LORD.

JOSHUA 24:15

How could anyone bow down before a golden calf? It might seem ridiculous, worshipping an object you had just created while ignoring the mighty God who had just saved you. But before we judge the Israelites, we must look at ourselves. Do we worship a paycheck? A job that consumes us? A position of power we long to attain? Just as ridiculous!

After leading the Israelites into the promised land, Joshua gathered the people together and challenged them to choose for themselves to serve the Lord, the one true God. He charged them to remember the holy God who had delivered them and to worship no other.

We face the same challenge to choose to worship God throughout the day. It's a decision we must make every day as we get out of bed, go to work or school, serve at church, interact in the community, select activities for our free time, and perhaps even decide what to eat.

Will you serve God—or will you serve yourself or some idol you have created to replace the only One who deserves your worship and praise?

> **"I BELIEVE THE GOD OF THE BIBLE IS THE ONLY TRUE GOD—FATHER, SON, AND HOLY SPIRIT."**

PERSONAL GOD

> *"As for me, this is my covenant with you: You will be the father of many nations."*

GENESIS 17:4

Have you ever done something you regretted so much you thought God's blessing would be withheld from you? Abraham and Sarah doubted God's promise to give them a son and took matters into their own hands. Instead of waiting on God, Abraham slept with one of their slaves, and that union produced a son. But when Sarah gave birth to Isaac, trouble arose, and Sarah demanded Abraham send the slave, Hagar, and her son, Ishmael, away. Surely Abraham's heart ached as he watched Ishmael leave and realized the damage they had done. Would God bless their lack of faith?

Originally, God promised Abraham he would make him *a* great nation. After the birth of Ishmael, the covenant was revised. God said, "I will make you the father of *many* nations." God continued to bless Abraham and Sarah, even though their faith was imperfect, and included Ishmael and Hagar in the blessing. Although there were consequences to pay, God's promise included them all.

Does your faith seem weak and insufficient at times? Do you wish you could turn back the hands of time because you tried to control situations or help God along instead of waiting? He's got you covered.

"I BELIEVE GOD IS INVOLVED IN AND CARES ABOUT MY DAILY LIFE."

SALVATION

They led him away to crucify him.

MATTHEW 27:31

I t was Palm Sunday, and the kindergarteners had just walked down the center aisle of "Big Church" waving palm fronds, shouting "Hosanna!" Back in their Sunday school classroom, they heard the story of that important day in Jesus' life when he loved us so much that he allowed himself to be nailed to the cross because of our sin. Now these precious boys and girls each sat with crisscross legs on the floor facing the TV. It was time to see the events of Holy Week unfold in animated color.

They watched as Jesus overturned the tables in the temple, washed his disciples' feet, shared the cup and bread with the Twelve, prayed in the Garden of Gethsemane, and then was arrested. The drama and tension built as they knew the loving Jesus was about to be killed.

As the Roman soldiers dragged Jesus to the cross, little Brett jumped up and yelled, "Don't hurt Jesus!" He didn't know about the resurrection story to be told next week!

When you read the story of Jesus' death and consider his crucifixion, remember Jesus hung on a cross that was meant for you. Be awestruck and humbled by the tremendous sacrifice Love made for you. But don't forget his resurrection! Because this is how Love wins!

> "I BELIEVE A PERSON COMES INTO A RIGHT RELATIONSHIP WITH GOD BY GOD'S GRACE THROUGH FAITH IN JESUS CHRIST."

THE BIBLE

We did not follow cleverly devised stories when we told you about the coming of our Lord Jesus Christ in power, but we were eyewitnesses of his majesty.

2 PETER 1:16

What can you believe? TV news or information on the Internet and in magazines? Everything that's tweeted or Instagrammed? Who can you believe? This radio host or that talk-show pundit? CNN or Fox?

The world is full of information we should be skeptical of, but there is one source of truth we can always rely on: the Word of God. We can trust God's Word because God himself preserved these writings and promises; they will last until the end of time as we know it (Mark 13:31). Eyewitnesses wrote these words through the inspiration of God's Spirit. And the people who contributed to or are mentioned in its pages were not just creating stories to gain attention; many willingly died rather than deny that Jesus was the Son of God, that he was crucified and buried, and that he rose again. Few people would be willing to give up their lives for something that isn't true!

There isn't much in our world today you can hang your hat on, let alone allow to determine what you believe and how you live. But you can depend on the truth of Scripture for just that!

"I BELIEVE THE BIBLE IS THE WORD OF GOD AND HAS THE RIGHT TO COMMAND MY BELIEF AND ACTION."

DAY 47

IDENTITY IN CHRIST

"I pray also for those who will believe in me through their message."

JOHN 17:20

Are you facing a difficult illness, or is someone you love facing one? Are you struggling to decide which job to take? Maybe you need wisdom to know whether you should end a relationship. Whatever the source of pain or anxiety, we can find great comfort in knowing someone is praying for us. Even more important than counsel or advice is having someone lift us before the Lord, asking that his good and perfect will be done in our lives.

More than two thousand years ago, in one of the last prayers Jesus prayed before his death, he expressed his passionate love for us. He prayed for "those who will believe in me" as a result of the life-saving message the disciples would soon proclaim about his victory over sin and death. Jesus prayed for you and me!

The Bible also tells us that Jesus is now at the right hand of God, the Father, advocating for us, reminding him that he died for us so we could have his gift of eternal life.

How does it make you feel to know you are important enough to have Jesus, God's Son, pray for you, both then and now?

> **"I BELIEVE I AM SIGNIFICANT BECAUSE OF MY POSITION AS A CHILD OF GOD."**

CHURCH

Two are better than one, because they have a good return for their labor: If either of them falls down, one can help the other up. But pity anyone who falls and has no one to help them up.

ECCLESIASTES 4:9–10

Well, um, we don't attend church anymore. We used to, but now we just worship at home. After so many years, we figured we'd learned everything we needed to know." This was my neighbor's response when I asked her where she went to church.

Over the next two years, our kids played together and we got to know each other a little. One day she showed up on my doorstep and said, "My husband lost his job, and we are having trouble making ends meet. We were wondering if you know of anyone at church who is hiring. We could use some help."

Trouble had come, and they knew exactly where to turn for help—the church. But they had cut themselves off from the relationships God designed to provide life-sustaining support, called the body of Christ, which has blood circulating through it to heal and restore.

Don't cut yourself off from the life-giving fellowship of the church. When you fall down and get injured, and we all do from time to time, you'll need that blood flow to help you before gangrene sets in.

"I BELIEVE THE CHURCH IS GOD'S PRIMARY WAY TO ACCOMPLISH HIS PURPOSES ON EARTH."

DAY 49

HUMANITY

Certain individuals . . . have secretly slipped in among you. They are ungodly people, who pervert the grace of our God into a license for immorality. . . . Woe to them! They have taken the way of Cain.

JUDE VV. 4, 11

This description of immoral humanity is not pretty. And this two-thousand-year-old picture is, sadly, a reflection of our culture today.

Consider Jude's reference to "the way of Cain." A son of Adam and Eve and the murderer of his brother, Abel, Cain displays selfishness, greed, and—as illustrated by God's rejection of his sacrifice—a superficial faith. How many of us are merely going through the motions of our faith? Are our hearts truly bowed before Lord Jesus? And which one of us—forgiven sinners that we are—doesn't struggle with selfishness? In our materialistic society, who doesn't wrestle with envy and greed?

"The way of Cain" also involved hatred and murder. Every one of us murders, not necessarily with guns and daggers, but with our anger and our words, as Jesus taught in Matthew 5:21–22. Our judgment of Cain—"How could he have murdered his brother?"—should be directed toward ourselves. How can we murder—gossip, rage, taunt, belittle—someone whom Jesus himself died for?

Teach me to love, Lord.

"I BELIEVE ALL PEOPLE ARE LOVED BY GOD AND NEED JESUS CHRIST AS THEIR SAVIOR."

COMPASSION

"The King will reply, 'Truly I tell you, whatever you did for one of the least of these brothers and sisters of mine, you did for me.'"

MATTHEW 25:40

When did we see you needing someone to drive your kids to school, to help cover the monthly bills, or to bring over a meal?" "When did we see you broken from divorce, crushed by a wandering child, or desperate for someone to listen?" "When did we see you need your lawn mowed , the oil in your car changed, or help with your taxes?"

Those were the kinds of questions the Lord was asked. Now look again at his answer: "Whatever you did for one of the least of these brothers and sisters of mine, you did for me." This will be the King of kings's response to us as well when we stand before him. Our acts of compassion have eternal consequences of either reward or punishment.

Looking at your life, note any evidence that you have served Jesus by showing compassion to others. Ask God to open your eyes to all the needs around you. No matter how small the gesture, every act of kindness is a reflection of your love of Christ and brings a smile to God's face.

"I BELIEVE GOD CALLS ALL CHRISTIANS TO SHOW COMPASSION TO PEOPLE IN NEED."

DAY 51

STEWARDSHIP

*Who knows but that you have come to your royal position
for such a time as this?*

ESTHER 4:14

The word *stewardship* probably first calls to mind concrete things like money and the planet. But the Bible teaches us to steward, or manage, every area of our lives so that we bless others. The call to good stewardship also applies to opportunities God gives us.

The beautiful young Esther became the queen of Persia while her Jewish heritage remained secret. When a new decree put the life of every Jew in jeopardy, Esther's role in God's plan for his people became evident. Her uncle Mordecai pointedly asked Esther whether it was possible that God had allowed her to become queen "for such a time as this." Esther had a job to do that required risking her life, and she bravely jumped in. She boldly approached the king to save her people—without having been summoned, which broke cultural rules and spelled danger. And God blessed her and many others through her.

Think about opportunities that you have—in your family, neighborhood, church, or workplace—to honor God and do his work. Ask God to show you how he wants to use you. He may call you to serve others in a way that's a little scary, but if he does, he will supply the courage you need to act bravely.

> **"I BELIEVE EVERYTHING I AM AND
> EVERYTHING I OWN BELONG TO GOD."**

ETERNITY

*"Between us and you a great chasm has been set in place,
so that those who want to go from here to you cannot, nor
can anyone cross over from there to us."*

LUKE 16:26

et's be honest—hell is not an easy subject to broach. But with bold, loving compassion, Jesus didn't shy away from discussing the agony of an eternity apart from God, nor should we.

In Luke 16 Jesus describes the spirits of a beggar named Lazarus and a rich man after their death. Lazarus rests peacefully at Abraham's side, a place reserved for the righteous. The rich man, who had known a life of luxury, is in hades, a place of torment for the wicked.

Finally accepting he will spend an eternity apart from God, the rich man asks Abraham to let Lazarus warn his five brothers about the reality of hades so they will repent. Abraham shakes his head and says, "If they do not listen to Moses and the Prophets, they will not be convinced even if someone rises from the dead" (v. 31).

Let the harshness of Jesus' story fuel in you a loving boldness to share your faith with those in your life who need him. Our time on earth is our only opportunity to hear and repent.

> "I BELIEVE THERE IS A HEAVEN AND A HELL AND THAT JESUS WILL RETURN TO JUDGE ALL PEOPLE AND TO ESTABLISH HIS ETERNAL KINGDOM."

DAY 53

GOD

The fire of the LORD fell and burned up the sacrifice, the wood, the stones and the soil, and also licked up the water in the trench.

1 KINGS 18:38

Yes, you read that right! God's fire "licked up the water" after the prophet Elijah had calmly prayed, asking him to let the pagan onlookers witness the incredible power of the one true God.

The showdown had been intense. From morning until noon, the followers of Baal had petitioned him to bring down fire on their offering. They shouted for him and danced for him. They even "slashed themselves with swords and spears . . . until their blood flowed" (v. 28), and nothing happened. Baal did not respond.

The God whom Elijah worshipped did not, however, need to be asked a second time. The fire burned the intended sacrifice and went on to devour the stone altar that had been drenched in water. Elijah clearly wanted to prove a point—and he did: "When all the people saw this, they fell prostrate and cried, 'The LORD—he is God! The LORD—he is God!'" (v. 39).

Thank God for the times when he has clearly made his presence known to you, and look for him to do so again today.

> **"I BELIEVE THE GOD OF THE BIBLE IS THE ONLY TRUE GOD—FATHER, SON, AND HOLY SPIRIT."**

PERSONAL GOD

"You must go to everyone I send you to and say whatever I command you. Do not be afraid of them, for I am with you and will rescue you."

JEREMIAH 1:7–8

When God calls us to do something, he empowers us to carry out his plan. Few of us get the specifics for our assignment from God the way the prophet Jeremiah did, but we are all called to be as faithful to our assignment as this man known as "the weeping prophet." The message he had to deliver grieved his heart because he knew his people were about to be exiled into Babylonian captivity. Doing exactly as God commanded him, Jeremiah warned the Southern Kingdom of Judah about the Lord's pending discipline in response to their unfaithfulness.

Jeremiah knew the people of Judah would not heed his warning. In fact, God told him the people would "fight against" him (v. 19). But his task was to faithfully and courageously deliver God's message. He rested in God's promise that he would be with him in every step of obedience he took.

What has God called you to do? It's surely an assignment tailored for you, but it is probably one you can't do apart from God's enabling strength. Don't be afraid. Obey and know that your Lord says, "I am with you."

"I BELIEVE GOD IS INVOLVED IN AND CARES ABOUT MY DAILY LIFE."

SALVATION

In him we have redemption through his blood, the forgiveness of sins, in accordance with the riches of God's grace.

EPHESIANS 1:7

When I visited South Africa for the first time, I was moved by the beauty of the land and the beauty of the body of Christ there. However, most of the poorest of the poor in South Africa live in shanties: horrific, unsafe, unsanitary places unfit for dogs, let alone humans, and certainly unhealthy places for children to be raised.

Charities attempted to help and built beautiful, safe houses. Surprisingly, once the impoverished took possession of these new homes, they sold them, pocketed the money, and moved back to their shanties!

It made me think of what Christ did for us. He did not purchase our freedom, our redemption, so we would continue to live in spiritual poverty. Because of Christ, we don't have to live in the dilapidated shanty of destitution anymore—not in oppression, in discouragement, in anxiety, in doubt, in fear, in depression, in humiliation, or in defeat.

You are covered in the riches of God's grace. Don't allow yourself to go back to where you once were. Don't pocket his grace. Use it to live a victorious life over sin and death!

> "I BELIEVE A PERSON COMES INTO A RIGHT RELATIONSHIP WITH GOD BY GOD'S GRACE THROUGH FAITH IN JESUS CHRIST."

THE BIBLE

*I have hidden your word in my heart that I might not
sin against you.*

PSALM 119:11

I once wrote an article for a major Christian magazine with my mentor, the late Dallas Willard. The interviewer asked Dallas which practice had been the most effective for him, based on his extensive work and writings on spiritual disciplines. We all expected him to cite some exotic practice from the ancient desert fathers. He didn't. He simply said, "Scripture memory has helped me the most." The interviewer was unimpressed, and it didn't make the final cut of the article.

I, however, took careful note. I had considered Scripture memory an ineffective exercise, but since that day I have taken it seriously. I now know what Dallas was talking about. There is something about the process of memorization that drives God's truth into our long-term memory and creates instant recall for daily living.

For God's Word to actually govern our beliefs and actions, we must have it embedded deep into our minds and in our hearts. Memorizing God's Word can be a painful process, but in the end it helps keep us from harmful sins and leads us in his good direction for our lives.

Why not start by memorizing Psalm 119:11 today?

**"I BELIEVE THE BIBLE IS THE WORD OF
GOD AND HAS THE RIGHT TO COMMAND
MY BELIEF AND ACTION."**

DAY 57

IDENTITY IN CHRIST

" . . . *your heavenly Father is perfect.*"

MATTHEW 5:48

When you think about the term *father*, what comes to mind? Were you blessed with a father who did not hesitate to show you how much he loves you; a father who earned your respect and devotion; a father you unhesitatingly ran to for comfort and reassurance, help and protection?

Not everyone has that kind of earthly father. Sometimes Dad wasn't on the scene at all. Some have fathers who are alcoholics, or are angry and abusive. The abuse may have been physical, emotional, or sexual, and home was not a safe place. Unfortunately, earthly fathers don't always fulfill their role in a proper manner.

God is our perfect Father, and what the name and role of father mean to you may depend on your personal experiences. If your earthly father makes it hard for you to trust and draw near to your heavenly Father, know that by God's grace you can experience great healing and grow in trust. There can be a day when you run into his arms, feel his perfect peace, love, and protection, and know that he will hold you close always.

> **"I BELIEVE I AM SIGNIFICANT BECAUSE OF MY POSITION AS A CHILD OF GOD."**

Here is a trustworthy saying that deserves full acceptance:
Christ Jesus came into the world to save sinners—of
whom I am the worst.

1 TIMOTHY 1:15

Do you have friends or family members who refuse to hear the truth about Jesus? Who is on your "Least Likely to Accept Jesus" list? In the early church, Saul of Tarsus was probably at the top of many people's lists. He had stood by calmly, coldly, as Stephen, one of seven deacons chosen to care for widows in the church, was stoned to death after challenging the religious leaders. Saul passionately pursued Jesus-followers on his mission "to destroy the church" (Acts 8:3).

But on his way from Jerusalem to Damascus, where he planned to continue persecuting believers, Saul encountered the risen Jesus. In that moment, Saul surrendered his life to Christ, who changed Saul's name to Paul. The remainder of his days were spent building Christ's church instead of destroying it. Paul took the gospel to the Gentiles even as he explained to fellow Jews how Jesus fulfilled Old Testament prophecies.

Is there someone you think will never be a part of God's family, the church? Never give up praying for them! You may be wrong, just as people were wrong about Saul. Who knows how God may use that person to advance his kingdom!

"I BELIEVE THE CHURCH IS GOD'S PRIMARY WAY TO ACCOMPLISH HIS PURPOSES ON EARTH."

HUMANITY

*"When Israel was a child, I loved him, and out of Egypt
I called my son. But the more they were called, the more
they went away from me."*

HOSEA 11:1–2

Randy and I were blessed to have wonderful parents whose acceptance and love made our heavenly Father's love very real to us.

Yet, as much as we thought we understood God's love, becoming parents rocked our world. We never imagined such powerful love! We would've taken a bullet for our six-pound person whom we really didn't know yet. We went without sleep, got spit up on, and ate lukewarm food in order to care for her.

No child understands the intense love of a parent until they have their own. Those of us who've had children turn away from us can hear God's heartache in Hosea 11. Just as a parent keeps loving even as the prodigal walks away, God keeps loving us when we, his children, turn away from him.

Experiencing love for your children enables you to understand God's amazing statement a few verses later: "All my compassion is aroused. I will not carry out my fierce anger" (vv. 8–9).

Your heavenly Father loves you—loves all people—with the unending and undeserved love of a parent.

> **"I BELIEVE ALL PEOPLE ARE LOVED BY GOD
> AND NEED JESUS CHRIST AS THEIR SAVIOR."**

COMPASSION

"Which of these three do you think was a neighbor to the man who fell into the hands of robbers?"

LUKE 10:36

The man had been robbed, beaten, and left for dead on the lonely road. The pastor of a local megachurch saw the man and passed by on the other side. He didn't want to be late to preach the first of eight sermons that weekend.

The worship leader of the same megachurch also noticed the bleeding man and he, too, passed by on the other side. Without him to help his congregation prepare their hearts for worship, how could they possibly hear the truth God had for them at church that day?

Then a janitor from a church of another denomination—one that some Christians criticized—walked by. He took pity on the injured man, drove him to a local hotel, and left a credit card at the front desk.

The expert in the law to whom Jesus was telling the story of the good Samaritan answered Jesus' question correctly: the neighbor was "the one who had mercy." And Jesus then spoke words that apply to us as well: "Go and do likewise" (v. 37).

Don't make excuses. Don't rationalize why you can't help. And don't let serving God keep you from serving your neighbor.

"I BELIEVE GOD CALLS ALL CHRISTIANS TO SHOW COMPASSION TO PEOPLE IN NEED."

DAY 61

STEWARDSHIP

I prayed for this child, and the LORD has granted me what I asked of him. So now I give him to the LORD. For his whole life he will be given over to the LORD.

1 SAMUEL 1:27–28

Every child conceived has been knit together by our heavenly Father, fearfully and wonderfully made. God entrusts children to their parents' care, but the children ultimately belong to him. Parents are trusted stewards of these precious little humans.

Hannah, whose story appears in the Old Testament, completely understood this concept of stewardship. For years, Hannah could not have children, and she pleaded earnestly with the Lord for a child. When God granted Hannah's request, she named her son Samuel. Once he was weaned, Hannah physically returned him to the Lord, to whom Hannah realized he truly belonged. How hard it must have been for her to say good-bye to the precious son she waited years for.

Have you had to say good-bye to a son or daughter? When they leave our nest, no matter the reason, we must turn them back over to God and acknowledge that they are his.

Take heart in the fact that God loves your precious child even more than you do. You won't always be with them, but God, their heavenly Father, will be!

> **"I BELIEVE EVERYTHING I AM AND EVERYTHING I OWN BELONG TO GOD."**

ETERNITY

The Spirit and the bride say, "Come!" And let the one who hears say, "Come!" Let the one who is thirsty come; and let the one who wishes take the free gift of the water of life.

REVELATION 22:17

Hydration is essential to running and recovering from a marathon. Those 26.2 miles make a body thirsty!

The marathon of life can also make us thirsty and can make us long passionately for something to satisfy our souls. Sometimes we don't know what we want; we just know something is missing. We stay married, we launch our kids into life, we achieve success in the workplace, and the house and cars suggest we've arrived. But we are still thirsty.

Just as a physical thirst indicates the need for water, the unsatisfied thirst prompted by a full-but-empty life can only be quenched by Living Water and an eternal life with Jesus. C. S. Lewis offered this insight: "If I find in myself a desire which no experience in this world can satisfy, the most probable explanation is that I was made for another world."[13]

God created human beings to be in relationship with him. And it will not be until you enter heaven that the thirst for perfect fellowship with him will finally be quenched.

"I BELIEVE THERE IS A HEAVEN AND A HELL AND THAT JESUS WILL RETURN TO JUDGE ALL PEOPLE AND TO ESTABLISH HIS ETERNAL KINGDOM."

DAY 63

GOD

Jesus was baptized. . . . The Holy Spirit descended on him in bodily form like a dove. And a voice came from heaven: "You are my Son, whom I love."

LUKE 3:21–22

The word *trinity* isn't found in the Bible, but we see suggestions that God is plural in the very beginning of his story. In the creation account we read, "God said, 'Let *us* make mankind in *our* image, in *our* likeness'" (Genesis 1:26, emphasis added).

At Jesus' baptism three distinct Persons show up: the Son was baptized, the Holy Spirit descended like a dove on the Son, and the Father spoke. It is therefore completely logical that, throughout the centuries, followers of Jesus have come to call the one true God "the Trinity," acknowledging three Persons who share one being.

When we embrace God with our whole hearts and worship him with every aspect of our lives, we experience the fruit of the Spirit's presence within us. Those Christlike traits of love, joy, peace, patience, and self-control materialize so that we, as well as those around us, reap the benefits.

Worship God the Father, make sure Jesus your Savior truly is Lord of every area of your life, and yield to the Holy Spirit's ability to transform you to become more like Jesus.

> **"I BELIEVE THE GOD OF THE BIBLE IS THE ONLY TRUE GOD—FATHER, SON, AND HOLY SPIRIT."**

PERSONAL GOD

When I consider your heavens, the work of your fingers,
the moon and the stars, which you have set in place, what
is mankind that you are mindful of them, human beings
that you care for them?

PSALM 8:3–4

When have you been most aware of God's presence with you? Of his power and his love? Of the hope and strength you can find in him? How did you respond? If you're a songwriter, these times can inspire songs of thanksgiving and joy.

David was a songwriter throughout his life. He wrote psalms when he was a shepherd boy gazing at the billions of stars God created, when he was a successful warrior being chased down by jealous Saul, and when he was the king of Israel. The songs of David and the other psalmists express a personal, intimate relationship with God, the kind of relationship that can be yours as well, if it isn't already.

Like a shepherd, the Lord longs to protect you, provide for you, guide you, rescue you, and comfort you, so that, like David, you can proclaim, "The LORD is my shepherd, I lack nothing" (Psalm 23:1). Our good Shepherd longs to have his "goodness and love . . . follow [us] all the days of [our] life" (v. 6). What a blessing!

> **"I BELIEVE GOD IS INVOLVED IN AND CARES ABOUT MY DAILY LIFE."**

SALVATION

The serpent was more crafty than any of the wild animals the LORD God had made.

GENESIS 3:1

Satan, the great deceiver, clothed himself as a serpent and set out to trick Adam and Eve into disobeying their good and gracious God. The Enemy's ploy succeeded: Adam and Eve willfully rejected God and disobeyed his single command to them.

And what were the consequences? Adam and Eve realized they were naked. They hid from God. Adam blamed the woman for his sin; the woman blamed the serpent. And the two were sent out of the garden of Eden. But consider the grace in that scene.

God didn't kill Adam and Eve when they broke the first and only rule in the garden. Grace? Check.

God cursed the snake and promised that a time would come when the woman's offspring would crush its head (v. 15). Grace? Check.

God replaced their fig leaves with the longer-lasting skins of animals. Grace? Check.

The killing of the animals signaled that it would take the blood of another to cover the sins of humankind. And in Jesus, those sins would in fact be covered forever. Grace? Check.

> **"I BELIEVE A PERSON COMES INTO A RIGHT RELATIONSHIP WITH GOD BY GOD'S GRACE THROUGH FAITH IN JESUS CHRIST."**

THE BIBLE

*The LORD thunders over the mighty waters. The voice of
the LORD is powerful; the voice of the LORD is majestic.*

PSALM 29:3–4

For several centuries the King James Version was the only source of
God's Word in the English language. Now we twenty-first-century
readers have multiple translations and paraphrases, leather-bound Bibles
and paperbacks, electronic and audio versions. Some are designed specifically for men, women, teens, tweens, or children; there are some that
offer study tips, and others with practical applications for living out the
commands of Scripture.

What is the impact of all these choices? Have we become numb to
the amazing fact that the words on these pages are God's actual majestic voice directed to us? Do we forget that people around the world and
throughout the ages have given—or would give—their lives for even a
chapter of Scripture to read?

Don't let easy access to God's Word cost you a sense of awe, wonder, or respect for this treasure. Scripture is indeed the passionate and
powerful voice of the Lord! It is God's divine love story to you in a
world full of rough waters. Let his thunderous voice guide you through
every storm in your life.

> **"I BELIEVE THE BIBLE IS THE WORD OF
> GOD AND HAS THE RIGHT TO COMMAND
> MY BELIEF AND ACTION."**

IDENTITY IN CHRIST

Those who are led by the Spirit of God are the children of God. . . . The Spirit you received brought about your adoption to sonship. And by him we cry, "Abba, Father."

ROMANS 8:14–15

Lots of people can call us by our first names. Our parents, our teachers, our friends, our coworkers. We have heard them all our lives— throughout elementary school, during our high school years, in the neighborhood, at the gym, in the office, at church.

Only a few people, however, call us "Mom" or "Dad." Only our children use those names for us. And it's the sweetest name we can hear. *Mama. Dada.* These precious words are among the first children speak, and every parent waits expectantly to hear their little one utter those words for the first time.

Similarly, only those who belong to God can call the almighty God, the Creator and Sustainer of life, the Author of history, "Daddy."

The Greek word *Abba* is used as a term of endearment from a loving, dependent child. Celebrate that privilege and joyfully cry out to *Abba.* He is waiting to hear you say his name.

> **"I BELIEVE I AM SIGNIFICANT BECAUSE OF MY POSITION AS A CHILD OF GOD."**

CHURCH

Through the gospel the Gentiles are heirs together with Israel, members together of one body, and sharers together in the promise in Christ Jesus.

EPHESIANS 3:6

The Gentiles are heirs together with Israel." Is this like the Hatfields and the McCoys laying down their rifles after generations of feuding? Is it comparable to the various Protestant denominations uniting under a single biblical theology? Is it like the Catholic Church, the Protestants, and the Orthodox coming together as a single body of believers to proclaim Jesus crucified, dead, and risen?

God's great plan is for the church to be the community of Christ. Along with reconciling individuals to himself, God has reconciled saved individuals to one another. Through his death, Christ broke down the barriers in order to unite believers in one body, the church.

Paul taught that the Jews were to embrace the Gentiles, who had long done things considered unclean and had previously worshipped idols rather than the one true God. The Gentiles were to embrace the Jews, whose ways had seemed strange and whose rituals seemed bizarre.

What brother or sister in Christ who is a little different from you is God asking you to embrace? The world will know you are his child by your love for others.

> "I BELIEVE THE CHURCH IS GOD'S PRIMARY WAY TO ACCOMPLISH HIS PURPOSES ON EARTH."

HUMANITY

I am already being poured out like a drink offering, and the time for my departure is near.

2 TIMOTHY 4:6

When I cook I often make a reduction sauce to go with the meat. After browning the meat, I remove it from the pan and add a cup of wine to loosen the bits of meat left behind. In only a few seconds, the wine evaporates. But oh what wonderful depth of flavor it adds to that sauce!

Paul referred to himself as a drink offering. A drink offering was a portion of wine poured over an animal sacrifice. Unlike the animal, which left ash behind, the drink offering did not leave any residue behind. It was completely consumed. Yet it gave a sweet aroma to the offering. That aroma was the only thing left.

Paul spent his life consumed with helping people understand that Jesus' blood had been poured out like a drink offering so all could become children of God. Both Paul and Jesus left everything behind and poured out their lives before God as a sweet aroma for the sake of others.

May we offer ourselves up as drink offerings before God for the sake of others and become a sweet aroma to him.

> "I BELIEVE ALL PEOPLE ARE LOVED BY GOD AND NEED JESUS CHRIST AS THEIR SAVIOR."

COMPASSION

When you are harvesting in your field and you overlook a sheaf, do not go back to get it. Leave it for the foreigner, the fatherless and the widow.

DEUTERONOMY 24:19

The mother who watches her children playing with their toys and notices they are having trouble sharing takes the time to sit down and give them specific instructions about how to share and be kind.

We aren't much different from little children who need to learn how to behave and act in a loving manner. We are self-centered human beings who need rules spelled out. Our Father knows this and took the time to give us guidelines on how to live a life that honors him.

As simple an instruction as Deuteronomy 24:19 is, it suggests much about the denial of self when we choose to act compassionately. After all, if we don't pick up every sheaf, we might worry whether there will be enough for our families. An act of compassion may require making a personal sacrifice and taking a step of faith.

The compassion of Christ-followers today is just as important as the compassionate testimony of God's people in the Old Testament. As Jesus said, "Everyone will know that you are my disciples, if you love one another" (John 13:35). To whom will you extend compassion today, even if it costs you something?

> "I BELIEVE GOD CALLS ALL CHRISTIANS TO SHOW COMPASSION TO PEOPLE IN NEED."

DAY 71

STEWARDSHIP

There was food every day for Elijah and for the woman and her family. For the jar of flour was not used up and the jug of oil did not run dry.

1 KINGS 17:15–16

When Elijah met the widow, she was preparing to make her last meal. After that she would be out of ingredients and money, and she and her son would die. Nevertheless, Elijah asked her to make a small loaf of bread for him first and then one for herself and her son. What appeared to be the prophet's selfish and thoughtless request came with a promise from God: her flour and oil would "not run dry until the day the LORD sends rain on the land" (v. 14).

The woman had a decision to make. Would she believe this man, trust in the promise of the Lord, and share her remaining food, or would she hold tightly to the last few morsels for her and her son? The woman boldly entrusted all she had to the Lord.

Stewardship of anything calls for a step of faith. We wonder, *Will we have enough if we give some away—if we give food to strangers, money to the church, time to serve in a ministry, our will to God's guidance?*

Like the widow, take that step of faith and watch God provide.

> **"I BELIEVE EVERYTHING I AM AND EVERYTHING I OWN BELONG TO GOD."**

ETERNITY

The angel showed me the river of the water of life, as clear as crystal, flowing from the throne of God and of the Lamb down the middle of the great street of the city.

REVELATION 22:1–2

I could finally afford a lavish gift for my mom, who had sacrificed everything for my three siblings and me. Excited, I made reservations at an opulent hotel facing the beautiful Niagara Falls. But tragically, days before our scheduled departure, Mom passed away from pancreatic cancer. I missed getting to honor her with this special gift. I was devastated on so many levels.

Delving into God's Word seeking comfort, I read the passage above describing God's future kingdom with a grand river containing the water of life flowing from the very throne of God. Hmm! Surely this river will rival Niagara Falls.

As it turns out, our trip wasn't canceled; it was postponed. The upcoming trip will not be paid for by her son, but by the Son of God. We will not be staying in a hotel, but in a permanent residence prepared by Jesus. And we will be together not for days, but for all eternity.

I look forward to seeing you there. You'll find me by the river. Stop by. I want to introduce you to my mom.

"I BELIEVE THERE IS A HEAVEN AND A HELL AND THAT JESUS WILL RETURN TO JUDGE ALL PEOPLE AND TO ESTABLISH HIS ETERNAL KINGDOM."

DAY 73

GOD

Since the creation of the world God's invisible qualities—
his eternal power and divine nature—have been clearly
seen, being understood from what has been made, so that
people are without excuse.

ROMANS 1:20

One evening when my daughter's family spent the night at our house, my granddaughter asked her mother, "Mommy, will you wake me up in the *night morning* when Nona gets up?" My daughter and I were confused until I realized she had made up an oxymoron to describe when I get up, which is usually before the sun rises.

Oxymora and paradoxes are fun! They are words or phrases with opposite meanings put together: "jumbo shrimp," "virtual reality," "clearly confused," "busy doing nothing." Whether used in writing or speaking, they wake up your ears and make you think.

Paul gets our attention in a similar way in the verse above. If he were writing today, he might say God is "hidden in plain sight." While sin does not allow us to see God in all his glory now, God does want you to know him. His invisible qualities glare at you through creation. And not only does he want you to know him, he wants to be with you.

If you look, he's hidden in plain sight!

> **"I BELIEVE THE GOD OF THE BIBLE IS THE ONLY TRUE GOD—FATHER, SON, AND HOLY SPIRIT."**

PERSONAL GOD

> *Consider it pure joy, my brothers and sisters, whenever you face trials of many kinds, because you know that the testing of your faith produces perseverance.*

JAMES 1:2–3

Trials and joy—James offered a puzzling contrast here. And he said "trials of *many* kinds." It's a little scary, quite honestly, to know that we will face any number of trials in the course of our lives.

But whatever the challenge, God doesn't require us to be joyful because of the *trial*. Instead, we can experience joy because of what our heavenly Father is doing for us and within us, teaching us to depend on him and persevere because we know he loves us.

All of us have undoubtedly experienced many athletic, academic, business, relational, or financial challenges. As we look back, we can see that God blessed our perseverance by strengthening our faith and making us more like Christ, who pressed on through the trials of life, even to death, for us.

Is there a struggle in your life right now? Take time to reflect on previous trials in your life and how God got you through; remember how they built your perseverance and what lessons you learned. Trials offer us chances to grow and become more like the Savior. Any adversity you face will pale in comparison with the trial Jesus faced for you.

"I BELIEVE GOD IS INVOLVED IN AND CARES ABOUT MY DAILY LIFE."

SALVATION

*The LORD God made garments of skin for Adam and his
wife and clothed them.*

GENESIS 3:21

Imagine if Michelangelo were forced to shatter the *Pietà*, his masterpiece of Mary holding Jesus' limp, expired body, or if Handel was ordered to burn the first and only copy of his Hallelujah Chorus. What heartbreak for the creator to have to destroy one of his masterpieces by his own hand!

Yet that is what God did after Adam and Eve sinned. After cursing the serpent and explaining to the man and woman the consequences of their sin, God destroyed one of his masterpieces. An animal had to die to provide new clothes to protect Adam and Eve in the world they would be entering outside the garden.

This animal sacrifice—the shedding of blood in order to cover Adam and Eve's sin—foreshadowed God's plan for redemption: the blood of Another would have to be shed to cover the sins of humankind.

God allowed his beloved Son to be brutally beaten and crucified so that you would be able to live in his presence forever. But God did not consider that cost too high, for it would restore his relationship with yet another one of the masterpieces he created and loved—you!

> "I BELIEVE A PERSON COMES INTO A RIGHT
> RELATIONSHIP WITH GOD BY GOD'S GRACE
> THROUGH FAITH IN JESUS CHRIST."

THE BIBLE

The grass withers and the flowers fall, but the word of our God endures forever.

ISAIAH 40:8

As Isaiah rightly observes, "The grass withers and the flowers fall." Such is the transitory nature of creation. Seasons come and go, and change is part of life. But there are some changes we should guard against.

We rewrite history and write God out. We dismiss traditional values and label them repressive. We decide to be more "progressive" and accept same-sex marriage. We no longer base our actions on the truth of the Bible and think we can do whatever we want as long we as we are not "hurting" anyone.

Despite what the world says, God's eternal Word has not changed since the first scribes wrote it down—from the time Moses wrote Genesis to when John wrote Revelation to this very moment. Its historical accounts, theological teachings, values for life, and godly morality have remained the same age after age. It is, after all, the expression of our unchanging God!

Need a strong foundation for life? Thank God that you need look no further than his Word.

> **"I BELIEVE THE BIBLE IS THE WORD OF GOD AND HAS THE RIGHT TO COMMAND MY BELIEF AND ACTION."**

IDENTITY IN CHRIST

You are a chosen people, a royal priesthood, a holy nation, God's special possession, that you may declare the praises of him who called you out of darkness into his wonderful light.

1 PETER 2:9

We all have memories of when we were chosen—and when we were *not* chosen. Not picked until last to be on the kickball team. Not chosen to be in the high school play. Not accepted by your dream college. Not selected for the promised promotion. Not asked to be a spouse . . .

These experiences shape who we are and how we approach life. The experience of being chosen by God also shapes us in the same way. Peter described us as "a chosen people . . . a holy nation, God's special possession." What amazing grace to be chosen to recognize Jesus as God's Son and our Savior! What a privilege to be "holy," to be set apart to serve our God! And what an honor to be special to the King of kings!

The beautiful thing about God's kingdom is that all those who welcome Jesus as their Lord are given the opportunity to accept a new identity through him. Let the reality that you are chosen by God give you unshakable joy as you live each day secure in his love. Choose him in return!

"I BELIEVE I AM SIGNIFICANT BECAUSE OF MY POSITION AS A CHILD OF GOD."

> *When the sun had set and darkness had fallen, a smoking*
> *firepot with a blazing torch appeared and passed between*
> *the pieces [of a heifer, a goat, and a ram]. On that day*
> *the LORD made a covenant with Abram.*

GENESIS 15:17–18

Earlier in the day the childless Abram had asked God how his promise of heirs would be fulfilled. God directed Abram's gaze to the stars and said that through his "own flesh and blood" (v. 4), Abram would have heirs greater in number than the stars in the sky.

To confirm this promise, God made a covenant with Abram, the kind of covenant that was made between a king and a subject. Then, obeying God's instructions, Abram cut in two a heifer, a goat, and a ram. He arranged the pieces opposite each other and then fell asleep.

That's when God passed between the sacrificed animals, saying with his actions, "May I be torn apart like these animals if I fail to uphold my part of this covenant."[14]

What gracious condescension! The holy God initiated this covenant to reassure Abram of his faithfulness and begin a long and complicated relationship with the not-always-faithful nation of Israel. Praise God for remaining faithful to you and to his not-always-faithful church, his not-always-faithful people.

> **"I BELIEVE THE CHURCH IS GOD'S PRIMARY WAY**
> **TO ACCOMPLISH HIS PURPOSES ON EARTH."**

DAY 79

HUMANITY

"If you do what is right, will you not be accepted? But if you do not do what is right, sin is crouching at your door; it desires to have you, but you must rule over it."

GENESIS 4:7

Few of us can imagine killing someone. We don't plan on cheating on our spouse, embezzling funds from the company, abusing a child, or destroying someone's reputation with our words. Cain probably didn't see where his anger would take him, but God warned him that sin, like a wild animal, was crouched outside his door. He needed to slam the door on it. Instead, Cain cracked the door open by harboring his anger, and the beast burst in and took over.

The same sin nature evident in Cain is in each of us. Any one of us is capable of committing the most atrocious deeds. We must become keenly aware of sin crouching at our door. It's waiting to pounce on us and take control if we so much as open the door a crack with gossip, anger, envy, jealousy, fear, or bitterness in our hearts.

Slam the door in the face of sin by continually shutting down evil thoughts, which unchecked will cause terrible, sometimes irrevocable, consequences.

> **"I BELIEVE ALL PEOPLE ARE LOVED BY GOD AND NEED JESUS CHRIST AS THEIR SAVIOR."**

COMPASSION

*All have sinned and fall short of the glory of God, and all
are justified freely by his grace through the redemption that
came by Christ Jesus.*

ROMANS 3:23–24

When a plague hit the Roman Empire in the third century, killing countless people, many fled to escape the illness. Pagans
and doctors left, but Christians stayed to help the sick. People were
astounded by such compassion, and glorified the God of the Christians.

Throughout history God has graciously shown compassion for his
people, with the ultimate demonstration being the sacrifice of his Son.
When we were his enemies—sinful and deserving death—he put his
grand mercy on display. He sent Jesus to step in and take on our death
sentence. We, the guilty ones, are justified by the sacrificial death of
the only Person who was completely righteous.

You serve and are loved by a compassionate God, and you reflect
his nature when you show compassion to others. Come alongside
people who are suffering and suffer with them so they are not alone.
That doesn't have to mean we can fix the problem, but it does mean
we enter into their pain.

Who in your world today needs a touch of compassion from the
God of all compassion through you?

> "I BELIEVE GOD CALLS ALL CHRISTIANS TO
> SHOW COMPASSION TO PEOPLE IN NEED."

STEWARDSHIP

They exceeded our expectations: They gave themselves first of all to the Lord, and then by the will of God also to us.

2 CORINTHIANS 8:5

A five-year-old was given the opportunity to sit in "Big Church" with her parents for the first time. When the offering plate was passed, this little girl took hold of it and walked into the aisle, put the offering plate on the floor, and stepped into it. Embarrassed, her parents asked her under their breath, "What in the world are you doing?" She replied, "We learned in Sunday school that God wants us to offer ourselves to him."

To inspire the Corinthians to give an offering to the hurting believers in Jerusalem, Paul cited the example of the Macedonian believers. He didn't refer to them because they gave the most money. They didn't have as much as the people in Corinth. What moved Paul was that they gave of themselves first. They said to God and to the hurting people of Jerusalem, "We are all in. Besides our money, what else would be helpful to you?"

So don't just drop a few bucks in the offering plate the next time it comes by; place it on the floor and jump on in. You may get a few strange looks, but it will put a smile on the face of God.

> **"I BELIEVE EVERYTHING I AM AND EVERYTHING I OWN BELONG TO GOD."**

ETERNITY

Christ died for our sins . . . he was raised on the third day . . . he appeared to [Peter], and then to the Twelve.

1 CORINTHIANS 15:3–5

The tomb was empty! What had happened to Jesus' body?

The Jews' chief priests paid the soldiers who had been guarding the tomb to say that the disciples had stolen the body. If that was indeed what happened, would these soldiers not have lost their lives for failing at their assignment? Besides, are we really to believe that those not-so-brave disciples—who had fled after Jesus' arrest in Gethsemane and were in hiding after the crucifixion—suddenly mustered the courage to confront the Roman soldiers and steal Jesus' body?

Also, Paul reported that the resurrected Jesus appeared to Peter, to the disciples, "to more than five hundred of the brothers and sisters at the same time" (v. 6), and to Paul himself. Why did no one among those hundreds deny Paul's report of seeing the resurrected Jesus if it was a fabrication?

Jesus did indeed die and rise again, defeating death and bringing life to all of us who were dead in our sin! Be encouraged in your faith and be emboldened to share the gospel. Your resurrected Lord has opened the door to eternity.

> "I BELIEVE THERE IS A HEAVEN AND A HELL AND THAT JESUS WILL RETURN TO JUDGE ALL PEOPLE AND TO ESTABLISH HIS ETERNAL KINGDOM."

GOD

In the beginning God created the heavens and the earth.

GENESIS 1:1

Imagine God Almighty gazing at the blank canvas of what was soon to be the universe. The Artist has his tools ready—but instead of a palette, paint, and brushes, his tools are creativity, love, and joy.

He has a plan: first create the setting for the story of redemption that will play itself out through the ages. God forms the heavens and the earth, light and darkness, day and night, land and seas, plants and trees, the sun and the moon. More specifically, he makes galaxies, planets, the northern lights, sunrises, sunsets, the Grand Canyon, Kilimanjaro, the Pacific Ocean, Niagara Falls, sequoias, and orchids.

Then comes God's formation of blue whales and hummingbirds, the buffalo and the tarantula, the kangaroo and the platypus, sea otters and elk, man and woman. God fashions a myriad of somethings from absolutely nothing!

As nineteenth-century American clergyman Henry Ward Beecher said, "Every artist dips his brush in his own soul, and paints his own nature into his pictures." Indeed, you can see God's nature reflected in his creation. You can peek at parts of his very soul, his glory, power, majesty, creativity, and joy.

> **"I BELIEVE THE GOD OF THE BIBLE IS THE ONLY TRUE GOD—FATHER, SON, AND HOLY SPIRIT."**

PERSONAL GOD

Who shall separate us from the love of Christ? . . .
Neither death nor life, neither angels nor demons, . . .
nor anything else in all creation, will be able to separate us
from the love of God.

ROMANS 8:35, 38–39

We enjoy watching HGTV's *Tiny House Hunters*, which is a show about people searching for tiny homes, some of which are only one hundred square feet. These people want to simplify and enjoy life more. Great idea! It's fascinating to see the houses, but we have commented several times, "They must really love each other if they're going to live in those close quarters!" These couples will never be apart!

God your Father loves you so much he sent his Spirit not to live *with* you in a tiny house but to live *in* you. His Spirit indwells you, his follower, 24/7. That's even closer than a one-hundred-square-foot home. What overwhelming love!

Space between humans is a good thing. Our idiosyncrasies can drive another person crazy, and that person may leave us, either for a short time or permanently. That won't happen with God. He knows you, idiosyncrasies included, and he loves you anyway. He promises nothing "in all creation" can separate you from him. Absolutely nothing.

Soak in this promise! You'll enjoy life more!

"I BELIEVE GOD IS INVOLVED IN AND CARES ABOUT MY DAILY LIFE."

SALVATION

"The fire and wood are here," Isaac said, "but where is the lamb for the burnt offering?"

Abraham answered, "God himself will provide."

GENESIS 22:7–8

Really, God? Abraham and Sarah had waited twenty-five years for you to give them the son you had promised. (That's a long time for us humans!) They waited, and, yes, you came through. But then you asked Abraham to do the absolutely unimaginable. You asked him to kill his own son—his beloved and long-awaited son—and to offer him as a burnt offering. Really, God?

Years later, your people had waited centuries for the Messiah, the Promised One who would bring healing and redemption, and they had Jesus ministering among them for only three years. They waited, and, yes, you came through. But then you did the absolutely unimaginable. You allowed people to kill your own Son—your beloved and only Son. You gave up your Son—he yielded himself—as an offering for our sin. Really, God?

Yes, really, because I love you.

> **"I BELIEVE A PERSON COMES INTO A RIGHT RELATIONSHIP WITH GOD BY GOD'S GRACE THROUGH FAITH IN JESUS CHRIST."**

THE BIBLE

Take the helmet of salvation and the sword of the Spirit,
which is the word of God.

EPHESIANS 6:17

S words were the most common weapon in a king's army for centuries, but in this age of drones and air strikes we have lost the
richness of this metaphor. Eighteenth-century commentator Matthew
Henry helps us appreciate what this sword—God's Word—can do for a
believer. As for its sharpness, God's Word "cuts off ignorance from the
understanding, rebellion from the will, and enmity from the mind. . . .
The word will turn the inside of a sinner out, and let him see all that
is in his heart."[15]

Henry is telling us the Bible has the power to remove hatred,
supply understanding, and change our will. It has the ability to let us
see how we need to change from the inside out.

No wonder the apostle Paul charged believers to take up "the
sword of the Spirit, which is the word of God." Skill with the sword of
God's Word will help you become a more effective and powerful follower of King Jesus.

> **"I BELIEVE THE BIBLE IS THE WORD OF**
> **GOD AND HAS THE RIGHT TO COMMAND**
> **MY BELIEF AND ACTION."**

IDENTITY IN CHRIST

Blessed are those who are invited to the wedding supper of the Lamb!

REVELATION 19:9

Columbia University conducted research several years ago, attempting to discover why some kids join gangs and others don't. The most significant factor reported was that kids who avoided gangs shared dinner with their families at least five nights a week. Apparently, a family dinner satisfies an innate sense of belonging and gives children an identity that keeps them from seeking it in an unhealthy place. So strong is the desire to belong that even though most kids who join gangs know it is extremely dangerous, they are willing to put their lives on the line rather than risk losing that sense of belonging they crave.[16]

There's no doubt God created us with a "connection requirement." From the very beginning God said, "It is not good for the man to be alone" (Genesis 2:18). When we accept Jesus' gift of salvation, we gain a new identity—children of God.

Jesus wants to satisfy your "connection requirement." He wants you to know you have a seat at his Father's table in the new kingdom. Until that ultimate, heavenly dinner, hang out with the other children of God. Let them help to form your new identity.

Don't risk your eternal life; accept your seat at God's table.

> **"I BELIEVE I AM SIGNIFICANT BECAUSE OF MY POSITION AS A CHILD OF GOD."**

I appeal to you, brothers and sisters, . . . that all of you agree with one another in what you say and that there be no divisions among you.

1 CORINTHIANS 1:10

Have you ever put your face into a headless frame painted to represent a muscle man, a clown, or even a bathing beauty? Maybe you had your picture taken this way. These photos are humorous because the head doesn't fit the body. If we could picture Christ as the head of our local body of believers, would the world laugh? Or would they stand in awe of a human body so closely related to a divine head?[17]

Paul reminded the church at Corinth that God was not pleased with the divisions among them. They were bickering and fighting among themselves, which was not good for a watching public that was supposed to look at them and experience Jesus' love.

The church today could use a similar reminder. We should put aside our differences (personal and denominational) and unite in showing a desperate world that Jesus is the only way to have a relationship with God. After all, "the church is the only cooperative society in the world that exists for the benefit of its non-members."[18]

Let's create a compelling picture of the body of Christ that Jesus will be proud to put his head on.

"I BELIEVE THE CHURCH IS GOD'S PRIMARY WAY TO ACCOMPLISH HIS PURPOSES ON EARTH."

DAY 89

HUMANITY

The LORD said to Cain, "Where is your brother Abel?"
"I don't know," he replied. "Am I my brother's keeper?"

Why was God not pleased with Cain's offering? Most scholars think his heart attitude was not right, and what Genesis 4 shows us supports that theory. Cain's murder of his brother is horrific, but then he lies about not knowing Abel's fate; his "Am I my brother's keeper?" drips with disrespect. And Cain was talking to his Creator, the Holy One, the Almighty!

But before we cast the first stone, we should ask ourselves how we are like Cain. Jesus taught that if we are angry with someone, we are subject to judgment just as if we had murdered that person (Matthew 5:21–22). When have we said, "I don't know" when in fact we did know? And when have we not treated our brother the way we would have wanted to be treated?

We all are infected by the effects of sin, and we all need Jesus Christ as our Savior. Examine the condition of your heart today and ask the Lord to show you where you are dishonoring him.

> **"I BELIEVE ALL PEOPLE ARE LOVED BY GOD AND NEED JESUS CHRIST AS THEIR SAVIOR."**

COMPASSION

Everyone should be quick to listen, slow to speak and slow to become angry.

JAMES 1:19

You've probably seen those rustic plaques that list family rules like "Clean up after yourself," "Laugh a lot," "Say please and thank you," "No whining," or "Love each other always."

James offered members of God's family some rules as well: "Be quick to listen." We need to be willing to take the time to truly hear someone's heart. Be "slow to speak." We should—as Mom always said—"think before we talk." Be "slow to become angry." Remember when you were told to count to ten before reacting with angry words or actions? Living according to these rules for God's family makes a difference in the lives of those we are called to love.

Here are some other how-tos from James: "Religion that God our Father accepts as pure and faultless is this: to look after orphans and widows in their distress and to keep oneself from being polluted by the world" (1:27). "If you really . . . 'Love your neighbor as yourself,' you are doing right" (2:8). "If [you say], 'Go in peace; keep warm and well fed,' but [do] nothing about their physical needs, what good is it?" (2:16).

Be alert to ways you can practice the kind of compassion your heavenly Father and his Son have shown you.

> **"I BELIEVE GOD CALLS ALL CHRISTIANS TO SHOW COMPASSION TO PEOPLE IN NEED."**

STEWARDSHIP

"The man who had received one bag of gold came. 'Master,' he said, 'I knew that you are a hard man, harvesting where you have not sown and gathering where you have not scattered seed. So I was afraid and went out and hid your gold in the ground. See, here is what belongs to you.'

His master replied, 'You wicked, lazy servant!'"

MATTHEW 25:24–26

An artist reflecting back on her lackluster career reported that her failure to succeed was due to fear. She feared the risk of committing herself completely to her art and of sacrificing in the short term to achieve the long-term goal of success. She had reasoned, *If I risk and it does not turn out, then all the effort is wasted.* So she played it safe.

We all know that where there is no sacrifice, there is no success; where there is no risk, there is no reward. The lazy servant in this verse played it safe just like the artist. They both suffered the loss of what might have been had they only ignored their fears and risked.

Use your gifts and talents for the Lord. He will give you the strength and courage to live boldly for him. Nothing you do in his name will ever be in vain, and it will always be worth the risk.

"I BELIEVE EVERYTHING I AM AND EVERYTHING I OWN BELONG TO GOD."

*[God] will wipe every tear from their eyes. There will be
no more death or mourning or crying or pain.*

REVELATION 21:4

How many homes have you lived in? Were you a military child who never lived in a house for very long? Or are you still living in the house you grew up in? Maybe you moved a few times; maybe just once. Were those relocations exciting or traumatic? Whenever you moved, however many times, you probably longed for the day the new house felt like a home.

How at home do you feel on earth? We should appreciate the natural beauty God created, the relationships he has blessed us with, and the material things he has given us. More than likely, though, you have also had moments of restlessness when you feel unsettled and you aren't exactly sure why. One possibility is set forth by the writer of Hebrews: "Here we do not have an enduring city, but we are looking for the city that is to come" (13:14). In other words, our real home is heaven.

In your new home, God promises no more death or crying or pain. As you enjoy the home you are settled in now, just think how much better your new home in the presence of Jesus will be. You'll feel at home immediately!

"I BELIEVE THERE IS A HEAVEN AND A HELL AND THAT JESUS WILL RETURN TO JUDGE ALL PEOPLE AND TO ESTABLISH HIS ETERNAL KINGDOM."

DAY 93

GOD

Joshua made a covenant for the people . . . he reaffirmed for them decrees and laws. . . . Then he took a large stone and set it up there under the oak near the holy place of the LORD.

JOSHUA 24:25–26

When God has just done something amazing for us, we can be completely sincere in recommitting our lives to him. We vow to change a behavior or attitude, to become a more faithful student of the Bible or person of prayer, and to walk a different path than the one we've been on. Our spirit may be willing to make that change for the better, but our flesh is often weak. As time goes by, we may simply forget either his goodness or our commitment.

Aware of this tendency, Joshua "took a large stone and set it up" in a place where the people would see it and remember their covenant with their merciful and gracious God. He said, "This stone will be a witness against us. . . . It will be a witness against you if you are untrue to your God" (v. 27).

Nothing in your life is more important than your relationship with the almighty God. What will you use to remind yourself of God's faithfulness and encourage your faithfulness to him?

"I BELIEVE THE GOD OF THE BIBLE IS THE ONLY TRUE GOD—FATHER, SON, AND HOLY SPIRIT."

PERSONAL GOD

What great love the Father has lavished on us, that we should be called children of God! And that is what we are!

1 JOHN 3:1

Jason had many doubts and questions about God. His best friend had been killed in a freak accident, and his parents got divorced. He wondered, *How can I trust God and his love if he allows these things to happen?* These doubts and questions kept him from God until he experienced the birth of his first child.

As Jason held his newborn son in his arms for the first time, he was overcome with unexpected emotion. He looked into the face of his child and said, "Son, you have no idea how much I love you. I would give my life for you right now if I had to."

In that moment, a question suddenly came to his mind: *Could God feel about me the way I feel about my child? Could God possibly love me this much?* Jason then became a child of God.

Your heavenly Father is looking at you now, saying, "You have no idea how much I love you." Life will not always make sense, and tragic events will occur, but you can rest, knowing God has a good plan for your life. Trust him. He gave his life for you.

"I BELIEVE GOD IS INVOLVED IN AND CARES ABOUT MY DAILY LIFE."

SALVATION

Everyone who believes that Jesus is the Christ is born of God.

1 JOHN 5:1

Twelve men met for their weekly morning Bible study. Upon reading the verse above, a man named Chuck declared, "I want that! How do I get it?"

Steve, one of the other men, answered, "Chuck, it is really simple. Jesus says it is all yours if you believe in him."

Chuck asked, "What does it mean to believe?"

Sitting on the table between the men was a glass of orange juice. Steve explained, "There's a difference between believing *about* that glass of juice and believing *in* it. You believe it exists, but until you accept it into your body, it can't nourish you or help you."

Then Steve picked up the glass of juice and took a big gulp. "Now the juice can do something for my body it could never do while just sitting there on the table. Believing in Christ is not only to believe he exists but to commit to take him in." Chuck was quiet for a moment and then, slapping the table, declared, "I believe! I do believe!"

Have you believed *about* Christ or believed *in* Christ? There's an eternal difference!

> **"I BELIEVE A PERSON COMES INTO A RIGHT RELATIONSHIP WITH GOD BY GOD'S GRACE THROUGH FAITH IN JESUS CHRIST."**

THE BIBLE

His divine power has given us everything we need for a godly life through our knowledge of him.

2 PETER 1:3

By simply looking at the natural world around us, we can conclude there is a God. (The towering mountains and vast oceans cry out the existence of an awesome Creator.) But how do we learn *about* God, about his plans and purposes for us, about the principles he wants us to live by? We learn these things and much more in God's revelation to us: his written Word, the Bible.

The apostle Peter stated that God has provided us with "everything we need for a godly life through our knowledge of him." The Bible offers us knowledge of God, and also knowledge of ourselves. Through it we learn that we are sinners in need of a Savior so we can be forgiven for our sin. We learn the extent of his love for us and his immense desire to be in relationship with us. And we can be empowered to lead a godly life.

Knowledge of God, the Bible reveals, leads to his "grace and peace . . . in abundance" (v. 2). Commit to spending time in his Word today, and marvel at your loving Father who gave you all you need to know and follow him.

> **"I BELIEVE THE BIBLE IS THE WORD OF GOD AND HAS THE RIGHT TO COMMAND MY BELIEF AND ACTION."**

DAY 97

IDENTITY IN CHRIST

I have been crucified with Christ and I no longer live, but Christ lives in me.

GALATIANS 2:20

The Legend of Bagger Vance is a story about a golf prodigy named Junah who returns from World War I wounded and broken-down, and is asked to play in an exhibition match against golf superstars Walter Hagen and Bobby Jones. Bagger Vance, the Christ figure in the story, mystically appears to caddie for Junah.

Bagger helps Junah rediscover not only his authentic swing but, more importantly, his authentic self. At one point in the story, Bagger says to Junah, "He [the golfer] comes to realize that the game is not against the foe, but against himself. His little self. That yammering fearful ever-resistant self that freezes, chokes, tops, nobbles, shanks, skulls, duffs, flubs. This is the self we must defeat."[19]

Christ came to defeat our insecure, self-promoting, envying, lusting, never-satisfied, greedy, false self. How is it defeated? By being crucified with Christ and buried with him so that you can be raised with Christ who now lives in you to transform you into his image.

Bagger helped Junah find his authentic self to play his authentic game. Christ restores your authentic self to live your God-created identity.

> **"I BELIEVE I AM SIGNIFICANT BECAUSE OF MY POSITION AS A CHILD OF GOD."**

CHURCH

Just as a body, though one, has many parts, but all its many parts form one body, so it is with Christ.

1 CORINTHIANS 12:12

It is estimated that the average human body consists of about a hundred trillion individual cells, which have different forms and functions. But what is it that causes all the individual cells to work together for the common good of the body? The answer is locked away in a strand of DNA in each cell. On each strand of DNA in each cell is the genetic code containing enough information (it is estimated) to fill a thousand, six-hundred-page books. Each cell receives its individual instructions from its indwelling DNA, and thus all cells work together for the good of the whole body. Each cell finds its sense of belonging, identity, meaning, and purpose from its membership in the body.[20]

The analogy is profound, isn't it? Each of us is a valued member of the body of Christ indwelled by Jesus' Spirit who is our spiritual DNA—Divine Nature from Above. You no longer have to question who you are or why you are here. You find your sense of belonging, identity, meaning, and purpose as a member of Christ's body, his church.

"I BELIEVE THE CHURCH IS GOD'S PRIMARY WAY TO ACCOMPLISH HIS PURPOSES ON EARTH."

DAY 99

HUMANITY

Jesus declared, "I am the bread of life. Whoever comes to me will never go hungry, and whoever believes in me will never be thirsty. . . . I am the living bread that came down from heaven. Whoever eats this bread will live forever."

JOHN 6:35, 51

Our ordinary, daily lives are filled with living illustrations of the most profound spiritual truths. For instance, consider your most recent meal. You *chose* what you would eat. You brought the bite of food to your mouth, you put it into your mouth, you chewed the food, and then you swallowed it. That food is now in your body, and whether it will do something healthy or unhealthy depends on what you *chose* to eat. Your will, informed by your mind, was active in the whole process. So it is with our spiritual lives. Biblical believing is an act of the will in response to God's offer in Jesus.

Did you notice that Jesus equates believing in him with ingesting him? Will you by an act of your will unconditionally receive Christ to nourish your God-hungry, God-thirsty soul? Jesus invites you to choose him. This is not a one-time act but a way of life, a daily act of choosing, so that you might be truly alive with Christ and live with him forever.

> **"I BELIEVE ALL PEOPLE ARE LOVED BY GOD AND NEED JESUS CHRIST AS THEIR SAVIOR."**

COMPASSION

If you really keep the royal law found in Scripture, "Love your neighbor as yourself," you are doing right.

JAMES 2:8

Adele Gaboury's neighbors were very attentive. When her front lawn became overgrown, they mowed it for her. When her pipes burst, they had the water turned off. When the mailbox was full to overflowing, they called the police. The only thing they didn't do was knock on her front door to see if she was alive. She wasn't.

When authorities found Adele's skeletal remains, they discovered the seventy-three-year-old woman had been dead for possibly as long as four years.

Do you stare at an overgrown yard in your neighborhood and think, *They should take care of that?* Perhaps you are like Adele's neighbors and you address the surface problem, but never knock on the door to get to know the person.

Behind every front door is a story waiting to be shared with a caring neighbor. Perhaps those living around you are lonely or depressed; maybe one neighbor is a single mom or dad struggling to get everything done. Maybe the person hoping or needing you to reach out will be your new best friend.

Why don't you take the time to walk over and knock?

"I BELIEVE GOD CALLS ALL CHRISTIANS TO SHOW COMPASSION TO PEOPLE IN NEED."

DAY 101

STEWARDSHIP

"I have no need of a bull from your stall or of goats from your pens, for every animal of the forest is mine, and the cattle on a thousand hills."

PSALM 50:9–10

If God sounds angry in those verses, it's because he was. Oh, he saw his people's offerings to him, but he also saw their hearts. Yes, they were doing what he had told them to do, but he knew all too well that they were only going through the motions. Often the Israelites offered sacrifices, but only out of habit; then they lived however they wanted. No sincere thanksgiving motivated their actions before, during, or after they performed the sacrifice.

We can be guilty of the same today. Are we merely going through the motions when we go to church on Sunday and then ignoring God's commands for how we are to live the rest of the week? Are we obeying God's commands and living in a way that honors him? God wants our devotion and complete adoration, not our recited prayers and empty gestures.

Because everything you have belongs to God, you are to live with gratitude and in obedience to him. Praise him with your whole heart and live your life in a way that reflects your understanding of the awesome gifts God has entrusted you with.

> **"I BELIEVE EVERYTHING I AM AND EVERYTHING I OWN BELONG TO GOD."**

102

ETERNITY

*You ought to live holy and godly lives as you look
forward to the day of God. . . . Make every effort to be
found spotless, blameless and at peace with him.*

2 PETER 3:11–12, 14

Maybe you've heard this cynical comment about Christians: "They're so heavenly minded that they're no earthly good." Is it possible, though, to be too heavenly minded?

Consider the positive impact that heavenly minded followers of Christ have had on the world. Through the centuries, Christians have stood for human rights, campaigned for basic freedoms, influenced America's constitutional government, cared for society's needy and outcast, started schools, built hospitals, protected the unborn, established orphanages, inspired the arts, and encouraged science by maintaining that rational truth can be discovered because a rational God exists. Christianity continues to impact our society in positive ways today.

Clearly, even this partial overview of both past and present-day activity supports what C. S. Lewis wrote in *Mere Christianity*: "If you read history you will find that the Christians who did most for the present world were precisely those who thought most of the next."[21]

Makes you want to get your head in the heavenly clouds, doesn't it?

> **"I BELIEVE THERE IS A HEAVEN AND A HELL AND THAT JESUS WILL RETURN TO JUDGE ALL PEOPLE AND TO ESTABLISH HIS ETERNAL KINGDOM."**

GOD

Every good and perfect gift is from above, coming down from the Father.

JAMES 1:17

I remember as a teenager the first time I had dinner with one family from the church I had recently begun attending. It happened without warning. Everyone bowed their heads, and the father prayed. With genuine simplicity, he thanked God for the food. I had been raised in an unchurched home, so this was a new experience for me. In my home, we understood our dad was the sole provider of the food. What made this moment even stranger was the humble man praying owned a grocery store. This seemed so unusual that I decided to peek. All four children and the wife still had their heads bowed, and they were nodding and smiling in agreement. They appeared grateful for the man praying, and even more grateful for the God he was praying to.

Smitten by this encounter, I whispered my own prayer: "God, if I get married and have children, I want to be like this man." I decided the best way to pull this off was to marry his oldest daughter. We've been married for over thirty years and have raised four children. Every evening I assume the honor of acknowledging the God behind all our blessings.

Do you acknowledge the God who provides every good gift you have in your life?

"I BELIEVE THE GOD OF THE BIBLE IS THE ONLY TRUE GOD—FATHER, SON, AND HOLY SPIRIT."

PERSONAL GOD

You created my inmost being; you knit me together in my mother's womb. I praise you because I am fearfully and wonderfully made. . . . Your eyes saw my unformed body; all the days ordained for me were written in your book before one of them came to be.

PSALM 139:13–14, 16

Have you ever wondered why a husband and wife desire to have children? After all, children take up a lot of time, energy, and money with no guarantees of how they will turn out, or if they will appreciate all the sacrifice and effort spent to raise and love them.

So why do we long to have children? Could it be the same reason that God—Father, Son, and Spirit—created us? Could it be that a husband and wife, like the Trinity, are not content to have only each other to love, but want to have children to love and care for?

This points you to a great truth about God. God created each of us because he loves us and wants a relationship with us, even knowing we may not choose him or appreciate all he did and does for us.

Every part of your being was intimately and carefully crafted, and every moment of your life planned and ordained. He loves you like a good parent. Will you choose him?

> **"I BELIEVE GOD IS INVOLVED IN AND CARES ABOUT MY DAILY LIFE."**

SALVATION

He was pierced for our transgressions, he was crushed for our iniquities; the punishment that brought us peace was on him, and by his wounds we are healed.

ISAIAH 53:5

When we enjoy a meal of steak, chicken, or fish, our bodies are nourished. But how often do we stop to think about the living thing that died in order for us to live? And how unfortunate it would be if the sacrifice was placed in front of us, but we never ate it to receive the gift of life it provides.

Because of sin, you deserve to die. But God loves you and wants a relationship with you, so something, or rather Someone, had to die in your place in order for that to happen. Not just anyone, but a perfect sacrifice, so that you could be reunited with a perfect God. Jesus' blood, shed to cover your sins, allows you to have a relationship with God and gives you the gift of eternal life if you will only receive him. Don't ignore the offering he has set before you.

For you to live eternally, Someone had to die. Receive the precious gift of Jesus' sacrifice for you today.

"I BELIEVE A PERSON COMES INTO A RIGHT RELATIONSHIP WITH GOD BY GOD'S GRACE THROUGH FAITH IN JESUS CHRIST."

THE BIBLE

"I am the God of your father, the God of Abraham, the God of Isaac and the God of Jacob."

EXODUS 3:6

The Bible repeatedly records that God revealed himself to his people, sometimes audibly and sometimes through dreams or visions. He loves people and wants them to know him.

While tending his father-in-law's flock, Moses noticed a burning bush and heard his name being called. Having captured Moses' attention, God introduced himself and told Moses the plan to rescue his people, who had been trapped in slavery for more than four hundred years.

God gave Moses a key role in this divine rescue mission. When Moses asked God how he was going to explain to the people God had sent him, God replied, "This is what you are to say to the Israelites: 'I AM has sent me to you'" (v. 14). God was going to make himself known in a mighty way to the Hebrews, and to Pharaoh as well.

God still loves people and wants to introduce himself. He doesn't seem to be using burning bushes anymore. Mostly he uses his Word, the Bible. The God of Abraham, Isaac, Jacob, and Moses wants you to know him. He longs to make your acquaintance through what he says in his Word, and to mightily rescue you from a life of slavery to sin.

> **"I BELIEVE THE BIBLE IS THE WORD OF GOD AND HAS THE RIGHT TO COMMAND MY BELIEF AND ACTION."**

IDENTITY IN CHRIST

If the Spirit of him who raised Jesus from the dead is living in you, he who raised Christ from the dead will also give life to your mortal bodies because of his Spirit who lives in you.

ROMANS 8:11

There are only two ways to live: performance-based identity or identity-based performance. The first is a treadmill for the weary whose formula in life is "my performance plus what others think of me equals who I am." These people live under the heavy burden of pleasing the world and trying to be good enough. How exhausting!

The other philosophy for life is "my performance is an expression of my relationship with the indwelling Spirit of God." For those who live this way, their lives and actions reflect their faith in Christ and the Spirit of God within them. They are released from the need to please the world and can rest in the peace of belonging to a heavenly Father who loves them, not for what they do, but because they are his children.

Jesus lived his life as an expression of his relationship with his Father. He calls you to do the same. When you do this, you can declare, "I am free to be who I am in Christ, as I allow Christ to be himself in me. This is my true identity."

> "I BELIEVE I AM SIGNIFICANT BECAUSE OF MY POSITION AS A CHILD OF GOD."

CHURCH

> *God placed all things under his feet and appointed him to be head over everything for the church, which is his body, the fullness of him who fills everything in every way.*

EPHESIANS 1:22–23

One of the many casualties of the German bombings in England during World War II was a large statue of Jesus with his arms outstretched. Its inscription read "Come unto Me." A group of students were able to restore the beautiful statue, but the hands had been demolished. The students debated whether they should try to reshape Christ's hands, but in the end they chose not to repair them. The inscription now reads, "Christ has no hands but ours."

Jesus said to his disciples, "As the Father has sent me, I am sending you" (John 20:21). We are the body of Christ. Our high calling is to make the invisible God visible through our very human but Christ-indwelt lives. We are to be his loving hands to a hurting and frightened world. May we reach out to all who are suffering and show the world his love. Ask the Lord to show you who needs his healing touch today.

> **"I BELIEVE THE CHURCH IS GOD'S PRIMARY WAY TO ACCOMPLISH HIS PURPOSES ON EARTH."**

HUMANITY

*As for you, you were dead in your transgressions and sins,
in which you used to live when you followed the ways of this
world. . . . But because of his great love for us, God, who is
rich in mercy, made us alive with Christ.*

EPHESIANS 2:1–2, 4–5

If you enter through security at an airport in Argentina, you will see a sign that has big red letters saying *SIN*. Beside the word are pictures of different objects such as sunglasses, wallets, and belts. The sign is telling all passengers they must pass through the security checkpoint but *sin*, meaning "without," any of these objects. To enter into a relationship with God, we need to be without sin—or, *SIN* sin.

Paul tells us that because of our sins we are spiritually dead without God. "For the wages of sin is death," as Paul put it in Romans 6:23. Trying to have a relationship with God as a sinful human is like trying to get through security at the airport with forbidden contraband. But, thank God, Paul goes on to finish his statement in Romans with: "but the gift of God is eternal life in Christ Jesus our Lord."

Christ came to make it possible for you to become alive through God indwelling your life. Your sins are forgiven through Jesus' death. If you accept his free gift, you can now enter into this relationship because he sees you as *SIN* sin.

> **"I BELIEVE ALL PEOPLE ARE LOVED BY GOD
> AND NEED JESUS CHRIST AS THEIR SAVIOR."**

COMPASSION

When they cried out to you again, you heard from heaven, and in your compassion you delivered them time after time.

NEHEMIAH 9:28

Throughout their history, the Israelites struggled to stay true to God. Sometimes they followed God, but after those periods of faithfulness came times of sin and rebellion. The pattern was evident. Israel followed God. Israel turned from God; God sent enemies. Israel repented and cried for help; God rescued. Israel followed God. Israel turned from God; God sent enemies. Israel cried for help; God rescued. Israel followed God . . . Israel turned from God . . . Does this pattern sound familiar in our own lives?

No matter how often Israel "did what was evil in [his] sight," prompting the Lord to "[abandon] them to the hand of their enemies," he responded with compassion whenever they cried out to him (v. 28). The God who calls you to show compassion is not asking you to do anything he himself hasn't done since history began. God showed compassion to Israel again and again, and he shows you that same compassion again and again.

He asks us to show compassion to others who may offend us over and over—even though it is hard for us! He knows exactly how hard it is.

> **"I BELIEVE GOD CALLS ALL CHRISTIANS TO SHOW COMPASSION TO PEOPLE IN NEED."**

STEWARDSHIP

"Be fruitful and increase in number; fill the earth and subdue it. Rule over the fish in the sea and the birds in the sky and over every living creature that moves on the ground."

GENESIS 1:28

If you're a parent, think back to the first time you left your newborn in someone else's care. Maybe it was Grandma while you ran to the grocery store or a worker at church while you worshipped. It can be hard to relinquish someone as precious as your baby to another's safekeeping.

God created a very intricate, amazing, and good world, and he has entrusted its care to humankind. I wonder if it was hard for him to relinquish its care to a people who can be so careless. We are to be respectful and diligent stewards of his exquisite design and the creatures that are a part of it. That is our responsibility, and it is a great honor as well as a huge job!

But, as the adage goes, many hands make light work. Caring for the Lord's creation is a job all of us are to be involved in. Does that make using energy-efficient lightbulbs and minimizing the use of your car more meaningful—even redemptive? Doing your part to be respectful of God's creation is one way you honor your Creator God.

> **"I BELIEVE EVERYTHING I AM AND EVERYTHING I OWN BELONG TO GOD."**

ETERNITY

> *We fix our eyes not on what is seen, but on what is unseen, since what is seen is temporary, but what is unseen is eternal.*

2 CORINTHIANS 4:18

We see in our children that their limited perspective intensifies life's painful disappointments. The birthday party invitation that didn't come, the prom date that never materialized, the college acceptance letter that never came—these moments are extremely painful. Yet we know, in the grand scheme of things, a missed birthday party and prom will fade into relative unimportance. We know that God's sovereign plan is better than our first choice for college.

Just as age gives us perspective on our children's disappointments, we need to let the hope of eternity give us perspective on ours. The hurts we experience, the struggles we suffer, the losses that were unfair and painful can consume our joy and hope. Yet, in the verse just before the one above, Paul maintained that "our light and momentary troubles are achieving for us an eternal glory that far outweighs them all."

Admit that your limited perspective intensifies life's disappointments. Fix your eyes on the hope of an eternity with your Father who sees the beginning from the end and loves you with an everlasting love.

"I BELIEVE THERE IS A HEAVEN AND A HELL AND THAT JESUS WILL RETURN TO JUDGE ALL PEOPLE AND TO ESTABLISH HIS ETERNAL KINGDOM."

SALVATION

We all, like sheep, have gone astray, each of us has turned to our own way; and the LORD has laid on him the iniquity of us all.

ISAIAH 53:6

Have you ever crossed a line in life you thought you would never cross? A professional golfer did the one thing he thought he would never do: he cheated in a tournament by kicking his golf ball back in bounds to avoid a penalty. The moment he cheated he was overcome with guilt and shame. After thirty years of crossing all other kinds of lines, it was only in this moment of blatant cheating that he finally saw his true nature. He acknowledged that he was capable of doing almost anything if he would cheat at the game he loved most in the world.

We have all gone astray. We have all made choices we never thought we'd make. We have given in to the sinful nature we all have inside us that leads us away from God. Thankfully, God in his great mercy provided us, his sheep, a way back to him through his Son, Christ Jesus, who bore our sins so that we might be forgiven and healed. Without him we are all capable of just about any sinful action.

Have you accepted God's offer of salvation through Jesus, his Son? He is waiting for you to cross *that* line.

> "I BELIEVE A PERSON COMES INTO A RIGHT RELATIONSHIP WITH GOD BY GOD'S GRACE THROUGH FAITH IN JESUS CHRIST."

PERSONAL GOD

> *"I know the plans I have for you,"* declares the LORD,
> *"plans to prosper you and not to harm you, plans to give*
> *you hope and a future."*

JEREMIAH 29:11

How many times do we disobey God, turn away from his wisdom and make a mess of our lives, and then reap the consequences of not following God's truth?

The kingdom of Judah had done just this. The prophet Jeremiah warned them about the Lord's pending discipline for their unfaithfulness, but they ignored him, and the Babylonians attacked Jerusalem and carried some of the people off to captivity. God told Jeremiah to write a letter to those exiles to remind them that God had an awesome plan for their lives and one day he would restore them to their homeland.

Did the exiles receive this message with relief or skepticism? Were they willing or afraid to hope in these words? What about you? What situations are you facing because of your own or another's unfaithfulness? Do you hear Jeremiah 29:11 with joy or unbelief? Are you willing or afraid to hope in the promise that God's good plan will prevail?

Let God's faithfulness in fulfilling his promises to Judah, and his promise-keeping through the ages, encourage you to hope in his promise to restore you, in his time.

> **"I BELIEVE GOD IS INVOLVED IN AND**
> **CARES ABOUT MY DAILY LIFE."**

DAY 115

IDENTITY IN CHRIST

The law of the Spirit who gives life has set you free from the law of sin and death.

Pick up any object and let it go. The inexorable law of gravity will cause the object to fall. Try it again, except this time as the object falls, catch it with your other hand and lift it high. The law of gravity was just overpowered by a stronger force. Paul wrote that the divinely powerful law of the Spirit of God within us is more powerful than the ever-persistent law of sin and death.

Are you struggling with the law of sin and death in some area of your life? Do you suffer defeat time and time again? Paul was feeling frustrated, too, when he cried out, "What a wretched man I am! Who will rescue me . . . ? Thanks be to God, who delivers me through Jesus Christ our Lord!" (Romans 7:24–25). Paul knew that as a child of God he had access to the awesome power of God.

When you feel the strength of temptation and the downward pull of sin and death, humbly yield to the Spirit of God within you, which you received when you became his child. As you do, you'll be giving yourself over to a stronger force than that which tempts you.

> **"I BELIEVE I AM SIGNIFICANT BECAUSE OF MY POSITION AS A CHILD OF GOD."**

CHURCH

The wedding of the Lamb has come, and his bride has made herself ready.

REVELATION 19:7

What a beautiful picture of the church John gives us here. He describes believers collectively as the bride of Christ who will be presented to Jesus when the new kingdom is established. Like an earthly bride, we should be preparing ourselves as we wait for the big day.

An earthly bride "makes herself ready" by choosing her gown, planning her hairstyle, and perhaps getting herself in shape physically. Her desire is to be as beautiful as she can when she presents herself to her groom. In Bible times, she also brought a dowry, a gift for him.

Instead of physically preparing ourselves, we, the bride of Christ, should be spiritually adorning ourselves with beautiful character that honors and glorifies our groom. The pursuit of godly character should fill our days.

Our dowry to Jesus will be those we have brought into the new kingdom through sharing our faith.

Many grooms are overwhelmed with joy as they see their brides finally coming down the aisle to stand at their side. Imagine Jesus as he sees his beautiful bride, the church, coming to be by his side forever! He's waited a long time!

> **"I BELIEVE THE CHURCH IS GOD'S PRIMARY WAY TO ACCOMPLISH HIS PURPOSES ON EARTH."**

HUMANITY

God said, "I give you every seed-bearing plant on the face of the whole earth and every tree that has fruit with seed in it. They will be yours for food."

GENESIS 1:29

We want it all. Just one more thing, one more promotion, and then we will be happy. But will we ever be truly content?

God gave Adam and Eve everything there was in the world. They had dominion over all the creatures and could use the rest of his creation as they pleased. Other than one tree, which he asked them not to eat from, everything was theirs to enjoy. That tree offered them a choice, the choice to love God or not. To obey or not. But they wanted it all. Wanting the one thing they shouldn't have wanted ended up robbing them of the only thing they truly needed: a relationship with God.

What will you pursue next? Genuine satisfaction comes only through a relationship with God. Everything is given to you through Jesus Christ. The only thing you need to pursue is a relationship with him, and your contentment is sure for all eternity.

> **"I BELIEVE ALL PEOPLE ARE LOVED BY GOD AND NEED JESUS CHRIST AS THEIR SAVIOR."**

SALVATION

If, while we were God's enemies, we were reconciled to him through the death of his Son, how much more, having been reconciled, shall we be saved through his life!

ROMANS 5:10

What does salvation mean to you? Is it just about being saved from hell and getting to be with God forever? Yes, salvation does change our eternal destination, but Paul informs us that our sins are forgiven through Christ's death so that we might be reconciled to God and saved through his life.

Paul would have us know that the result of saving faith in Christ's life and death is having the God of the universe indwelling our lives, making us brand-new, born-again children of God.

If we think of salvation primarily as a ticket to heaven, we will miss the blessings God offers us in this life: unconditional love and acceptance, the power of his Spirit living in us, his peace that surpasses all understanding, plus so much more. When we accept Christ and become his, we are indwelled with the Spirit of God, who enriches our lives and gives us the passion to make his love known to the world.

Don't give up the life Christ offers you now by just getting a ticket to secure eternal life. Live the life Jesus died to give you now!

> "I BELIEVE A PERSON COMES INTO A RIGHT RELATIONSHIP WITH GOD BY GOD'S GRACE THROUGH FAITH IN JESUS CHRIST."

DAY 119

IDENTITY IN CHRIST

"No longer will you be called Abram; your name will be Abraham."

GENESIS 17:5

In Bible times, a person's name was more than simply a reference to one's family or a way to identify someone; typically, the chosen name characterized something about the person. In the Old Testament, for instance, we find that Esau's name, which means "hairy," was a trait significant in his life story (Genesis 27:11–23), and in the New Testament, Barnabas's name, which means "son of encouragement," reflected an important aspect of his character (Acts 4:36).

Whenever we read that God gave a person a new name, we know that he was establishing for them a new identity. God changed *Abram* (meaning "exalted father") to *Abraham* (meaning "father of many"). Abraham would be father not only to his own children but also to the great nation of Israel.

Now consider some of the new names you have received since Jesus became your Savior. You are Forgiven, Redeemed, Chosen, Child of God, Light of the World, Salt of the Earth, and Beloved. God has given you a new identity in him. How are you living out the truth of your new names?

> **"I BELIEVE I AM SIGNIFICANT BECAUSE OF MY POSITION AS A CHILD OF GOD."**

COMPASSION

Suppose a brother or a sister is without clothes and daily food. If one of you says to them, "Go in peace; keep warm and well fed," but does nothing about their physical needs, what good is it? In the same way, faith by itself, if it is not accompanied by action, is dead.

JAMES 2:15–17

There is a significant difference between sympathy and compassion. *Sympathy* is feeling sorry about someone else's trouble;[22] *compassion* is the desire to *help* someone who is sick, hungry, or in trouble.[23] Sympathy is only a feeling, but compassion takes action to meet the needs of a hurting brother or sister.

James calls us to a faith that is alive and goes beyond sympathy to compassion. A dead faith offers only an empty sentiment. A compassionate heart is actively stirred to alleviate the physical or emotional needs of others. Sometimes we provide meals, sometimes we give shelter, and sometimes we take the time to lend a listening ear and give a hug to bring a breaking heart peace.

Living faith moves us to action and produces opportunities for the love of Jesus to be shared. Will you let Jesus' compassionate love move through your hands and feet?

"I BELIEVE GOD CALLS ALL CHRISTIANS TO SHOW COMPASSION TO PEOPLE IN NEED."

PART 2: ACT

What Should I Do?

THE TEN KEYS OF "ACT"

Worship

Prayer

Bible Study

Single-Mindedness

Total Surrender

Biblical Community

Spiritual Gifts

Offering My Time

Giving My Resources

Sharing My Faith

LEARNING TO ACT LIKE JESUS

Brothers and sisters, whatever is true . . . think about such things. Whatever you have learned or received or heard from me, or seen in me—put it into practice. And the God of peace will be with you.

PHILIPPIANS 4:8–9

Becoming a great reader begins with learning the foundational principles. There are countless rules and numerous phonograms to memorize if you are to read the English language properly. Becoming a lifelong reader begins by learning these basic axioms.

But just thinking about what you have learned won't make you a great reader. You have to practice these key principles over and over again by sitting down with a book and actually reading it. You start with something simple like *See Spot Run*. Over time you progress to great reads like *War and Peace* by Leo Tolstoy. To *be* a great reader, you must first *think* and then *act*.

The same is true of the Christian life. If you want to *be* like Jesus, you must first *think* like Jesus. You just finished reading about the ten key beliefs that drive the Christian life. Now you must practice your faith or *act* like Jesus. Look more closely at the verse above and you will see the pattern.

The devotionals in the pages to come will introduce you to the ten key practices of the Christian life. Read them, but most importantly, give them a try.

DAY 122

WORSHIP

Come, let us sing for joy to the LORD; let us shout aloud to the Rock of our salvation. Let us come before him with thanksgiving and extol him with music and song.

PSALM 95:1–2

I love to hear my father share memories of his days as a US Air Force staff sergeant in Morocco during the Korean War. His duty started at Lackland Air Force Base in San Antonio, Texas, and sixty years later, I made a point of taking my dad back to that base for a visit.

An active lieutenant colonel graciously offered to provide us with access to the base and to give us a personal tour. We saw restored fighter planes from WWI to the present. When we came to the Korean War plane, the lieutenant colonel stopped us, looked my father straight in the eyes, and said these heartfelt words: "Al, as an officer and representative for the United States Air Force, I want to thank you for your dedication and service to our great nation." He finished with a strong salute.

Overwhelmed by this display of honor and respect, my dad saluted back, his eyes filled with tears.

Do you think our heavenly Father becomes overwhelmed, his eyes filled with tears of joy, when we salute him with our heartfelt worship?

"I WORSHIP GOD FOR WHO HE IS AND WHAT HE HAS DONE FOR ME."

PRAYER

If I had cherished sin in my heart, the Lord would not have listened; but God has surely listened and has heard my prayer. Praise be to God, who has not rejected my prayer or withheld his love from me!

PSALM 66:18–20

Asking for forgiveness is one of the hardest things to do, mostly because it requires admission of guilt. If you have wronged a friend—and whether or not your friend knows you have wronged them—you naturally avoid eye contact or avoid their presence altogether. You certainly would not be calling on them to do you any favors.

If you knew approaching your friend with an apology would mean reconciliation, you might be more likely to attempt the hard conversation, but most of the time your chances are fifty-fifty at best.

With God, you never need to fear rejection if you approach him with a repentant heart. He's your loving heavenly Father who wants nothing more than to be in a relationship with you, to hear your requests, and to grant the desires of your heart. The chances of reconciliation with God are 100 percent. He already knows what you have done. He even knows your motives, and he loves you anyway. So you might as well come clean.

> "I PRAY TO GOD TO KNOW HIM, TO FIND DIRECTION FOR MY LIFE, AND TO LAY MY REQUESTS BEFORE HIM."

DAY 124

BIBLE STUDY

The word of God is alive and active. Sharper than any double-edged sword, it penetrates even to dividing soul and spirit, joints and marrow; it judges the thoughts and attitudes of the heart.

HEBREWS 4:12

A surgeon determines that you need surgery by evaluating your symptoms. He may treat your symptoms, but this only masks them. The illness is caused by a deeper problem. Until the root problem is cut out, the symptoms will not permanently disappear.

Living the Christian life without reading the Bible is like treating the symptoms of a disease instead of removing the actual cause. Symptoms like anger, bitterness, depression, or hatred are indications of a deeper problem and can be masked for a time, but they always return.

Studying God's Word is like being under a surgeon's scalpel. During this surgery, however, you're awake, peering in a mirror. You see the deeper problems—insecurity, doubt, sin. Reading Scripture daily will bring healing and comfort for deep wounds, reinforce beliefs where doubt has crept in, and lead you in practices that will strengthen your faith.

The very best surgeon in the universe is available to you. Put your trust in the Great Physician!

"I STUDY THE BIBLE TO KNOW GOD AND HIS TRUTH AND TO FIND DIRECTION FOR MY DAILY LIFE."

SINGLE-MINDEDNESS

"Seek first his kingdom and his righteousness, and all these things will be given to you as well."

MATTHEW 6:33

M ax Lucado tells the story of a little girl who earns enough money to buy a pretty faux pearl necklace. One night her daddy comes to tell her good night and asks her, "Do you love me?"

The daughter replies, "Oh, yes, you know I love you!"

"Then give me your pearls," he says.

"Oh, not my pearls, Daddy! You know I love my pearls."

Kissing her good night, he says, "I understand."

Several nights pass, then one evening the dad sees tears filling up his little girl's eyes. He asks, "What's wrong?"

Holding out her hand, she opens it and offers her strand of pearls to her dad, explaining, "I love my pearls, Daddy, but I love you more."

The dad accepts the pearls, then reaches into his pocket. He pulls out a beautiful genuine pearl necklace and places it in his daughter's hand.[24]

Your heavenly Father wants you to open your hand and let go of the temporal things of your world so he can replace them with the genuine, eternal things of his kingdom.

"I FOCUS ON GOD AND HIS PRIORITIES FOR MY LIFE."

TOTAL SURRENDER

I urge you, brothers and sisters, in view of God's mercy, to offer your bodies as a living sacrifice, holy and pleasing to God—this is your true and proper worship.

ROMANS 12:1

The problem with living sacrifices is that they keep trying to crawl off the altar. Surrendering to someone else's will brings about tremendous fear, even when it is God's will.

What will he ask you to do? Stay in a tumultuous relationship or marriage for the good of the other person? Walk away from a relationship that is not honoring or pleasing to him? Watch your spouse or child head overseas to serve their country? Move your family halfway across the country for a new job?

Fear associated with surrendering to uncertainty can cause a living sacrifice to wiggle right off the altar and try to take back control. Sometimes you can't even muster the courage to get on there in the first place!

When you are tempted to wiggle off the altar, God asks you to stay on it, rely on his mercy and grace to get you through, and believe his promise that he is working out all things for your ultimate good.

"I DEDICATE MY LIFE TO GOD'S PURPOSES."

BIBLICAL COMMUNITY

All the believers were together and had everything in common. They sold property and possessions to give to anyone who had need.

ACTS 2:44–45

The members of the early church did not devote themselves to evangelism. They devoted themselves first to each other and to God. They saw each other every day and often shared a meal together, eating with "glad and sincere hearts" (v. 46). How did they do that? Between bites they chatted about the wonderful life they now had in Christ, and they praised God for it.

Once they finished their meal, they walked through the neighborhood streets and simply met the needs of the people around them from a heart of gratitude. Before people knew the doctrine that drove these believing neighbors, they experienced it. The result? People were added to the community of Christ every day. Evangelism was a result of their community.

Happy and kind people are contagious. You may only be a great meal away from seeing another person come to Christ.

> **"I FELLOWSHIP WITH CHRISTIANS TO ACCOMPLISH GOD'S PURPOSES IN MY LIFE, IN THE LIVES OF OTHERS, AND IN THE WORLD."**

DAY 128

SPIRITUAL GIFTS

We have different gifts, according to the grace given to each of us. If your gift is prophesying, then prophesy in accordance with your faith.

ROMANS 12:6

"That person has charisma." We make this kind of statement about someone who arouses enthusiasm in others. Did you know that if you are a Christian, you have charisma? It's absolutely true.

The Greek word for *gifts* that Paul used in the verse above is *charismata*. It is literally translated "grace gift," and it refers to at least one special gift the Holy Spirit deposited in you when you gave your life to Christ. Maybe it is the gift of leadership, or mercy, or administration, or teaching, or simply being a good helper. When we know our spiritual gifts and humbly use them in concert with other Christians to fulfill God's purposes, good things happen in the lives of other people. When good things happen in the lives of other people, it arouses enthusiasm in them. Voilà: charisma!

So, next time you hear someone say, "That person has charisma," see who they're talking about—it just may be you.

> **"I KNOW MY SPIRITUAL GIFTS AND USE THEM TO FULFILL GOD'S PURPOSES."**

OFFERING MY TIME

Whatever you do, whether in word or deed, do it all in the name of the Lord Jesus, giving thanks to God the Father through him.

COLOSSIANS 3:17

The clock is no respecter of persons. Every single human who has ever lived on the earth has exactly 168 hours a week. And most of us find that after spending time sleeping, working, eating, and commuting, there just isn't much left over. So when someone requests a piece of your time, you can feel tension in your gut.

God, however, doesn't want just a piece of your time; he wants it all. Yikes! Now, he is not asking you to go without sleep, quit your job, or stop eating. He is asking for a total shift in attitude. As you do the things you need to do, want to do, and are compelled to do because of your faith, offer them up to God in a way that pleases him.

You see, the time God wants you to offer him doesn't have to be spent only sitting in church or serving in a ministry. If you are peeling a potato, peel it in excellence for God. If you are holding a baby, hold that baby for God, offering the child love and the warmth of a caring heart. If you run into a friend in the store, offer that conversation up to God and see what a difference it might make.

What are you going to do next? Offer it up to God.

"I OFFER MY TIME TO FULFILL GOD'S PURPOSES."

GIVING MY RESOURCES

Since you excel in everything—in faith, in speech, in knowledge, in complete earnestness and in the love we have kindled in you—see that you also excel in this grace of giving.

2 CORINTHIANS 8:7

History tells us that during the Middle Ages, whenever a soldier was baptized he would leave his right hand extended above the water. Why? This was the hand he carried his sword in, and he was not offering it up to God. Today we might see a person with that same hand extended above the water, but with a wallet in it.

Paul challenged the Corinthian believers to drop that hand with the wallet into the water and excel in the "grace of giving." Notice he didn't say the "obligation of giving." We often miss this. In the opening words of 1 Corinthians Paul wrote, "I always thank my God for you because of his *grace given* you in Christ Jesus" (1:4, emphasis added). Aren't you glad that when Jesus was baptized, his whole body went down into the water? Aren't you glad his whole body went on the cross?

So grab your wallet and baptize it along with the rest of you, so you can excel in offering the same kind of grace Christ offered to you.

"I GIVE MY RESOURCES TO FULFILL GOD'S PURPOSES."

SHARING MY FAITH

Pray also for me, that whenever I speak, words may be given me so that I will fearlessly make known the mystery of the gospel, for which I am an ambassador in chains. Pray that I may declare it fearlessly, as I should.

EPHESIANS 6:19–20

A husband came home from work after a very long and terrible day. Everything had gone wrong. He said to his wife, "I've had nothing but bad news at the office today. If there is one thing I don't want, it is more bad news."

His wife gently replied, "In that case, you'll be glad to know that three of your four children did not break their arms today."

There is a real art to learning how to share bad news. But delivering good news is so much fun. Why, then, is it so hard for us to share our faith? Without question, Paul goes down in history as one of the most aggressive evangelists ever to walk the planet. Yet he confesses that it is easy to hold back and that even he needs courage. If it is true for Paul, then it is likely true for you.

Maybe it helps to remember that the gospel is good news. Try this on for size: "You'll be pleased to know that four out of every four people who ask for forgiveness and for eternal life in Jesus will receive them."

> **"I SHARE MY FAITH WITH OTHERS TO FULFILL GOD'S PURPOSES."**

WORSHIP

> [Jesus] took bread, gave thanks and broke it, and gave it to
> [his disciples], saying, "This is my body given for you; do
> this in remembrance of me."

LUKE 22:19

Seriousness and joy are not mutually exclusive. For example, a wedding is a solemn occasion that should honor God and the covenant of marriage, but it should also be full of joy and laughter and a celebration of the joining of two hearts.

We should experience the sacrament of Communion in the same manner. First Corinthians 11:26 reminds us, "Whenever [we] eat this bread and drink this cup, [we] proclaim the Lord's death." Jesus was completely innocent, yet his death was indescribably brutal. He hung on the cross, bled, and gasped for breath because of your sin and mine. We killed the holy Son of God. Nothing is more serious than that.

Yet there is no greater reason for genuine joy than the cross. Jesus let himself be crucified in order to save you from the death of eternal separation from God. Furthermore, Jesus did not stay dead! When you approach the bread and wine, you proclaim Jesus' death until he comes again, the glorious resurrected conqueror of sin and death.

You should never approach Communion "in an unworthy manner" (v. 27), but neither should you approach it without heartfelt joy.

> "I WORSHIP GOD FOR WHO HE IS AND
> WHAT HE HAS DONE FOR ME."

PRAYER

God is in heaven and you are on earth, so let your words be few.

ECCLESIASTES 5:2

Ever get so carried away talking to God that you realize you didn't spend any time listening to him? Yes, your heavenly Father wants to hear from you. He desires you to be open and honest with him. He cares about your hurts and disappointments, even your disappointments in him. You can spill your heart to him. Yet heeding Solomon's words is wise.

Solomon reminds us that we should make listening a priority. God longs to hear from us (2 Chronicles 7:14; Psalm 88:2; Luke 18:1), but he also wants us to hear from him (2 Timothy 3:16–17).

We have the privilege of prayer only because he grants us access, so we should not approach him with hollow words, frivolous or rote prayers, or promises made lightly. *Prayer is an intimate conversation with God and should be treated as such.* Letting your words "be few" can help you pray more simply and sincerely. It can also help you be more attentive to whatever he wants you to hear him say.

Share your heart with God, but save some time to listen with your soul.

> **"I PRAY TO GOD TO KNOW HIM, TO FIND DIRECTION FOR MY LIFE, AND TO LAY MY REQUESTS BEFORE HIM."**

BIBLE STUDY

Your word is a lamp for my feet, a light on my path.

PSALM 119:105

The road ahead of us often seems twisty and mysterious. There are forks and detours and confusing signs. We can feel like Dorothy on the yellow brick road, not knowing which way to go, and the only one to guide us is a scarecrow pointing both directions who doesn't have a brain.

Thankfully, God has graciously supplied us with his Word to light our path and show us the way. In Psalm 119—the longest chapter in the Bible—the psalmist wrote with gratitude about the value of reading and studying God's Word to understand his will. God's Word provides light in this world darkened by sin, lies, and upside-down values.

One more detail. The lamp the psalmist referred to was not a high-powered flashlight like ours today. This lamp shed just enough light for his next step so he could avoid obstacles, holes, and bumps right in front of him. Since Jesus doesn't want us to worry about tomorrow (Matthew 6:34), that's enough light.

Do you have the light you need to take your next step?

> **"I STUDY THE BIBLE TO KNOW GOD AND HIS TRUTH AND TO FIND DIRECTION FOR MY DAILY LIFE."**

SINGLE-MINDEDNESS

> *When [Peter] saw the wind, he was afraid and, beginning to sink, cried out, "Lord, save me!" Immediately Jesus reached out his hand and caught him.*

MATTHEW 14:30–31

"Mom, the whole team is having their number shaved in the hair! Can I pleeeeeease do it too?" my son requested.

This seemed a bit extreme . . . but I'm all for team spirit, and well, what harm would it do? The young girl at Pro-Cuts cut his hair really short and then took the guard off the clippers to shave #3 in the back of his head. While she was working on him, she complained about her awful date the evening before to the girl next to her. When she was done, you could barely make out the #3. Apparently she hadn't been completely focused.

A lack of focus can have much worse consequences, especially if we let our single-minded focus on Jesus lapse.

Peter learned that lesson when he boldly stepped out of the boat and started walking toward Jesus, who was walking on the water. All went well for Peter—until he was distracted by the wind and the waves. When he started to sink, Jesus reached out and saved him.

We can start to sink, too, unless we remain focused on Jesus during the storms of life.

"I FOCUS ON GOD AND HIS PRIORITIES FOR MY LIFE."

DAY 136

TOTAL SURRENDER

I will go to the king. . . . And if I perish, I perish.

ESTHER 4:16

The Aucas were a fierce, murderous tribe who never hesitated to kill outsiders. Aware of the danger, missionary Jim Elliot was convinced meeting Jesus was the only way they would stop killing. He noted in his journal, "He is no fool who gives what he cannot keep to gain what he cannot lose."

After months of dropping gifts from their plane, Jim decided it was time to meet the Aucas face-to-face. He and four companions set up camp, and everything was fine until day six. They saw Auca women crossing the river toward them, looking unfriendly. Hearing a blood-curdling cry behind them, the men turned and saw Auca warriors with spears raised. Within seconds all five men were killed.[25]

Queen Esther was willing to take that same risk. Approaching King Xerxes without being summoned could cost her life, but the date for the kingdom-wide massacre of her people was near. Esther chose total surrender to protect her people, and God protected her.

When Elliot chose total surrender, he perished; however, his wife and his son returned to the Aucas with forgiveness, courage, and the same total surrender Jim had. The Aucas who took his life are now believers in God.

For whom are you willing to totally surrender?

"I DEDICATE MY LIFE TO GOD'S PURPOSES."

BIBLICAL COMMUNITY

The LORD God said, "It is not good for the man to be alone. I will make a helper suitable for him."

GENESIS 2:18

It must have been some parade! God brought every living creature he had created to Adam to be named. But among all these creatures there wasn't a "suitable" helper for him. Not the Brahma bull. Not the ostrich. Not the giraffe. Not even the ole reliable canine! Yet God knew community would be essential for Adam to live a godly and healthy life. So he made Eve.

Our need for community hasn't changed, though it can be challenging at times, because we are sinful creatures in need of a Savior. We are, as someone has observed, like porcupines in a snowstorm: we need to get close to be warm, but we hurt one another when we do!

God intended for people to have rich, life-giving relationships with one another, relationships energized and motivated by the presence of God among them. But that can only come when grace and compassion are extended.

Don't be afraid to be in community; you need it! When the porcupine needles prick, offer the grace and compassion you want others to show you when yours flare.

> **"I FELLOWSHIP WITH CHRISTIANS TO ACCOMPLISH GOD'S PURPOSES IN MY LIFE, IN THE LIVES OF OTHERS, AND IN THE WORLD."**

DAY 138

SPIRITUAL GIFTS

But to each one of us grace has been given as Christ apportioned it.

EPHESIANS 4:7

A fellow pastor's wife came to me with tears of exhaustion. Abbey wanted so badly to simplify her life, but she was in a small church. She chaired the missions committee, led the women's ministry, taught Sunday school, conducted the children's choir, and coordinated potlucks—in addition to being a wife and mother of three.

My response? "Why do you feel you need to do all of that?"

"Because if I don't, no one will, and these ministries can't die."

You don't need to be a pastor's wife to get life out of balance and get caught up in the rat race of overcommitment. While there's no doubt serving others is a sacred responsibility, many of us say yes way too often. We feel similar to Abbey: *If we don't, who will?*

No one person possesses all the spiritual gifts. God's grace apportions, or divides, them among his whole body, and therefore calls us to the sacred race of fulfilling his purposes together. He's not calling you to do it all alone. Saying no gives others opportunities to use their gifts.

Use your *yes* when you can, but also accept God's grace and use your *no*—as my friend and author Susie Larson might put it—to get out of the rat race and join the sacred race.[26]

> **"I KNOW MY SPIRITUAL GIFTS AND USE THEM TO FULFILL GOD'S PURPOSES."**

OFFERING MY TIME

> [The sailors asked Jonah,] "What have you done?" (They knew he was running away from the LORD, because he had already told them so.)
>
> JONAH 1:10

It was a rematch between boxer Joe Louis and challenger Billy Conn. Louis had defeated Conn in the thirteenth round of the 1941 fight. After World War II, in June of 1946, the two met again. Before the fight, a sportswriter pointed out Conn's speed and asked Louis what his strategy would be in the ring. To that, Louis reportedly said, "He can run, but he can't hide."[27]

In a well-known Old Testament story, Jonah ran from an assignment he didn't want. He didn't like God's plan, so he took off to Joppa and got on a ship headed for Tarshish. He went in exactly the opposite direction the Lord had instructed him to go.

A mighty storm arose, the ship was threatened, and Jonah convinced the crew to throw him overboard. He had to camp out in the belly of a fish for three days. Jonah ran, but he couldn't hide.

Are you—like Jonah—running from God, or are you going the direction God wants you to go? Honor God with your time by using it as he directs.

P. S. Billy Conn ran, but couldn't hide. In the eighth round, Joe Louis knocked him out.

"I OFFER MY TIME TO FULFILL GOD'S PURPOSES."

DAY 140

GIVING MY RESOURCES

In everything I did, I showed you that by this kind of hard work we must help the weak, remembering the words the Lord Jesus himself said: "It is more blessed to give than to receive."

ACTS 20:35

Ever had an honest conversation with yourself about giving? *Why do I struggle with giving? Why do I feel a nagging resistance to let go of my stuff? When it comes to giving back to God, why do I ask what is the least I can give and still stay in God's good graces? Why is my natural inclination toward getting, keeping, and hoarding?*

These soul-tormenting questions bear witness to our allergic reaction to giving.

Our inner battles with releasing our resources might cease if something else were first given to God—our very selves. We tend to forget that even the very air we breathe is a gift from our loving Creator. God doesn't want our stuff; he already owns it all. He wants us. Why? Because it is only when God fully has us that we can fully have God.

So the next time you feel an inner allergic reaction to giving, try this: Remind yourself it all belongs to God anyway. It's always easier to give someone else's money and stuff away! You may find yourself willing to give it all. Then how blessed you will be!

> **"I GIVE MY RESOURCES TO FULFILL GOD'S PURPOSES."**

SHARING MY FAITH

[God] has committed to us the message of reconciliation. We are therefore Christ's ambassadors.

2 CORINTHIANS 5:19–20

After a demanding campaign season, incumbent Harry Truman went to bed early on Election Day. He didn't know whether he had been reelected.

Neither did the people at the *Chicago Daily Tribune*. Returns were slow coming in, and the deadline for getting the paper out was fast approaching. Based on early returns and their sense of what the results would be, they printed "Dewey Defeats Truman." After the paper was delivered, more returns showed the gap closing and, eventually, that Truman had won. Not the finest moment for the *Tribune* editors.

When we're a trusted messenger, we want to be sure we get the message right. Especially when that message is the most important message in history. Here are the basics: all of us are sinners; Jesus, God's Son, who was without sin, took the punishment for our sins when he died on the cross; Jesus rose from the dead, having defeated sin and death; believing in this amazing truth means forgiveness for sins and eternal life. Rehearse what this means to you right now—you want to be sure to have the message right!—and when the opportunity presents itself, share how this message has changed your life.

> **"I SHARE MY FAITH WITH OTHERS TO FULFILL GOD'S PURPOSES."**

WORSHIP

I will praise you, Lord my God, with all my heart; I will glorify your name forever.

PSALM 86:12

Our *Daily Bread* gives an account of a Christian man late in life, a great singer, preparing for a surgery to remove his tongue because of cancer. He understood that afterward he would never be able to sing again. Moments before the procedure began, he asked if he could sit up and then said, "I have one song that will be my last. It will be of gratitude and praise to God."[28]

How sad this man was losing his ability to sing. But the joyful truth is that even without a singing voice, he would be able to continue to praise God the rest of his days. His heart could still be full of love for God, and he could express that beautifully through the way he lived. True worship means living out the fruit of the Spirit with our whole life.

Dallas Willard wrote, "The life we live out in our moments, hours, days and years wells up from a hidden depth. What is in our heart matters more than anything else."[29]

So sing if you can, but make sure everything you do flows from a heart of praise.

"I WORSHIP GOD FOR WHO HE IS AND WHAT HE HAS DONE FOR ME."

PRAYER

I will consider all your works and meditate on all your mighty deeds.

PSALM 77:12

Sometimes we just need to get something off our chest. We need to vent and process. After we do, we tend to feel better.

In Psalm 77, Asaph unloaded or—to use a biblical word—lamented. We find anguish and grief in verses 7–9: "Will the Lord reject forever? Will he never show his favor again? Has his unfailing love vanished forever? . . . Has God forgotten to be merciful?" Asaph didn't hold back!

But we also see in verse 12 above that, as he vented and ranted, Asaph came to remember who God is and what he had done for him. The same can happen to you. You can start by sharing your pain with God, but as you talk to him, you will be reminded of who he is and all he has done for you. You'll see his good involvement in your life, and your lamentations will become declarations of hope and trust. After all, prayer is not to be some kind of eloquent performance. Prayer is a personal conversation with your heavenly Father who loves you.

Don't hesitate to lament and vent. But like Asaph, choose to consider God's good works in your life and meditate on his mighty deeds.

> **"I PRAY TO GOD TO KNOW HIM, TO FIND DIRECTION FOR MY LIFE, AND TO LAY MY REQUESTS BEFORE HIM."**

DAY 144

BIBLE STUDY

Put on the full armor of God, so that you can take your stand against the devil's schemes.

EPHESIANS 6:11

The Word of God is so powerful it's compared to a sword in what's known as the "armor of God" passage, and it's the only offensive weapon in the entire arsenal. Defensive weapons can protect a soldier if he's blindsided (temptation doesn't usually warn us when it's coming), but without an offensive weapon, he cannot fight back and conquer his enemy.

Someday Jesus will return to defeat his enemies. When he does, a "sharp, double-edged sword" will come out of his mouth (Revelation 1:16). Jesus' weapon of choice? Words. They are powerful enough to win the final victory!

Before he goes into battle, a soldier must know his weapon well. He must train with it daily. Conquering our enemy also requires we know our offensive weapon well. Jesus' weapon can be yours too. When you draw on God's words, it's not you speaking. His words carry the same authority as the One who originally spoke them.

Get on the offensive and draw your sword; the ambush of temptation is approaching. God's Word is your best tool to conquer the Enemy.

> **"I STUDY THE BIBLE TO KNOW GOD AND HIS TRUTH AND TO FIND DIRECTION FOR MY DAILY LIFE."**

SINGLE-MINDEDNESS

Day after day, in the temple courts and from house to house, they never stopped teaching and proclaiming the good news that Jesus is the Messiah.

ACTS 5:42

They couldn't get it on Facebook fast enough . . . the pregnancy test was positive! Liz and Sam had been trying to get pregnant for what felt like an eternity. Lots of heartache and fertility testing had been their single-minded focus, and it had been hard on their marriage. But they had remained hopeful, and now there was a baby coming. They wanted the world to know and to share in their joy! The good news was tweeted, texted, telephoned, Instagrammed, and Facebooked.

Are we that excited—or even half that excited—about sharing the news that brings joy now and for eternity? Could it be that we let many things distract us from sharing with others that Jesus died for our sins and rose from the dead, victorious over sin and death? We can enter into a relationship with our holy God. We can live with the hope of eternal life. Would anyone say we "never stopped teaching and proclaiming the good news that Jesus is the Messiah"?

Jesus, make me bold and excited to tell people about my risen Savior and Lord!

"I FOCUS ON GOD AND HIS PRIORITIES FOR MY LIFE."

DAY 146

TOTAL SURRENDER

"You shall not make for yourself an image in the form of anything. . . . You shall not bow down to them or worship them; for I, the LORD your God, am a jealous God."

EXODUS 20:4–5

Early in our marriage, we saw two other marriages within our church fail. We were sure these couples never meant to be unfaithful, but hadn't taken careful precautions to prevent it. Randy suggested we set up guidelines to protect our relationship and to avoid putting ourselves in situations that could make us vulnerable. We made a commitment to share all computer and phone passwords with each other, and not to have lunch alone with someone of the opposite sex. Randy also had a window installed in the door to his church office.

Marriage is meant to be an exclusive relationship. God wants the same kind of exclusive relationship with his people. When he calls himself a *jealous* God, he means the *Merriam-Webster* definition: "intolerant of rivalry or unfaithfulness" and "vigilant in guarding a possession."[30] This passionate self-description comes out of a love language similar to the marriage covenant. God is totally committed to us and requires total commitment from us. He won't share our allegiance.

What threatens the exclusivity of your relationship with God? Take steps to remove it!

"I DEDICATE MY LIFE TO GOD'S PURPOSES."

BIBLICAL COMMUNITY

> *[Jesus] got up from the meal . . . poured water into a basin and began to wash his disciples' feet, drying them with the towel that was wrapped around him.*

JOHN 13:4–5

It was the top of the seventh inning. Two outs. Eckerd College sophomore Kara Oberer stepped up to the plate and hit a three-run home run. But when she tried to get around the bases, she blew out her knee. That's when Florida Southern College pitcher Chelsea Oglevie and second baseman Leah Pemberton carried Kara, their struggling opponent, around the bases to home plate.[31]

It was Passover, and the master had been looking forward to sharing the special meal with his closest followers. Imagine the disciples' surprise when Jesus stood up from the table and proceeded to wash their feet. Imagine your Bible study leader or your pastor washing your feet.

The unexpected makes for a powerful lesson. Chelsea and Leah served a rival. Jesus washed the feet of friends who would desert him, deny him, and betray him. Jesus served, and like him, his followers today who live in a biblical community seek to serve, not to be served.

Where are you serving? Where do you think God wants you to be serving? Figuratively speaking, whose feet does Jesus want you to wash?

"I FELLOWSHIP WITH CHRISTIANS TO ACCOMPLISH GOD'S PURPOSES IN MY LIFE, IN THE LIVES OF OTHERS, AND IN THE WORLD."

DAY 148

SPIRITUAL GIFTS

From [Christ] the whole body, joined and held together by every supporting ligament, grows and builds itself up in love, as each part does its work.

EPHESIANS 4:16

M uch can be accomplished by teamwork when no one is concerned about who gets the credit."

So spoke John Wooden, the legendary UCLA basketball coach who led the school to seven straight championships, with three undefeated seasons and an eighty-eight-game winning streak along the way. Much was accomplished by college students who heeded their coach's wisdom and played as a team.[32]

The church can learn from Coach Wooden too. Just as Wooden had centers, guards, and forwards, the church has pastors, teachers, and evangelists. Just as Wooden worked on basketball fundamentals like passing, shooting, and dribbling, the body of the church can focus on prayer, the Word, and service. And when everyone pulls together, UCLA gets victories, and the church shines God's light of love and hope.

Whatever your gifts, God has a place for you to serve. Each part of the body has its work to do. Jesus enables both the sharpening and the exercise of those gifts to be done in love, resulting in joy for the body, and a witness to the world, to bring glory to himself.

> **"I KNOW MY SPIRITUAL GIFTS AND USE THEM TO FULFILL GOD'S PURPOSES."**

OFFERING MY TIME

Be very careful, then, how you live—not as unwise but as wise, making the most of every opportunity.

EPHESIANS 5:15–16

Chronos and *kairos* are two of the words in the Bible translated as "time." *Chronos* is time measured by minutes and hours. Time marches on, and we must march with it. *Kairos* is different. *Kairos* is time as a gift or opportunity. Living in *chronos*, we ask, "What time is it?" Living in *kairos*, we ask, "What is this time for?" The word translated as *opportunity* in Ephesians comes from *kairos*.

Time is a mystery, isn't it? We move through our days and time seems to move so slowly, but looking back we're amazed at how quickly life has rushed by and wonder, *Where did it all go?* Time as a master wields a cruel whip. Ah, but time from our Maker is his precious gift. Each day is a present we open, full of opportunities to work and play and learn and serve our Father.

Time is a treasure, and your days on earth are numbered according to your heavenly Father. So don't worry about how much is left, fretting over when the end will come, but ask the Giver, "What is this time for?"

"I OFFER MY TIME TO FULFILL GOD'S PURPOSES."

GIVING MY RESOURCES

"Where your treasure is, there your heart will be also."

MATTHEW 6:21

Jane and Michael Banks from *Mary Poppins* were puzzled when the tall, singing men of Dawes, Tomes, Mousely, Grubbs Fidelity Fiduciary Bank desperately wanted Jane's and Michael's money to invest in their bank. Jane and Michael were not ready to let go of their coins. They wanted to feed the birds instead.

How ready are you to let go of the treasures you're holding on to? If you're reluctant, Jesus would ask you, "Are you serving God, or are you serving money? You can't serve both!"

Treasures here on earth offer fleeting pleasure at best. Moths and vermin can destroy; thieves can break in and steal. Overextended banks can go belly up; the retirement savings can fail to stretch as long as you expected them to or need them to.

We need to be ready to let go of our earthly coins so that we can invest wholeheartedly in God's eternal purposes and activities. Our treasures—as well as our efforts to amass or protect them—control our hearts.

Ask the Lord to help you see your heart for what it is—committed to the present or to him for eternity—and then, if necessary, ask him to transform it.

"I GIVE MY RESOURCES TO FULFILL GOD'S PURPOSES."

SHARING MY FAITH

Now I know that there is no God in all the world except in Israel.

2 KINGS 5:15

Atheist Lee Strobel was thinking it was time to get out of the marriage to his wife, a new follower of Jesus. He said, "I felt like a victim of bait and switch. I had married one Leslie—the fun-loving, risk-taking Leslie—and she was being transformed into someone different. . . . This isn't what I signed up for!"

Atheist-turned-Christian Lee recalls: "But before it was too late, Leslie learned how to live her faith in a way that began to attract me rather than repel me. She learned how to grow and even flourish in her relationship with Christ, despite discouragement from me."[33] As Leslie lived out her devotion to Jesus, Lee saw clear evidence that following Jesus was the best approach to life and soon became a Christian.

You may be able to name several people in your life who piqued your interest in Christianity. Thank God for those people—and then think about how you can be such a person in others' lives.

Today's verse is Naaman's response because of the behavior of a servant girl. Lee Strobel's response to God came because of his wife's actions and attitudes. Someone may notice how you live and go in search of the God who is revealing himself through you.

> **"I SHARE MY FAITH WITH OTHERS TO FULFILL GOD'S PURPOSES."**

DAY 152

WORSHIP

The jailer called for lights, rushed in and fell trembling before Paul and Silas. He then brought them out and asked, "Sirs, what must I do to be saved?"

They replied, "Believe in the Lord Jesus, and you will be saved."

ACTS 16:29–31

What a random question for a jailer to ask two prisoners. But these weren't just any two prisoners.

Paul and Silas had been arrested, flogged, and thrown into a prison cell, yet with their feet in stocks, they were "praying and singing hymns to God" (v. 25). As if their behavior wasn't strange enough, an earthquake shook the prison, causing every prisoner's chains to fall off, but remarkably, no prisoner fled. After all, this guard's life would have been on the line if they had. No wonder the jailer wanted to know how he could be saved.

When we worship in the dark as Paul and Silas did—in the midst of pain, loss, fear, uncertainty, sickness, or death—people notice. When we bless the name of the Lord, whether he gives us the desires of our hearts or takes something precious from us, people notice. God can use our praise to move in their hearts, and we may find their voices joining ours in heartfelt worship of the one true God.

> **"I WORSHIP GOD FOR WHO HE IS AND WHAT HE HAS DONE FOR ME."**

PRAYER

"Father, if you are willing, take this cup from me; yet not my will, but yours be done."

LUKE 22:42

Does prayer seem useless to you? Perhaps you see others' prayers answered time and again while yours remain unanswered. Maybe you find yourself thinking, *God has everything set in motion to accomplish his plan, so what's the point of praying? It won't change his mind.*

Jesus feels your pain. Jesus' prayer in the Garden of Gethsemane failed to change God's mind. Jesus knew God's plan was set in stone before he prayed, but it didn't hinder him from pouring out his heart until he sweated drops of blood. Through humbling himself in prayer, Jesus surrendered to the Father's will. In turn, I believe the Father instilled in him the courage and strength he needed to accept the horrific death on the cross.

Keep fervently praying and asking God to answer your prayers. Even if he doesn't answer the way you had hoped, he will give you the courage and strength to face whatever challenge is before you.

"I PRAY TO GOD TO KNOW HIM, TO FIND DIRECTION FOR MY LIFE, AND TO LAY MY REQUESTS BEFORE HIM."

DAY 154

BIBLE STUDY

The unfolding of your words gives light; it gives understanding to the simple.

PSALM 119:130

L ast week a friend of mine shared a frustration. She awoke at 5:00 a.m. before her children stirred to have some quiet moments studying her Bible. As soon as she sat down and opened her Bible, her children emerged from their slumber and appeared by her side. "They're like little moths!" she said. "When I turn on the light, it's as if they are drawn to it."

All day the image of moths being irrepressibly drawn to light stayed in my head. These tiny creatures, lured out of the dark, fly incessantly in circles until they can't help but land on the light source. God's Word is a lamp, drawing us from the dark into the illuminated, life-giving guidance we so desperately need to stay on course. The more captivated you become by his Word and learn what it says, the clearer your path becomes.

Facing a heavy decision? Trying to mend a broken relationship? Need encouragement? Want to become more like Christ? Oh, that you would be drawn to God's Word like a moth to light.

> **"I STUDY THE BIBLE TO KNOW GOD AND HIS TRUTH AND TO FIND DIRECTION FOR MY DAILY LIFE."**

SINGLE-MINDEDNESS

We do not know what to do, but our eyes are on you, [Lord].

2 CHRONICLES 20:12

Imagine the president of the United States addressing the nation about the imminent threat of enemies planning to pounce on our land with a vengeance. Then imagine him telling us that after many meetings, the military still didn't have a plan to protect our country, so we were all going to have to keep our eyes on the Lord.

Overwhelmed by the huge hostile army that was threatening Judah, this is exactly what young King Jehoshaphat did. He told his people the enemies were closing in and he did "not know what to do." Then he cried out to the Lord and reminded the people that they worshipped a powerful and mighty God who alone would protect them. He told them they were powerless to defeat their enemies, and then he led them to single-mindedly focus on God despite their fear.

God sent word back to them, "Do not be afraid or discouraged . . . for the battle is not yours, but God's. . . . You will not have to fight this battle. . . . Stand firm and see the deliverance the LORD will give you" (vv. 15, 17).

Are you overwhelmed by your circumstances today? Stand firm and single-mindedly keep your focus on God. He's got this!

"I FOCUS ON GOD AND HIS PRIORITIES FOR MY LIFE."

DAY 156

TOTAL SURRENDER

While they were stoning him, Stephen prayed, "Lord Jesus, receive my spirit." Then he fell on his knees and cried out, "Lord, do not hold this sin against them."

ACTS 7:59–60

A person's last words can be poignant, funny, wise, tragic, ironic, clever, puzzling, or indicative of their relationship with God. Death is the moment in our lives, like it or not, when we totally surrender to our Maker if we haven't before.

"I'd rather be skiing." So spoke Stan Laurel of the beloved Laurel and Hardy comedy team. When his nurse asked if he was a skier, his response was, "No, but I'd rather be skiing than doing what I'm doing."[34]

Philosopher, historian, and writer Voltaire was talking with a priest when the lamp at his bedside flared up. "The flames already?" Voltaire asked.[35]

Cofounder of Apple Computers, Steve Jobs died from pancreatic cancer in 2011. His last words were, "Oh wow. Oh wow. Oh wow."[36]

After a bold speech recounting the history of God's people from Abraham to the long-awaited Messiah, Stephen's last words honored God, the God to whom he had surrendered his life and to whom he was surrendering himself at the moment of his death.

May our words always honor God as we continue to entrust ourselves to him in total surrender.

"I DEDICATE MY LIFE TO GOD'S PURPOSES."

BIBLICAL COMMUNITY

Now you are the body of Christ, and each one of you is a part of it.

1 CORINTHIANS 12:27

A father told his rebellious teenage son, "One of these days you are going to have a Copernican revolution in your life." "What's that?" the boy slurred, his speech impaired from all the alcohol he'd consumed. "Copernicus is the man who discovered that the universe does not revolve around the earth," his father answered.

The young man had his Copernican revolution during marine corps boot camp. For three long, grueling months he was taught that what mattered most was the great mission of freedom for his country, and to accomplish the mission they had to work as a team. Each soldier had to find his identity and meaning as a part of the group. As each soldier did his part, the team worked to achieve the greater good of the mission.

As members of the body of Christ, we have an eternal mission to bring the good news of freedom in Christ to those oppressed by sin. Each individual must do their part so that our mission from God is achieved. We can't do it alone. We need each other. The mission depends on it.

> **"I FELLOWSHIP WITH CHRISTIANS TO ACCOMPLISH GOD'S PURPOSES IN MY LIFE, IN THE LIVES OF OTHERS, AND IN THE WORLD."**

SPIRITUAL GIFTS

*God has put the body together . . . that its parts should
have equal concern for each other. If one part suffers,
every part suffers with it; if one part is honored, every part
rejoices with it.*

1 CORINTHIANS 12:24–26

I've had an injured ligament in my foot for quite some time, and now my knee and the muscles in my shin and calf area ache every night as I get into bed. The doctor tells me the injury to my foot is causing the other parts of my leg to compensate and use their strength to support that damaged ligament. If they didn't, my leg would not hold me up. These other parts of my body have entered into the suffering to support my hurting foot.

God designed our bodies to work in such a way that when one of its own hurts, the other members step up and support it.

The body of Christ is designed to work the same way. When a brother or sister is injured, the rest of us enter into their suffering and use whatever spiritual gifts we have to support the hurting member. When we enter into a brother's or sister's suffering, we are living out God's design for his body.

If you are present in the pain, you can lighten the burden—and later share in the joy of recovery.

> **"I KNOW MY SPIRITUAL GIFTS AND USE
> THEM TO FULFILL GOD'S PURPOSES."**

OFFERING MY TIME

Teach us to number our days, that we may gain a heart of wisdom.

PSALM 90:12

As an Irish Proverb says, "God made time, but man made haste." The word *rushed* could describe how many of us get through our days—we actually put quite a bit of energy into hurrying. But try answering this: *Why* are we in such a hurry? Even if we are spending our time "doing good," are we doing those things in God's way? The whole point, after all, is to please him by using the days he gives us *well.*

We need to slow down and offer our time first to God, even before we help others. There is little chance of becoming all God wants us to be unless we take the time to hear his voice, read his Word, and fulfill his major purpose for our lives: a relationship with him.

"Hurry up!" says the world. "You are going to miss out on life!" There's wisdom in replying, "No, thank you! If I hurry, I'm going to miss the meaning of life and all that God wants me to see and know."

Do you remember reading about Jesus being in a hurry? Can't say that I do! If the Son of God, who came to earth to save all of humanity from sin and death, didn't rush, then why should you? Hurrying through life might be a big waste of time.

"I OFFER MY TIME TO FULFILL GOD'S PURPOSES."

GIVING MY RESOURCES

I have learned to be content whatever the circumstances.

PHILIPPIANS 4:11

How to Win Friends and Influence People by Dale Carnegie was published in 1936, and it's no surprise that a book by that title has sold fifteen million copies. Here is one bit of wisdom that the book contains: "It isn't what you have or who you are or where you are or what you are doing that makes you happy or unhappy. It is what you think about it."

That observation offers an interesting perspective on the apostle Paul's declaration that he "learned to be content whatever the circumstances . . . whether well fed or hungry, whether living in plenty or in want" (vv. 11–12).

Whether he was well fed or hungry, preaching the gospel or imprisoned, dining with friends or being flogged, what do you think Paul was thinking about? The one who wrote, "For to me, to live is Christ and to die is gain" (Philippians 1:21) was undoubtedly thinking about his Savior and trusting that his circumstances were in Jesus' capable hands.

Ask God to teach you to be content not by looking at the circumstances of your life but instead by looking—with trust—toward the One who is faithful.

> **"I GIVE MY RESOURCES TO FULFILL GOD'S PURPOSES."**

SHARING MY FAITH

"Let your light shine before others, that they may see your good deeds and glorify your Father in heaven."

MATTHEW 5:16

Light has been somewhat of a mystery to scientists. Does it move in waves, or does it move in particles?

Albert Einstein was the one who, in 1905, proposed that light—at that point thought to be a wave—is also a stream of particles. Experiments since then have proven that light behaves like waves *and* like particles. In March 2015, a research team at Switzerland's EPFL (Ecole Polytechnique Fédérale de Lausanne) took a picture of light behaving as both a wave and a stream of particles at the same time.[37]

Just as light in the physical world has mystified people, so has the supernatural light of the Lord that shines through his people. Why is there a constant stream of meals arriving for the family with the newborn? Who are those people who arrived at the widow's home to tend to her yard? How could Renee, the mother of Megan Napier, forgive the drunk driver who killed her precious daughter and plead for his early release from prison?

Like the scientists at EPFL looking long and hard at light, may the people who see your love in action keep looking until they figure out and embrace the Source.

"I SHARE MY FAITH WITH OTHERS TO FULFILL GOD'S PURPOSES."

DAY 162

WORSHIP

"These people honor me with their lips, but their hearts are far from me. They worship me in vain; their teachings are merely human rules."

MARK 7:6–7

Ouch! Jesus' words sting, don't they? Why? Because his remarks have, at some time or another, been true of all our lives. Our worship of God on Sunday somehow doesn't match the way we live Monday through Saturday. Sometimes we don't even get out of church before the hypocrisy takes place. Why is this so common? Consider at least two reasons.

First, our worship is just another item to check off—our worship is a matter of ritual. We worship, and then we move on to what's next. Second, we think of worship as a Sunday-morning church activity that has little relevance to the real world we live in during the week. In both cases we worship with our lips and not our hearts. And we wonder why our lives feel empty.

Jesus is telling us that true worship is offering our hearts to God. When you worship passionately and honestly, your heart becomes one with Christ, who lives within you. Your life then will be an expression of worship wherever you are, whatever you are doing, and whomever you are with. Remember, you don't leave God at church. He is with you always.

> **"I WORSHIP GOD FOR WHO HE IS AND WHAT HE HAS DONE FOR ME."**

PRAYER

When you ask, you do not receive, because you ask with wrong motives.

JAMES 4:3

Have you ever wondered why Jesus prayed? After all, wasn't he equal with God? Didn't he say that he and the Father were one?

That's true! But when Jesus chose to be born in human form, he temporarily emptied himself of his glory and majesty, and surrendered his all-knowing power. He became fully human and lived as we live.

He prayed for the same reasons we pray: to stay connected with his heavenly Father and to find direction for his next steps. However, many times in our prayers, we plead with God to conform to our will instead. That is praying with wrong motives. Jesus always prayed for God's will over whatever he asked. Even if it meant he had to die.

One theologian has said, "Prayer is surrender—surrender to the will of God and cooperation with that will. If I throw out a boat hook from the boat and catch hold of the shore and pull, do I pull the shore to me, or do I pull myself to the shore? Prayer is not pulling God to my will, but the aligning of my will to the will of God."[38]

Throw out the prayer hook, but remember to pull yourself toward God's desires. Not the other way around.

> **"I PRAY TO GOD TO KNOW HIM, TO FIND DIRECTION FOR MY LIFE, AND TO LAY MY REQUESTS BEFORE HIM."**

DAY 164

BIBLE STUDY

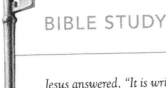

Jesus answered, "It is written: 'Man shall not live on bread alone, but on every word that comes from the mouth of God.'"

MATTHEW 4:4

Jesus had already been in the wilderness for forty days fasting. He was tired and hungry when Satan came to him on three occasions with temptations aimed directly at his weaknesses.

Satan's first attempt to bring down Jesus was, "If you are the Son of God, tell these stones to become bread" (v. 3). Oh, how good that bread would have tasted to the malnourished Jesus! He responded by quoting Scripture, Deuteronomy 8:3 to be exact: "Man shall not live on bread alone but on every word that comes from the mouth of God."

Satan came at him two more times; both times Jesus quoted Scripture. Jesus was modeling the spiritual practice of Bible study. He not only knew the teachings of Scripture but also drew on them to combat evil. After the third failed attempt, with his tail between his legs, Satan scrammed.

How will you overcome temptation and make good decisions for your life? Imitate Jesus by following every word that comes from the mouth of God. You can't live out what you do not know, so faithfully study God's Word.

> "I STUDY THE BIBLE TO KNOW GOD AND HIS TRUTH AND TO FIND DIRECTION FOR MY DAILY LIFE."

SINGLE-MINDEDNESS

"What I have heard from him I tell the world. . . . I do nothing on my own but speak just what the Father has taught me."

JOHN 8:26, 28

One morning I woke up to crime-scene tape surrounding the house across the street and police cars parked in front. Later I learned someone had been shot the night before in the backyard of that house—and our beagle, Lady, had slept through the excitement.

Later that day, our dog suddenly sprang up from her afternoon nap, barking and running to the window. Her perked-up ears showed us she was on high alert. Why? A squirrel was walking along the top of the wall surrounding our backyard. Lady slept through the gunshot, but woke up when a squirrel invaded her turf.

Do you, like our beloved pet, tend to hear only those things that you care about? A mom hears her child's cry in the midst of a room of crying children. Kids don't hear instructions to clean their room but hear parental whispers of plans to go get ice cream after dinner.

What are you hearing—or, perhaps better, what you are listening for? Ask God to teach you how to be tuned to his voice so you hear the important things, and to let you receive direction so you can "bark" or speak up for the things that matter to God.

"I FOCUS ON GOD AND HIS PRIORITIES FOR MY LIFE."

TOTAL SURRENDER

*Some time later God tested Abraham. . . . "Take your
son, your only son, whom you love—Isaac—and go to the
region of Moriah. Sacrifice him there as a burnt offering
on a mountain I will show you."*

GENESIS 22:1–2

Our son-in-law's father needs a liver transplant. His nephew's wife
felt led to offer part of hers. As I am writing this she is at the
Mayo Clinic in Minnesota to see if she is a match. Her attitude? "Why
would God so clearly lead me to do this if I am not a match?" She is
approaching it with total confidence that this is God's call on her life.
How selfless and inspiring.

Abraham had the same kind of experience. God called him to
sacrifice his only son. Abraham surrendered to God's will, and the
flint knife was in the downward motion to kill when God interrupted
him and said, "Do not lay a hand on the boy. . . . Now I know that you
fear God, because you have not withheld from me your son, your only
son" (v. 12).

Sometimes God asks us to make a sacrifice just to see if we are
totally surrendered to him. Whether or not this courageous gal turns
out to be a match, she has acted out her faith in the spirit of Abraham.
She has passed the total surrender test.

"I DEDICATE MY LIFE TO GOD'S PURPOSES."

BIBLICAL COMMUNITY

Every day they continued to meet together in the temple courts. They broke bread in their homes and ate together with glad and sincere hearts, praising God and enjoying the favor of all the people.

ACTS 2:46–47

There was a time when the word *screen* was commonly understood to be a lightweight, meshed-wire door designed to let fresh air in the house and keep bugs out. When a more solid, inner door was left open, the screen door was also a signal to neighbors that someone was home and others were invited to stop in for a visit.

In our frantic lives today, however, *screen* now means something else entirely. We set up screens around our lives, not to signal availability, but to keep people away. Our solid, inner doors are tightly closed and locked. Peepholes, caller ID, e-mail filters, and voice mail give us the option to say yes to those we want to speak with and no to those we do not.

One of the beauties of the early church was their simplicity and availability for each other to hang out, share a meal, laugh, and just spend an evening enjoying each other's company. We can't live in modern society without screens that keep people out, but I long for the screen that invites people in. How about you?

"I FELLOWSHIP WITH CHRISTIANS TO ACCOMPLISH GOD'S PURPOSES IN MY LIFE, IN THE LIVES OF OTHERS, AND IN THE WORLD."

SPIRITUAL GIFTS

"The Holy Spirit, whom the Father will send in my name,
. . . will remind you of everything I have said."

JOHN 14:26

always have trouble remembering three things: faces, names, and—I can't remember what the third thing is."—Fred Allen

"The advantage of a bad memory is that one enjoys several times the same good things for the first time."—Friedrich Nietzsche

"We'll be friends until we're old and senile. . . . Then we'll be new friends!"—Anonymous

Boy, can I identify with those statements! As forgetting becomes easier than remembering, you either laugh or cry at comments like those above. Yet sometimes we remember what we don't want to (the bully in second grade) but forget what we want to remember (I used to have Psalm 139 memorized!).

Jesus doesn't want us forgetting anything about him and what he taught, and that's where the Holy Spirit steps in. He empowered Peter (Acts 2), Stephen (Acts 7), and Paul (Acts 13), enabling them to spread the gospel message by reminding them of "everything [Jesus] said."

The Holy Spirit can enable you to be a powerful witness for Jesus. Be willing to be used for the Lord's work, take a step of faith, and trust that the Spirit will remind you of all God's truth.

"I KNOW MY SPIRITUAL GIFTS AND USE THEM TO FULFILL GOD'S PURPOSES."

OFFERING MY TIME

Is it a time for you yourselves to be living in your paneled houses, while this house [of the Lord] remains a ruin?

HAGGAI 1:4

Y ou make time to do what matters most to you." I squirm when I hear this because I know there's a good amount of truth in it.

So why the dry spell in date nights with my spouse? Why the neglected Bible study? Why can't I get all my work done by 6:00 p.m. and be home on time for dinner with my family? Far too often we get sidetracked from the good things we know we need to do and become occupied with lesser things. God wants us to use the time he's given us according to his priorities.

When the first exiles returned from Babylon to Judah, they made rebuilding the temple a top priority. They began strong, but they got distracted. The building project came to a complete halt and lay dormant for ten years.

Prompted by God, the prophet Haggai challenged the people of Israel to reconsider how they were prioritizing their time. Why, Haggai asked, were they building their own houses instead of the house of the Lord?

What question about the use of your time would Haggai ask you today? What activities—even ones that are good—are keeping you from doing what God wants you to do?

"I OFFER MY TIME TO FULFILL GOD'S PURPOSES."

GIVING MY RESOURCES

"Love your enemies, do good to them, and lend to them without expecting to get anything back. Then . . . you will be children of the Most High, because he is kind to the ungrateful and wicked."

LUKE 6:35

We are called to love our enemies, turn the other cheek, and go the extra mile. But did you realize Jesus asks you to lend money to your enemies without expecting anything in return? Isn't that pushing the envelope just a little too far? After all, if you lend money to your enemy, do you think you'll get it back?

If someone who has hurt you deeply loses their job, it is easier to say, "Well, I hope they find a new one" than it is to head to the grocery store, buy a gift certificate, and drop it off secretly at their house. But Jesus is looking for this kind of response, and here's why.

It's a matter of the heart. It's easy to say, "I love my enemies," but Jesus knows talk is cheap. He's asking us to put our money where our mouth is and show that our heart loves unconditionally.

Jesus loved us while we were his enemy, full of wickedness and ungratefulness. Is it so surprising he would ask his children to do the same for each other?

"I GIVE MY RESOURCES TO FULFILL GOD'S PURPOSES."

SHARING MY FAITH

*Make the most of every opportunity. Let your
conversation be always full of grace, seasoned with salt.*

COLOSSIANS 4:5–6

As a young boy I loved practical jokes. One evening before dinner I snuck to the table early and loosened the top of the saltshaker, then waited to see who would grab it first and be surprised with a plateful. It ended up being my dad! No one was laughing except me, but I quit when I saw my dad's face as he went to the trash to empty his plate. A sprinkle of salt makes food flavorful, but in large quantities it ruins the meal.

Paul is telling us our conversations can be the same: a little bit of salt or truth can make a person thirsty for God, but pushing too hard can turn them off.

Do you sometimes feel like you need to speak up about decisions your adult children are making even though you haven't been invited to share your opinion? This usually causes tension. Too much salt!

Sometimes we desperately desire someone to join the family of God so we determine to speak truth to them, even when they aren't willing to hear it. Our conversation puts them off. Too much salt!

May the Lord sensitize you to those moments and empower you during conversations to add the right amount of salt to your words.

> **"I SHARE MY FAITH WITH OTHERS
> TO FULFILL GOD'S PURPOSES."**

WORSHIP

"What fault did your ancestors find in me, that they strayed so far from me? They followed worthless idols and became worthless themselves."

JEREMIAH 2:5

Have you ever wondered why God wants to be worshipped? Is there some need in God that must be satisfied by our worship? Is God that insecure, that self-centered? And what is worship anyway? These unspoken questions and others can haunt our hearts. Is it possible we have the wrong idea about God and worship?

Perhaps our worship of God is not for his sake but for ours. God knows we strive to become like people we idolize or things we want to acquire. Make no mistake, we all worship something or someone. Anything we worship other than God is called an idol. Money, possessions, a popular or powerful person, prominence, and pleasure are only a few items on the list of what the Bible calls idols. God knows if we give our attention and devotion to idols, we will become as worthless as the idols we have deemed worthy of our focus.

Why worship the one true God from whom you received your being? Because when you give attention and devotion to him and worship him, you will strive to become like the One in whose image you have been created. Worship changes you.

> **"I WORSHIP GOD FOR WHO HE IS AND WHAT HE HAS DONE FOR ME."**

PRAYER

LORD, *you are the God who saves me; day and night I cry out to you. May my prayer come before you; turn your ear to my cry.*

PSALM 88:1–2

O h my God!" How often do these words fly from our lips at a surprise or shock, whether from something good or bad? Some people feel it is disrespectful to use God's name this way, but perhaps it is often a prayer rolling off our lips because we can't help ourselves. Could it be our first inclination when something good happens is to thank him or when tragedy strikes to spontaneously cry out to him for help?

Perhaps C. S. Lewis, when chided by his unbelieving friends for praying, said it best: "I pray because I can't help myself. I pray because I'm helpless. I pray because the need flows out of me all the time, waking and sleeping. It doesn't change God. It changes me."[39]

When the phrase "Oh my God!" flows from your lips, let it remind you of your gratefulness or your helplessness, and acknowledge your dependence on your Creator. Make those words a prayer from your heart, and let him change you.

> **"I PRAY TO GOD TO KNOW HIM, TO FIND DIRECTION FOR MY LIFE, AND TO LAY MY REQUESTS BEFORE HIM."**

BIBLE STUDY

The LORD gives wisdom; from his mouth come knowledge and understanding.

PROVERBS 2:6

The young man held his firstborn child in his hands for the first time and whispered to her, "Daughter, you don't even know who I am, but I am your father and it is up to me to teach you about life. And if it is up to me to teach you, I had better get on the stick and figure out what life is all about because it's not just about me anymore." The new father sought advice from an older man, "How do I teach my daughter about God?" The older man replied, "Simple. You will teach her by the kind of man you are. The question is, what will determine the kind of man you become?"

Where do we go to find needed truth about God and life, not just for our lives, but also for those whom we love? In God's Word, the Bible.

The Author of life inspired his Word, the Bible, to give you his wisdom, knowledge, and understanding. Could anything be more important to your life? You can't pass on what you yourself do not have. Learn to read it. Study it to learn. Live what you've learned so that others who depend on you may know God as well.

"I STUDY THE BIBLE TO KNOW GOD AND HIS TRUTH AND TO FIND DIRECTION FOR MY DAILY LIFE."

SINGLE-MINDEDNESS

*Hear, O Israel: The LORD our God, the LORD is
one. Love the LORD your God with all your heart and
with all your soul and with all your strength.*

DEUTERONOMY 6:4–5

In the first of the Ten Commandments, God instructed the Israelites to serve him exclusively. As the one who had rescued them from slavery, he was worthy of their worship. Later, just before Moses died and the Israelites entered the promised land, God inspired Moses to remind the people of their calling.

When asked what the greatest command was, Jesus replied, "Love the Lord your God with all your heart and with all your soul and with all your mind" (Matthew 22:37). These Old Testament words, reiterated by our Savior, remain the clarion call for believers today.

So how do you love the Lord with all that you are in a world with so many distractions? Only through the power of the Holy Spirit is such single-minded devotion possible. Ask the Holy Spirit to help focus your attention on the one true God in the midst of the many responsibilities, duties, and voices that clamor for your attention. Ask him to train you to notice evidence of God in your everyday life.

When the Holy Spirit makes you aware of God's presence, how could you respond with anything other than grateful love?

**"I FOCUS ON GOD AND HIS
PRIORITIES FOR MY LIFE."**

TOTAL SURRENDER

Just as you received Christ Jesus as Lord, continue to live your lives in him.

COLOSSIANS 2:6

Have you ever watched the electrifying spectacle of a high trapeze act? The flyer abandons the safety of the bar and soars through the air, trusting that she will be caught. Flyers will tell you that the star of the act is the catcher. All the flyer can do is let go. She surrenders her hold on the bar, stretches out her arms, and trusts the catcher. If the flyer doesn't let go, she remains alone, and the two never join each other on the catcher's bar. And there is no remarkable feat for the audience to applaud.

God, the trustworthy Catcher of souls, invites us to join him on his bar so that we might live together as one with him in life and purpose. But something is required of us, and it can be scary. God asks us to let go of the bar of our old life—our desires, our plans, our will—and surrender it all to his will. God wants us to let go and trust him.

Jesus surrendered his will to his Father. Will you? Is there something he's asking you to surrender? Let it go! You won't fall! Your heavenly Father will catch you every time.

"I DEDICATE MY LIFE TO GOD'S PURPOSES."

BIBLICAL COMMUNITY

There is one body and one Spirit, just as you were called
to one hope when you were called; one Lord, one faith,
one baptism; one God and Father of all, who is over all.

EPHESIANS 4:4–6

Imagine you are listening to an orchestra playing Handel's *Messiah*; hear in your mind the melodious sounds that fill your soul with heavenly delight. Two conditions make this rapturous experience possible. First, each player's instrument must be in tune. Second, each player must play in concert with the other players, following the lead of the conductor.

We are the body of Christ, a holy symphony, and we are called to play a song in tune with other believers that proclaims God's grace and joy to a listening world. There are two questions for us all. First, is my life in tune with my Creator? Second, is my life being lived in concert with my brothers and sisters in Christ?

The Eternal Composer sent his Son to bring our lives back in tune with his. Christ Jesus is leading his orchestra, teaching us to live in harmony with each other. Let's accept his invitation to play our parts in his symphony of joy. Let's get in tune with God and in harmony with each other. Remember, we have a listening audience.

> **"I FELLOWSHIP WITH CHRISTIANS TO ACCOMPLISH GOD'S PURPOSES IN MY LIFE, IN THE LIVES OF OTHERS, AND IN THE WORLD."**

SPIRITUAL GIFTS

God has placed the parts in the body, every one of them,
just as he wanted them to be. If they were all one part,
where would the body be?

1 CORINTHIANS 12:18–19

At the 1980 Winter Olympics, the US hockey team, made up of passionate college kids, pulled off a dramatic victory over the then-Soviet Union team, who were experienced professionals. The win was so stunning that *Sports Illustrated* named it the number one sports moment of the twentieth century.[40]

Teamwork was important to making the Miracle on Ice happen. The players on the roster couldn't all be goalies; they couldn't all be forwards; they couldn't all be defenders. All three roles were needed. Each person had a unique ability, and they worked together to accomplish an amazing feat.

God's body, the church, is no different. It can't be only made up of people with gifts of healing or gifts of guidance or gifts of teaching. God uses individuals with those gifts and many more to do the work he has for the church.

What gifts do you bring to the work of Christ's body in the world? When the body of Christ works together, God makes miracles happen. There's no sweeter victory.

> **"I KNOW MY SPIRITUAL GIFTS AND USE**
> **THEM TO FULFILL GOD'S PURPOSES."**

OFFERING MY TIME

"Why were you searching for me?" [Jesus] asked. "Didn't you know I had to be in my Father's house?"

LUKE 2:49

W here does the time go? Well, studies show where some of it goes. Based on an average life expectancy of 74.3 years, we'll spend a total of 3 days and 8 hours applying deodorant; 10 months and 17 days grocery shopping; 8 months opening junk mail; and 64 hours waiting to see doctors.[41]

But what about time devoted to matters of eternal significance— worshipping, praying, reading the Bible, going to church? It would be interesting, if not sobering, if someday we could see how much of our lifetime we invested in our relationship with God.

Be intentional about your schedule this week and block out time each day to be with Jesus, to study his Word, and to listen for his voice. It doesn't have to be the same time every day, although that works for some people. Make a daily appointment with your Shepherd—and don't forget to mute your cell phone. Those e-mails and texts can wait.

By the way, at the young age of twelve, Jesus understood how best to use his time. Follow his example and spend more time with your heavenly Father.

"I OFFER MY TIME TO FULFILL GOD'S PURPOSES."

GIVING MY RESOURCES

One person gives freely, yet gains even more; another withholds unduly, but comes to poverty.

PROVERBS 11:24

One dollar out of every ten. *Okay, I can do that.*

Ten dollars out of every one hundred. *Umm. Okay . . .*

A hundred dollars out of every thousand. *This is getting hard.*

A thousand out of every ten thousand? *That's a lot of money.*

Throughout the Old Testament, God's people set aside a tenth of their crops, herds, and flocks for God's purposes. This principle is called tithing. Giving a tithe started as a nonreligious, political tradition in the ancient world, where giving a tribute or tax of a tenth (a tithe) to the king was a demonstration of allegiance. When we give a tenth of our income to God's purposes, we declare our allegiance to God.

Of course, giving implies letting go, and letting go of money can be hard. Most people make the mistake of thinking that it will be easier when they have more to give. But the reality is, the more you have, the harder it is to let go. Giving brings great freedom as you exercise control over money rather than having it control you. Giving also brings great joy. Try it and see! With a tithe, declare allegiance to the King who deserves it more than any earthly king, and know his pleasure and blessing.

"I GIVE MY RESOURCES TO FULFILL GOD'S PURPOSES."

SHARING MY FAITH

"You will receive power when the Holy Spirit comes on you; and you will be my witnesses."

ACTS 1:8

During our engagement, Randy persuaded me to buy a cute sports car with manual transmission. I fretted because I had never driven a stick before. "Don't worry, I'll teach you!" he promised. And he tried!

The next day was my turn to drive carpool to work. I came up with all kinds of excuses: "What if I make us late?" "What if the car dies in the middle of the intersection?" "What if I stall the car getting on the highway?" I could have called my carpool friends and passed off the responsibility. Instead, I just got out there and did it—somehow we made it to work on time.

We find many excuses not to share our faith or to pawn off the responsibility on others. "I'm new at this Christianity thing." "What if I can't answer her questions?" "Witnessing isn't my spiritual gift."

Jesus doesn't say, "If it's in your comfort zone," or "If it's your gift," or "Only if no risk is involved." All believers are to share the truth about God's love and faithfulness, and the Holy Spirit promises to empower us.

If you have opportunity, just get out there and do it! Share what God has done in your life and let him use his power to do the rest.

> **"I SHARE MY FAITH WITH OTHERS TO FULFILL GOD'S PURPOSES."**

WORSHIP

Come near to God and he will come near to you.

JAMES 4:8

Our friends invited us to join them at their lake house for the weekend. The invitation included our son who was attending college not far from their home. I called our son and extended the offer for him to meet us at the lake, but was sad when I heard him say, "Well, Mom, I can't. I have too much studying to do before midterms next week." I told him, "No pressure, but you are more than welcome to just come and study the whole time." He told me he probably wouldn't.

On the appointed day, Randy and I headed to meet our friends. To our surprise, when we were about halfway to the lake, my cell phone rang and I heard, "Mom, I'm on my way to hang out with you all." We could not wait to see him!

He did study all weekend long, but we didn't care. We spent time together, and that was all that mattered. Our son chose to be in our presence!

I wonder if God feels the same way when we choose to "hang out" in his presence and worship him. Or better yet, when we choose to worship him continually as we take his presence with us into whatever we need to do. Homework included!

> "I WORSHIP GOD FOR WHO HE IS AND
> WHAT HE HAS DONE FOR ME."

PRAYER

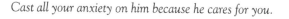

Cast all your anxiety on him because he cares for you.

1 PETER 5:7

One summer day when I was a kid, I made a bet with two boys I met at the local farmer's market. For every ball they hit over the fence, I'd give them fifty cents. For every ball I hit over the fence, they'd give me five dollars. Within minutes I was down five dollars. I said I'd have to go get money at home and return with it. But I didn't have five dollars at home, and I had no intention of coming back. I just ran off and hid in my bedroom with overwhelming anxiety, expecting to live out the rest of my days there.

Two hours later my dad asked me if I owed some boys five dollars. The thugs had tracked down where I lived. So I confessed. He informed me that he'd paid the bill in full, and he hoped I had learned my lesson. I walked out of that room relieved. I just wished I had gone to my dad two hours earlier and saved myself from such intense worry and anxiety.

God wants us to do the same thing. Whenever you feel anxiety or fear, don't delay. Take it to your Father, and find peace that transcends all understanding.

> **"I PRAY TO GOD TO KNOW HIM, TO FIND DIRECTION FOR MY LIFE, AND TO LAY MY REQUESTS BEFORE HIM."**

BIBLE STUDY

Direct me in the path of your commands, for there I find delight.

PSALM 119:35

The Bible is made up of 66 books: 39 in the Old Testament and 27 in the New. There are 1,189 chapters, 31,173 verses, and 773,692 words. Psalm 117 is both the middle chapter and the shortest chapter of the Bible, and Psalm 119 is the longest. The shortest verse is John 11:35 and the longest, Esther 8:9. Such information may be interesting, but it is hardly life changing.

What is life changing about the Bible is that its pages are filled with actual words given to us by God, our Creator, for purposes far greater than statistical, cultural, or linguistic analysis. The ancient stories and messages on these pages contain the grand love story of God's desire to have a relationship with us and to provide the wisdom we need to follow him. As we bask in these divinely spoken words, the Holy Spirit uses them to teach us; to transform us; to make us more like Jesus; to be more compassionate, kind, patient, and loving; to be more willing to serve; and to be obedient and yielded to God.

As you dive into the Word and apply it to your life, its life-changing power can make you more like Jesus.

> "I STUDY THE BIBLE TO KNOW GOD AND HIS TRUTH AND TO FIND DIRECTION FOR MY DAILY LIFE."

SINGLE-MINDEDNESS

*I consider everything a loss because of the surpassing
worth of knowing Christ Jesus my Lord, for whose sake
I have lost all things. I consider them garbage, that I may
gain Christ.*

PHILIPPIANS 3:8

Paul was deserving of every gold star imaginable in the Jewish
world—he'd spent his life earning his high standing. It would've
been absolutely radical for him to say that he'd come to consider all
he'd established with them "a loss"! By God's grace, this zealous Jew
had become a passionate preacher of the gospel of Jesus Christ. He had
come to value Jesus most, and so he'd identify and remove anything
that got in the way of him living every moment for Jesus. Otherwise it'd
be like he was running a marathon with ankle weights.

As Paul traveled from city to city teaching people about the gift of
salvation, he called believers to imitate his example of single-mindedly
following Christ. He said, "Forgetting what is behind and straining
toward what is ahead, I press on toward the goal to win the prize for
which God has called me heavenward in Christ Jesus" (vv. 13–14).

All kinds of things, good or bad, can keep you from running well
for Jesus. What are the "ankle weights" in your life that you can leave
behind?

**"I FOCUS ON GOD AND HIS
PRIORITIES FOR MY LIFE."**

DAY 186

TOTAL SURRENDER

Praise be to the God of Shadrach, Meshach and Abednego . . . ! They trusted in him . . . and were willing to give up their lives rather than serve or worship any god except their own God.

DANIEL 3:28

've wanted to ask you this for a while." Diane had been the family accountant for eight years. "You're living on a school teacher's salary. You have three kids. Why do you give so much money to your church? It seems that life would be easier if you didn't."

James smiled. "We're blessed, and God has been faithful and generous through the years. Supporting our church is a way to thank and worship him. It's also how we express trust in him to provide for us."

James and his family chose the furnace of financial frugality just as Shadrach, Meshach, and Abednego chose a blazing literal furnace instead of bowing to the statue of King Nebuchadnezzar. They chose loyalty to God over their own lives. When they emerged unharmed, the pagan king responded with praise for the young men's God.

Although the level of sacrifice is different, your countercultural ways may prompt some head scratching. When onlookers are puzzled about why you do what you do, they may find their attention directed to the God who prompts your loyalty. Some soul searching and soul saving may result.

"I DEDICATE MY LIFE TO GOD'S PURPOSES."

BIBLICAL COMMUNITY

Be completely humble and gentle; be patient, bearing with one another in love.

EPHESIANS 4:2

Merriam Webster's defines *entitlement* as "the feeling or belief that you deserve to be given something (such as special privileges)."[42] Sound familiar? That sentiment is rampant in our society. It seems both to arise from and fuel narcissism, which implies self-love and self-centeredness—hardly a mind-set for Christian community.

Consider Paul's words above. Humility, gentleness, and patience are traits we need as we interact with other people. "Bearing with one another in love" is hardly easy, especially if those "one anothers" are interfering with what you feel or believe you're entitled to!

But one of the marked differences between the church and the rest of society is Jesus' call to live for others. Throughout the New Testament, followers of Jesus were urged to look out for one another. When the early Christians did this, it created an irresistible attraction for outsiders to belong to God's family. Looking out for one another in the body of Christ could have the same impact on our society today.

So this week, start each day by asking God to show you which "one anothers" he wants you to look out for, help, and serve.

> **"I FELLOWSHIP WITH CHRISTIANS TO ACCOMPLISH GOD'S PURPOSES IN MY LIFE, IN THE LIVES OF OTHERS, AND IN THE WORLD."**

SPIRITUAL GIFTS

"To one [servant] he gave five bags of gold, to another two bags, and to another one bag, each according to his ability. Then he went on his journey."

MATTHEW 25:15

The pastor of the small church I grew up in came to me and said, "Our pianist is having some health issues and has decided to retire. Rozanne, would you consider being her replacement?" This wouldn't have been so strange, except I was thirteen years old, very shy, and not very accomplished. I raised every objection I could; then finally, reluctantly accepted the position, and for the next three years I was the church pianist.

Up to that time I had practiced only halfheartedly, but now I found myself motivated to practice diligently because I was actually using this gift God had given me. Who would have ever thought this shy little thirteen-year-old girl would one day marry a man who would become the pastor of a large church? Not me!

God created you and knows the talents, skills, and passions he knit into you. He offers you opportunities to use your gifts for his church body and his work in the world. Are you sharing your gifts generously and joyfully, or reluctantly like I did? You may be surprised what his plans are for you!

"I KNOW MY SPIRITUAL GIFTS AND USE THEM TO FULFILL GOD'S PURPOSES."

OFFERING MY TIME

Listen, my dear brothers and sisters: Has not God chosen those who are poor in the eyes of the world to be rich in faith and to inherit the kingdom he promised those who love him?

JAMES 2:5

Several years ago I was serving food with my neighbors at the local homeless shelter. I sat down to share a meal with the homeless when a member of our church joined us. I said, "Hey, man, great to have you here to serve with us tonight." His response: "Oh, I am not here to serve; this is where I live."

He knew it; everyone at the table knew it; I knew it. Instantly, I saw him differently. Instead of a self-sufficient member of my fairly affluent church, he was a poor, homeless man. It was in my eyes. It was in the tone of my voice throughout the rest of our conversation.

I left so ashamed of myself. I knew this was not how God saw him. In my desperation, God whispered, "I want you to go back to the shelter every month, not to serve the poor people, but to sit and talk with them until you can look them in the eye and see them the way I do."

It took two years, but it finally happened. When we offer our time to help others, God often uses that experience to help us become more like Jesus.

"I OFFER MY TIME TO FULFILL GOD'S PURPOSES."

GIVING MY RESOURCES

The people were restrained from bringing more, because what they already had was more than enough to do all the work.

EXODUS 36:6–7

Jack was a young pastor-to-be, newly married, and very poor. While he waited for a ministry position to open up, he was selling—or *trying* to sell—swimming pools in San Diego. His wife's minimum-wage job was better than nothing.

Frustrated, tired of the poverty, and wondering what God was doing and why he was taking so long, Jack gave the Lord a piece of his mind. "What do you want me to do? We need to pay rent. We need to eat. We're in survival mode! What else can we do?"

"Tithe" was the response, and "What?!" was the reaction. But that week Jack and his wife began the lifelong, faith-building practice of tithing. Ten percent of any amount of money that came in, whether earned or a gift, went to the Lord.

Years later, Jack was a pastor, father of four kids, and still tithing. He and his wife could tell some remarkable stories of God's financial faithfulness, and Jack spoke from experience when he said from the pulpit: "A 10 percent tithe is the starting point. Giving is a step of faith and a vote of confidence that God will provide. Give until it hurts—and then give until it stops hurting."

> **"I GIVE MY RESOURCES TO FULFILL GOD'S PURPOSES."**

SHARING MY FAITH

Those who had been scattered preached the word wherever they went.

ACTS 8:4

There's a remarkable pattern evident in history as well as around the world today: persecution can strengthen an individual's faith in Jesus and increase the number of people following the Lord. The church in China, for instance, has been marked as a symbol of strength in spite of increasingly brutal persecution; it continues to grow, even in extremely harsh conditions.

Sometimes such conditions prompt believers to flee their homelands and all that is familiar. That was certainly the case in the first-century church. None of Jesus' early followers left Jerusalem with the good news of their Lord's forgiveness and love until persecution forced them to leave the city. Rather than a setback to the growth of God's kingdom, it was actually a fulfillment of a prophesy Jesus made in Acts 1:8: "You will be my witnesses in Jerusalem, and in all Judea and Samaria, and to the ends of the earth." This was God's plan all along.

Do you see what seems to be a setback to the growth of God's kingdom? Since history tends to repeat itself, it could be the very thing God uses to advance his kingdom. Be encouraged!

> **"I SHARE MY FAITH WITH OTHERS TO FULFILL GOD'S PURPOSES."**

WORSHIP

*Set your hearts on things above, where Christ is, seated
at the right hand of God. Set your minds on things above,
not on earthly things.*

COLOSSIANS 3:1–2

Imagine doing all your tasks with your heart and mind "set . . . on
things above." Imagine approaching everything you do as an act of
worship, as an act of service that both pleases and glorifies the Lord.
What a redemptive perspective on the mundane, unlovely, and rote
aspects of life!

Cleaning up the dinner dishes, sitting in a meeting, raking the
leaves, changing a diaper, driving to work or to run errands, paying
bills, doing laundry—we can, as God's children, do these things as acts
of worship.

All that we do in the home and at the workplace, in our church
and out in the community, should be done with a sense of gratitude for
the task God has assigned to us, for the material goods he has given
us, and for the people he has put in our lives. And as we go about our
day, we can ask for the Lord's guidance, strength, and joy to accomplish
what our hands find to do. Whatever the activity, let your love for your
heavenly Father fuel an ongoing conversation with God. And *that* is
worship!

> **"I WORSHIP GOD FOR WHO HE IS AND
> WHAT HE HAS DONE FOR ME."**

PRAYER

Very early in the morning, while it was still dark, Jesus got up, left the house and went off to a solitary place, where he prayed.

MARK 1:35

When you think of people of prayer, who comes to mind? Someone you know personally? Famous writers you've read? Or people in the Bible? Often we think of people who pray eloquently, which can be intimidating. But God loves prayers that are simply a conversation.

We have no more perfect example than Jesus. Spending time with the Father in prayer gave him the strength and guidance he needed to fulfill his purpose in coming to earth. Jesus consistently sought direction and support from his Father. If Jesus needed to turn to his Father, how much more do we need to!

"Get up a little earlier and spend some time with the Lord!" "Set aside your coffee break at work to pray." "Before you read the newspaper, spend some time in prayer." The suggestions go on and on. Figure out the best time for you to just talk with your heavenly Father. It may be only ten minutes, but your heavenly Father longs to give you strength and guidance for life if you ask. Perhaps you'll find it's the best ten minutes of your day.

> **"I PRAY TO GOD TO KNOW HIM, TO FIND DIRECTION FOR MY LIFE, AND TO LAY MY REQUESTS BEFORE HIM."**

BIBLE STUDY

"You study the Scriptures diligently because you think that in them you have eternal life. These are the very Scriptures that testify about me, yet you refuse to come to me to have life."

JOHN 5:39–40

Have you ever read a book or watched a movie and felt like you missed something? Jesus is saying in John 5 that his listeners had done the same with God's Word. They read it. In fact, they searched it diligently because they wanted to have a relationship with God. But they missed the point. The Old Testament stories and prophesies all pointed to the coming of the Messiah. They knew the Scriptures well but refused to accept Jesus as the fulfillment of the promises.

Many of us attend church where we hear the Bible taught, we are involved in Bible studies, and we read the Bible daily during our quiet time. We do all this, and even apply the principles found to our lives, but sometimes we miss God's point: Jesus. If we never come to declare Jesus as the only way to have a relationship with our holy God, we have missed the whole point of his life, death, and resurrection.

As you diligently read God's Word, always remember to look for Jesus. He's the point. Don't miss him!

> **"I STUDY THE BIBLE TO KNOW GOD AND HIS TRUTH AND TO FIND DIRECTION FOR MY DAILY LIFE."**

SINGLE-MINDEDNESS

Pray continually . . . for this is God's will for you in Christ Jesus.

1 THESSALONIANS 5:17–18

P ray continually! Other translations read, "Pray without ceasing." Now there is a passage that will bury most people in a pile of guilt. Don't just pray once a day or twice a day; never stop praying. How is that even possible?

Here's my solution: I realized that I talk to myself all day about every situation I am in—a task, a meeting, a jog, planning the day, determining my next move, deciding on a purchase. So I decided I'd have that conversation with God instead. *God, I am about to go into this meeting. What do you want to accomplish? How can I encourage the person I am meeting with? God, I am so overwhelmed with things to do today. Where should I start? What should I eliminate? Give me your wisdom. God, I'm having trouble sleeping. I'm anxious. Can you stay up with me?*

I think this is what Paul, who led a busy life, must have had in mind in his command above. Pray on the go. Have a continuous conversation with God instead of yourself. You never say "amen" because the conversation is never over.

Have a conversation right now with God. Ask him, "God, is this something you want me to try?"

> **"I FOCUS ON GOD AND HIS PRIORITIES FOR MY LIFE."**

DAY 196

TOTAL SURRENDER

Many are the plans in a person's heart, but it is the
LORD's purpose that prevails.

PROVERBS 19:21

To-do lists give you a sense of accomplishment and success. But how often have you breathed a heavy sigh as you climbed into bed, remembering all the interruptions that hindered successful completion of your to-do list?

God asks you to surrender everything to him. That includes your to-do list. Proverbs 19:21 reminds us that people who do not surrender their lists see interruptions as a frustration; people who do surrender their lists allow for God's purposes to emerge and prevail. Interruptions become opportunities instead of frustrations. Did a distraught friend call? God used you to bring encouragement. Did your child wake up sick? God used you to bring them comfort, care, and security. Did your spouse call with a need, or want an impromptu lunch date? God deepened your relationship.

Try adding the interruptions to your to-do list in a different color and cross them off as well. At the end of the day, whatever you have crossed off indicates the to-do list God designed for you. Rest peacefully knowing you surrendered to God's plan.

"I DEDICATE MY LIFE TO GOD'S PURPOSES."

BIBLICAL COMMUNITY

[Jesus'] purpose was to create in himself one new humanity out of the two [Gentile and Jew], thus making peace, and in one body to reconcile both of them to God through the cross.

EPHESIANS 2:15–16

The local politics got very partisan—and very strange. Desperately wanting to win the election, a candidate arranged for a woman in his party to join the other party and run against him. He hoped to succeed by diluting the votes of the opposition. So this woman found herself fraternizing with the opposing party in order to help a candidate from her own party gain votes. Politics does make strange bedfellows.

In the early church, the new Christian faith also made for some strange bedfellows. God had sent his Son, the Messiah, through the family line of his chosen people, but Jesus' death and resurrection was for Gentiles as well as Jews (*all* have fallen short of God's standards). It was a jarring assignment, but a Jew was to embrace as "fellow citizens with God's people and also members of his household" (v. 19) those Gentiles who recognized Jesus as their Savior.

Who in your local fellowship do you need to embrace because you both have been reconciled "to God through the cross"?

> **"I FELLOWSHIP WITH CHRISTIANS TO ACCOMPLISH GOD'S PURPOSES IN MY LIFE, IN THE LIVES OF OTHERS, AND IN THE WORLD."**

SPIRITUAL GIFTS

Tongues of fire . . . separated and came to rest on each of them. All of them were filled with the Holy Spirit and began to speak in other tongues as the Spirit enabled them.

ACTS 2:3–4

"Surprise!"

Most birthday celebrations involve an element of surprise. Sometimes the party itself is a surprise. Sometimes it's the out-of-town daughter flown in for the special day. Maybe it's the gift you didn't think you'd receive. Perhaps it was the chance to try that new restaurant or even get away for a day or two. Whatever the birthday surprises, they are all motivated by love.

Similarly, the birthday of the church—that first Pentecost—had its surprises that left people amazed, perplexed, and bewildered. The promised gift of the Holy Spirit arrived with wind, fire, and the wonders of God being declared in many different languages. The Spirit's arrival was a gift motivated by God's love for his people.

Jesus sent the Spirit—whom he called the Counselor—to teach his followers the things of God and his kingdom and, when necessary, to help us recall what we've been taught.

Thank God for the gift of his Spirit! Watch for ways he will continually surprise you with his love and gifts. He wants to amaze you today.

> **"I KNOW MY SPIRITUAL GIFTS AND USE THEM TO FULFILL GOD'S PURPOSES."**

OFFERING MY TIME

"The LORD has given you the Sabbath; that is why on the sixth day he gives you bread for two days."

EXODUS 16:29

When Dave and Beth got married, they didn't argue about not putting the cap on the toothpaste or which way the toilet paper went. The challenge for them was vacations.

Raised in a military family, Beth traveled a lot as a child, moving from base to base. The family occasionally stopped at landmarks on the way to the new assignment, but that hardly made the traveling a vacation. Dave's family, on the other hand, intentionally took vacations. Everyone piled into the station wagon for long road trips to see all the aunts and uncles in Missouri. He had an abundance of "He's touching me!" and sandwiches at rest stops memories. It took Beth awhile to learn to value restful vacations, but thanks to Dave's patience and perseverance she did—and then she had to learn *how* to rest.

If that sounds strange, consider the fourth commandment: "Remember the Sabbath" (Exodus 20:8). If taking a day of rest came easily to us, God might have issued only nine commandments. God created you with the need for regular and intentional rest—and then mandated it. God knows if you don't find time to replenish, you just might fall apart. Why not start this week?

"I OFFER MY TIME TO FULFILL GOD'S PURPOSES."

DAY 200

GIVING MY RESOURCES

Whoever loves money never has enough; whoever loves wealth is never satisfied with their income.

ECCLESIASTES 5:10

The stories of what happens after people win the lottery are often tragic: gambling away millions—and now living in a trailer; losing friends; divorcing; going into debt or filing bankruptcy; a winner's brother hiring a hit man to kill him; being fleeced; being murdered; committing suicide.

These stories wouldn't have surprised Benjamin Franklin, who observed, "Money never made a man happy yet, nor will it. The more a man has, the more he wants. Instead of filling a vacuum, it makes one."

Jesus also knew that money doesn't mean happiness and—worse—it can mask a person's need for God. In his words, "It is easier for a camel to go through the eye of a needle than for someone who is rich to enter the kingdom of God" (Luke 18:25).

So what is the takeaway? Winning the lottery may not be as great a deal as you think; in fact, it might mean the death of you. But giving generously out of the financial resources God has blessed you with will help you avoid money's stranglehold, and you'll find satisfaction and contentment.

> **"I GIVE MY RESOURCES TO FULFILL GOD'S PURPOSES."**

SHARING MY FAITH

You are a Jew and I am a Samaritan woman. How can you ask me for a drink?

JOHN 4:9

Author of *Seeking Allah, Finding Jesus*, Nabeel Qureshi, PhD, was proud of his Islamic identity. Growing up in a devout Muslim home, he remembers reading the Quran in Arabic by the time he was five years old. His parents taught him to seek Allah.

But a close college friend shared the gospel with Nabeel and told him, "We can be very confident that Jesus Christ died on the cross and rose from the dead after having claimed to be God. . . . These three points would contradict the teachings of Islam, yet they establish the truth of Christianity." Nabeel went on to receive Jesus' love because this friend shared his faith. He hopes that after hearing about his personal experiences, people will be kinder to Muslims and quicker to share the gospel with them so they can discover Jesus' love.

Jesus reached out to the Samaritan woman (who would have been shunned by other Jews), much to her surprise—and to the disciples' as well! A college friend reached out to Nabeel. With whom does God want you to share your faith? Maybe you'll surprise that person by sharing Jesus' love—and maybe that person will surprise you by finding faith in Jesus!

> **"I SHARE MY FAITH WITH OTHERS TO FULFILL GOD'S PURPOSES."**

WORSHIP

> *"The multitude of your sacrifices—what are they to me?"*
> *says the* LORD. . . . *"I have no pleasure in the blood of*
> *bulls and lambs and goats."*

ISAIAH 1:11

The sacrificial system was God's design. He had instituted the principle that sin was removed only when blood from an acceptable sacrifice was shed—and now he was not pleased? What was God saying in Isaiah 1?

The holy and almighty God was well aware that the Israelites' sacrifices had become meaningless rituals, and he was both angry and heartbroken. The people brought God sacrifice after sacrifice, but he knew their hearts were cold, dispassionate. Their worship was anything but pleasing to him.

And just how pleasing to God is our worship? Have certain elements become mere rituals? Are we singing the words without much thought and listening to the truth with our ears but not our hearts?

Just as he was then, God is far more concerned with the state of your heart when you worship than the motions you go through. He longs for you to praise him with your heart, mind, and soul.

"I WORSHIP GOD FOR WHO HE IS AND WHAT HE HAS DONE FOR ME."

PRAYER

Will you forget me forever? How long will you hide your face from me?

PSALM 13:1

H ow long, O Lord?" "How long before the healing begins?" "How long before my child comes home?" "How long before the pain eases?" "How long, God, before you do something, anything?"

All of us can and should pray like David did, with total honesty, transparency, and vulnerability. That kind of prayer is not only encouraged but crucial to having a real and deep relationship with God.

Our God is not a distant, cosmic being, but a good Father who longs to interact with his children, even when they're hurting or angry, despairing or hopeless. We serve a God who is not threatened by our questions and doubts. We don't have to put on a false persona to please him. He permits us to be honest about our fears, our feelings of isolation, and our disappointments—even our disappointments in him.

So, like David in Psalm 13, pour out whatever is on your heart to the powerful God of the universe. Like David, you can be sure that God wants to know what you are experiencing and feeling. He longs to hear you speak to him from your heart.

"I PRAY TO GOD TO KNOW HIM, TO FIND DIRECTION FOR MY LIFE, AND TO LAY MY REQUESTS BEFORE HIM."

BIBLE STUDY

These commandments that I give you today are to be on your hearts. Impress them on your children.

DEUTERONOMY 6:6–7

We pass on nursery rhymes we learned as children. We recount fairy tales told to us by our own mothers and fathers as our little ones drift off to sleep at night. But do we take time to impress upon our children's hearts the wisdom and stories from God's Word?

For years, the words of God and the stories of his people were passed on to the next generation orally. Even after Moses wrote the first five books of the Old Testament, people still didn't have access to written words. So oral tradition remained, and before Moses died, he issued a command for parents to continue to teach their children God's principles. What an overwhelming responsibility, especially if you feel you don't know God's Word well yourself! But Moses' command doesn't allow us to relegate our parental responsibility to children's workers at church for one hour each weekend.

If you feel overwhelmed, simply start by reading stories from a children's Bible and applying one of the key ideas you are learning through *Believe* to each story with your kids. You can begin to give your children the foundation needed to build their own relationship with God.

> "I STUDY THE BIBLE TO KNOW
> GOD AND HIS TRUTH AND TO FIND
> DIRECTION FOR MY DAILY LIFE."

SINGLE-MINDEDNESS

"I am the LORD your God, who brought you out of Egypt, out of the land of slavery. You shall have no other gods before me."

EXODUS 20:2–3

It's far too easy to have spiritual ADD in this noisy, fast-paced world. With our powerful technology and ever-present social media, we can find it difficult to hear God's still, small voice. When we feel compelled to keep up with Facebook, Twitter, Instagram, and "old-fashioned" e-mail, we may struggle to have frequent time with the Lord. The responsibilities of life and the amount of time it takes to simply live can have us on a hamster wheel, exhausted, not thinking straight, just trying to keep up.

When we do sit down to spend time with God, we are easily distracted. God understands this. They had the same struggles in Old Testament times, so when God spoke to the people of Israel, the first thing he commanded was that they focus on him. That focus doesn't come easily for the naturally sinful, ADD-addled human beings. To be single-minded means to have one desire that trumps all others. From the beginning, God made it clear that his people's main focus should be him.

God wants you to remember that he brought you out of the land of slavery to sin and into eternal life. He deserves your focus.

> **"I FOCUS ON GOD AND HIS PRIORITIES FOR MY LIFE."**

DAY 206

TOTAL SURRENDER

"I don't know him," [Peter] said. . . . Just as he was speaking, the rooster crowed. . . . He went outside and wept bitterly.

LUKE 22:57, 60, 62

It was the biology classroom, and that meant microscopes, petri dishes, 3-D models of a DNA spiral, and Mr. Evans.

Everyone at school knew where Evans stood on the matter of evolution, but that didn't discourage Rob. He raised his hand as the lecture about evolution began and calmly said, "I know that's a popular theory, but it *is* just a theory—"

Then Mr. Evans's attack began—and it was hate-filled and personal. And I was quiet.

Like Rob, I believe God created the heavens and the earth. Like Rob, I had done enough research that I could have respectfully asked about the holes in evolutionary theory. But I was quiet. I was like Peter . . .

As the Twelve had shared the Passover meal with Jesus, Peter had declared his allegiance to the Lord and had vowed to follow him, no matter the cost. Now, fear overtook him, and he denied even knowing Jesus.

If you had been in the courtyard, would you have responded any differently than Peter did? It's easy to proclaim total surrender to our God and far more difficult to live out that loyalty. Live boldly for Jesus today.

"I DEDICATE MY LIFE TO GOD'S PURPOSES."

BIBLICAL COMMUNITY

Let us consider how we may spur one another on toward love and good deeds, not giving up meeting together, as some are in the habit of doing, but encouraging one another.

HEBREWS 10:24–25

S tatistics tell us that 0 percent of people who try to quit smoking on their own achieve success. If they add to their determination a tool, like a nicotine patch, the percentage rises to 5 percent. Add a support group or community and their chances jump to 40 percent. And with a support structure in place, they have a much better chance of staying smoke-free.[43]

It's not always easy to do what's right and to live with Jesus as our top priority, but it can be significantly easier when we have the built-in accountability, encouragement, and companionship of a friend—or of several friends, brothers and sisters in Christ—walking with us.

The right kind of support or community encourages us to live better physically and spiritually. But often our lives are too full to add a small group or Bible study or to get to know our neighbors. The writer of Hebrews encourages believers to make biblical community a top priority. His words are words for us: let's spur one another on and encourage one another to persevere in our faith!

"I FELLOWSHIP WITH CHRISTIANS TO ACCOMPLISH GOD'S PURPOSES IN MY LIFE, IN THE LIVES OF OTHERS, AND IN THE WORLD."

SPIRITUAL GIFTS

"The LORD does not look at the things people look at. People look at the outward appearance, but the LORD looks at the heart."

1 SAMUEL 16:7

Our family was visiting Washington, DC, one summer when a thunderstorm began. It was short-lived, and the crackle of lightning, the rumbles of thunder, and the pelting rain soon gave way to peace. When the skies cleared, we noticed a rainbow, but my little girl couldn't see it. Neither my pointing to it nor my telling her where to look helped. But when I picked her up, her perspective changed, and she saw the rainbow and giggled with delight.

The Holy Spirit can do for us what I did for my daughter—and what he did for Samuel. Samuel saw Jesse's eldest son, Eliab, and thought he must be God's choice for the next king of Israel. That's when the Lord reminded the prophet that he "looks at the heart." When young David returned from the flocks, Samuel heard the Lord tell him that he was the one. When Samuel looked at David, he only saw a shepherd boy; when God looked at him, he saw a king.

Thank God for a time he changed your perspective and gave you the wisdom and insight to see a person or a situation through his eyes.

"I KNOW MY SPIRITUAL GIFTS AND USE THEM TO FULFILL GOD'S PURPOSES."

OFFERING MY TIME

What you are doing is not good. . . . The work is too heavy for you; you cannot handle it alone.

EXODUS 18:17–18

We were raised in an era when the vast majority of moms stayed at home rather than working to bring home a paycheck. That meant Mom managed the house—and she did it pretty much on her own.

When Rozanne and I had our family, we were busy in different ways than our parents had been. We both became involved in ministry, and we had four kids. Need we say more?

The demands Rozanne and I felt between home and church soon made it clear we needed a new strategy. Our "Just do it!" approach was wearing us out. The work was too heavy, and we couldn't handle it alone. We had to learn how to work smarter, not harder. Our plan? Instead of taking on a car payment, we decided to hire people—someone to help me with lawn care and a "fun" junior high girl to play with our kids while Rozanne cleaned the house uninterrupted, allowing us more time as a family.

In what ways is your work too heavy? What can you let go of? What creative ways can you discover to save yourself time and help you fulfill more of God's purposes?

"I OFFER MY TIME TO FULFILL GOD'S PURPOSES."

GIVING MY RESOURCES

*"Bring the whole tithe into the storehouse . . . ," says
the LORD Almighty, "and see if I will not throw open the
floodgates of heaven and pour out so much blessing that
there will not be room enough to store it."*

MALACHI 3:10

One Sunday I spoke to the congregation on the spiritual practice of giving away our resources for God's purposes, and the next day a young woman dropped off a letter at the church telling her story.

She lived with her mom and brother. She was working hard to set aside money from her minimum-wage job to attend college in the hopes of becoming a nurse. She kept the money in a box hidden in her bedroom. One day she came home from work to discover that all but $10 had been stolen from her box. Her brother had used it to buy drugs. The next day, during the Sunday morning message on giving, she decided to forgive her brother and put the remaining $10 in the offering plate. Her letter ended with the words, "Thank you."

Inspired, the following Sunday I shared her story. A family was so moved they agreed to pay for her entire college education. Today she is married, a mom, and a full-time nurse.

"Test me in this," God said, "and see if I don't throw open the floodgates of heaven."

**"I GIVE MY RESOURCES TO
FULFILL GOD'S PURPOSES."**

SHARING MY FAITH

In your hearts revere Christ as Lord. Always be prepared to give an answer to everyone who asks you to give the reason for the hope that you have. But do this with gentleness and respect.

1 PETER 3:15

On the day my neighbor Kyle trusted Christ, I asked him when he had first thought Jesus might be the answer. He responded, "Oh, I remember exactly when it happened. You and I were golfing with Ted. We were walking down the second fairway when Ted's wife called. Ted picked up the call, and I eavesdropped on their conversation as we walked. I was struck by the way he talked to his wife—patiently listening, tenderly responding, with love on his lips. I remember thinking, *I don't listen and talk to my wife this way. What is different about Ted?* That's the day I started asking questions, which Ted freely answered."

You may have heard the phrase "Share the gospel and if necessary use words." You may have also heard the phrase "Our lives may be the only Bible people read." Both statements are true and illustrated beautifully in Ted's life. Let Christ live in and through you. Whenever an observer asks why you have so much hope, tell them about Jesus.

Oh, that our lives would be lived in such a way that people long to know Jesus.

"I SHARE MY FAITH WITH OTHERS TO FULFILL GOD'S PURPOSES."

DAY 212

WORSHIP

Miriam the prophet, Aaron's sister, took a timbrel in her hand, and all the women followed her, with timbrels and dancing.

EXODUS 15:20

When we worship God, we have an opportunity to express our love for our Creator and our Redeemer, the Sustainer of life and the Giver of all good gifts, our heavenly Father and the Father of our Savior. We can find no greater One to worship and no greater purpose in life than to, in the words of the seventeenth-century Westminster Catechism, "glorify God and enjoy him for ever."

So why don't we emulate Miriam and pour all that we are into worshipping God? Why don't we make more of an effort to develop a lifestyle of worship? Why do we hold back? Why do we hesitate to be bold about our devotion to almighty God? The reasons may vary from person to person, having to do with personality and upbringing or a false understanding of worship. No matter the excuses for our inhibitions, God can free us to truly worship him with abounding joy.

Maybe you long to grab a tambourine when you think about God's grace in your life. Maybe you wish you could celebrate God with the kind of wholehearted worship Miriam had, and to hold nothing back. Maybe the secret is . . . just do it!

> **"I WORSHIP GOD FOR WHO HE IS AND WHAT HE HAS DONE FOR ME."**

PRAYER

> *The Spirit helps us in our weakness. We do not know what we ought to pray for, but the Spirit himself intercedes for us through wordless groans. And he who searches our hearts knows the mind of the Spirit, because the Spirit intercedes for God's people in accordance with the will of God.*

ROMANS 8:26–27

Ashley was born lifeless, the umbilical cord wrapped tightly around her neck. Resuscitated quickly by the doctor, her tiny blue body became pink again, but too late to save much brain function. Unexpectedly, Ashley lived beyond the predicted two or three years and became a young woman. Though Ashley was unable to move, talk, or express herself, her mother loved her deeply and cared for her. Outsiders to the family couldn't distinguish Ashley's sounds or see any variances in her facial expression, but her mother could interpret every groan. Peering deep into her daughter's blue eyes, she could discern if Ashley felt happy, anxious, or fearful. She always knew what Ashley wanted or needed.

When you feel too weak to utter a sound, the pain is too hard, and all you can do is cry, remember God's love is greater even than a mother's love for her child. His Spirit looks deep into your eyes, straight to your heart, and makes sure your heavenly Father gets your message.

"I PRAY TO GOD TO KNOW HIM, TO FIND DIRECTION FOR MY LIFE, AND TO LAY MY REQUESTS BEFORE HIM."

BIBLE STUDY

"Keep this Book of the Law always on your lips;
meditate on it day and night, so that you may be
careful to do everything written in it."

JOSHUA 1:8

No matter how long you've been driving around in circles, seeing the same shops over and over, will you ever stop to ask for directions? Do you start putting together the bookcase or installing the light fixture without glancing at the instructions?

It's human nature to want to do things *our* way. We don't always find it easy to obey commands, follow instructions, or even heed wise counsel. When we try things our own way in this chaotic world, it can be a struggle, and we usually end up lost or in a mess. God knows this, and he knows exactly what we need.

After Moses died, Joshua was looking at some big shoes to fill as the leader of Israel. God paid Joshua a special visit, reminding Joshua how important it was to meditate on his truth, learn his law, and live it out. And today God calls you and me to do the same.

Stop stubbornly trying to do things your own way and instead search God's instruction manual. When you do, your life will be "put together" the right way, and you'll always be heading in the right direction.

> "I STUDY THE BIBLE TO KNOW GOD AND HIS TRUTH AND TO FIND DIRECTION FOR MY DAILY LIFE."

SINGLE-MINDEDNESS

Those who live in accordance with the Spirit have their minds set on what the Spirit desires.

ROMANS 8:5

What? How? Why? We ask these questions in all areas of our lives. Regarding our career we wonder, *What do I want to achieve? How am I going to achieve it? Why do I want to achieve it?* Asking these kinds of questions can give us focus, but are we fixing our eyes on the things that will truly satisfy our souls? Perhaps a better use of these questions is to ponder, *What kind of person do I want to become? How am I going to become this kind of person? Why do I want to become this kind of person?*

Paul's singular goal in life, above all others, was to honor God, and his desire was to become increasingly more Christlike. The world measures success by achievement in the roles you play and by the money you make and the possessions you gain. But God measures success by who you are and who you are becoming in Christ. Why? Because the more you transform into his image, the more your heart becomes aligned with the priorities of his heart and not the world's.

The major questions become, *What does God want?* and *Can I achieve this by who I am becoming?*

"I FOCUS ON GOD AND HIS PRIORITIES FOR MY LIFE."

TOTAL SURRENDER

Some Jews . . . Shadrach, Meshach and Abednego . . .
pay no attention to you, Your Majesty. They neither serve
your gods nor worship the image of gold you have set up.

DANIEL 3:12

If you were accused of being a Christian, would there be enough evidence to convict you?

For Shadrach, Meshach, and Abednego, evidence of their commitment to Yahweh could be seen in what they weren't doing—they weren't worshipping the Babylonian idols, gods, or king despite the deadly consequences of that decision. They were thrown into an incinerator, but Jesus saved them, miraculously showing up in the fiery furnace with them. Their clothes remained unburned, and their skin untouched!

The astonished king called, "Servants of the Most High God, come out!" (v. 26). When they emerged, there was no smell of smoke on them. Then the king declared that "no other god can save in this way" (v. 29). The faithfulness of these three men was evidence of their belief in God and their commitment to him.

What evidence of your commitment to Jesus might people see in you? As they look at your life, will they see your willingness to pay a price to stay committed to Jesus? Totally surrendering to Christ can have a huge impact on those looking into your fiery furnace. Will they see Jesus in there with you?

> **"I DEDICATE MY LIFE TO GOD'S PURPOSES."**

BIBLICAL COMMUNITY

> *[Believers] devoted themselves to the apostles' teaching and to fellowship, to the breaking of bread and to prayer.*

ACTS 2:42

Our first date was at The Spaghetti Company, the best Italian food in Cleveland, Ohio. But I don't remember what either of us ate. I do remember experiencing that special connection that happens over a shared meal.

Conversation can reach a deeper level when a meal is shared between believers. After all, Jesus promised if two or three gather in his name, he would show up! Somehow when bread is broken, hearts are knit together. Consider how God blessed the early church as they gathered for teaching, meals, and prayer. Their fellowship was enriched by Christ's presence in their midst, and as relationships between God's people developed, great things began to happen. The fellowship itself became a source of nourishment.

Maybe you already experience this in a church small group or Bible study. If you don't, follow the early church's example. Gather a small group of people together, share a meal, and devote yourselves to God's Word, fellowshipping, and praying. Jesus will be there, and when he shows up, great things happen.

> "I FELLOWSHIP WITH CHRISTIANS TO ACCOMPLISH GOD'S PURPOSES IN MY LIFE, IN THE LIVES OF OTHERS, AND IN THE WORLD."

SPIRITUAL GIFTS

There are different kinds of gifts, but the same Spirit distributes them. There are different kinds of service, but the same Lord.

1 CORINTHIANS 12:4–5

It's always nice to hear from strangers how polite and well-behaved our children are. We're glad when our sullen teens, moody tweens, and strong-willed toddlers act respectfully when they're out in public.

God also wants us to "behave well" with the gifts he's given us. Each of us receives a spiritual deposit when we accept Jesus as our Savior. He gives us our gifts not to build ourselves up but to benefit those he places in our lives, both in the body of Christ and outside of it. He doesn't want us just to go through the motions so we *look* like Christians (whatever that means!). Nor does he want us to use our gifts egotistically. God wants our hearts engaged in wholehearted service to him, using our gifts *in* love and *with* love.

Just as a piston engine requires pure gasoline to run smoothly, exercising our gifts must be fueled by love. Gifts driven by selfish ambition and pride will sputter and fail. Spiritual gifts extended without love are as disappointing to our Father as a rude child is to his parents.

Ask Jesus to love people through you as you use your spiritual gifts for his glory.

"I KNOW MY SPIRITUAL GIFTS AND USE THEM TO FULFILL GOD'S PURPOSES."

OFFERING MY TIME

She watches over the affairs of her household and does not eat the bread of idleness.

PROVERBS 31:27

The jobs that homemakers do range from private chef, housekeeper, and child caregiver, to chauffeur, laundry worker, and landscaper—roles that could altogether pay one substantial annual salary! And they do even more than that . . . what about being the personal shopper (food, clothes, stuff), the resident CEO, an unlicensed EMT (emergency medical technician), a tutor, a coach, and often a veterinarian? No idleness here!

Like the Proverbs 31 woman, twenty-first-century homemakers, whether they work at home full time or have another job outside the home, have more than enough responsibilities and activities for any given day. And like the Proverbs 31 woman, many women today do what needs to be done in a calm, measured, and gentle way. What worked in the day of Proverbs still works now.

The key to "noble character" (v. 10) and the ability to accomplish all that needs to be done—the ability to use wisely the time God gives—is knowing what the most important activity is: keeping God's purposes at the center of your life. But remember to keep the most important thing first—your relationship with the Lord.

"I OFFER MY TIME TO FULFILL GOD'S PURPOSES."

GIVING MY RESOURCES

> "A poor widow came and put in [the temple treasury] two
> very small copper coins, worth only a few cents. . . . Out
> of her poverty, [she] put in everything."

MARK 12:42, 44

No one expects a two-year-old to run a marathon, or a kindergartener to read and understand Plato's "Allegory of the Cave" from *The Republic*. No one expects a grandma to try out for the synchronized swimming Olympic team, or an eight-year-old to shop at Tiffany's for his mother's birthday.

And Jesus doesn't expect his people who have little income to put into the offering plate the same amount as those individuals who have much income. After all, Jesus looks at the heart of the giver. The heart of a successful businessman who puts in a few cents is very different from the heart of the woman whose few cents deposited in the offering plate are all she has to live on.

Which type of giving touches God's heart? The person with a heart like the widow, who gives everything, knowing God will provide for her. The only way to have a heart like the widow's is to believe in the God who has promised to meet all your needs according to his riches (Philippians 4:19) and has given everything for you!

**"I GIVE MY RESOURCES TO
FULFILL GOD'S PURPOSES."**

SHARING MY FAITH

I speak of your faithfulness and your saving help. I do not conceal your love and your faithfulness.

PSALM 40:10

I didn't freely share my testimony. After all, I had no radical conversion experience to relate; my life before I named Jesus my Savior was not much different from my life after. But then a friend told me that my birth into God's family was no less an act of grace: "When God helps a nice girl/good student/straight-arrow kid see her need for a Savior, the same grace is applied as when he helps an alcoholic, a prostitute, or a drug dealer acknowledge their need."

Sharing our faith is simply living a faithful life and telling about who God is and what he has done for us. Think about young David living out his faith in God when, with only a sling and some stones, he confronted and defeated the giant Goliath (1 Samuel 17). David shared his faith by the way he lived his life, but he also used his words to praise God's character. In Psalm 40, for instance, David celebrated the wonders, righteousness, faithfulness, and love of God he had experienced.

Like David, in addition to sharing our faith by how we live, we are also to share with words who God is and what great things he has done for us. What's your story?

> **"I SHARE MY FAITH WITH OTHERS TO FULFILL GOD'S PURPOSES."**

WORSHIP

Daniel learned that the decree had been published. . . .
Three times a day he got down on his knees and prayed,
giving thanks to his God, just as he had done before.

DANIEL 6:10

Daniel had heard about the king's new decree that stated the people's prayers could be directed only to him, the king, for thirty days. Daniel knew that this decree could not be altered or repealed. He was also aware that disobeying the law would mean being thrown into a den of hungry lions.

Yet we read that three times a day Daniel prayed to his God "just as he had done before." Despite the law forbidding it, Daniel was committed to worshipping the one true God. He would give his praise to no other. Daniel didn't waver in his faithful worship of Yahweh, despite the danger of doing so.

The potential cost of worshipping God and following Jesus is increasing these days. Around the world believers are losing their lives simply because they identify themselves as Christians. Will we who proclaim our faith in God and his Son, Jesus, continue to follow him, continue to serve him, worship him, and share the truth of his message, no matter the cost?

"I WORSHIP GOD FOR WHO HE IS AND WHAT HE HAS DONE FOR ME."

DAY 223

PRAYER

"When you pray, do not keep on babbling like pagans, for they think they will be heard because of their many words. Do not be like them, for your Father knows what you need before you ask him."

MATTHEW 6:7–8

If God knows what we need before we ask him, then why is it necessary to pray? It's a reasonable question. But what if prayer itself is the means to the fulfillment of our greatest need—that of God himself?

What if communion with God is the one need in our lives above all other needs, and it is through prayer that we experience God and he experiences us? This is what prayer is all about. Prayer is companionship with God. Prayer is offering to God a listening heart and a life that responds to what is heard. Prayer is including God in all aspects of our lives.

Maybe we are changed more by companionship with God than by anything else. Just as a child walks and talks like his father, and even picks up the same mannerisms, because he spends time with him, communion with God can change us. Perhaps this is the real value of prayer. Do you want to experience God and know him? Then pray.

> "I PRAY TO GOD TO KNOW HIM, TO FIND DIRECTION FOR MY LIFE, AND TO LAY MY REQUESTS BEFORE HIM."

BIBLE STUDY

We also thank God continually because, when you received the word of God, which you heard from us, you accepted it not as a human word, but as it actually is, the word of God, which is indeed at work in you who believe.

1 THESSALONIANS 2:13

How often do you check your cell phone? Do you regularly peek at the time, make calls, glance at it before scheduling appointments, check the weather, or surf the web to gather information to make decisions or purchases?

Studies show the average person looks at his cell phone 150 times per day or over 9 times per hour, assuming you sleep for 8 hours.[44] It appears we don't make a move without consulting our phones.

The Bible is God's direct line to us. Through it, he speaks to us. It has the power to change our very nature, give us courage to make decisions, and equip us for life, but most of us don't turn to it nearly as often as we should.

What if for one week you exchanged your cell phone for your Bible? Anywhere you normally take your phone, take your Bible instead. Anytime you normally look at your phone, look into God's Word instead. If you do, it will indeed begin working in you.

> **"I STUDY THE BIBLE TO KNOW GOD AND HIS TRUTH AND TO FIND DIRECTION FOR MY DAILY LIFE."**

SINGLE-MINDEDNESS

This is what the LORD says: "Stand at the crossroads and look; ask for the ancient paths, ask where the good way is, and walk in it, and you will find rest for your souls."

JEREMIAH 6:16

A line from the 1993 movie *Jurassic Park* aptly applies to our lives today if we are not careful in keeping God's priorities before us.

In the movie, a group of people are sitting around a table discussing the genetic wonder world of prehistoric dinosaurs reconstructed from the DNA of their blood extracted from ancient mosquitoes. The paleontologists are caught up in the marvel of actually seeing flesh on the bones they have been digging up for years; the lawyer sees dollar signs. Only one character offers a stern word of caution and concern, saying that the scientists were so focused on what they *could* do, they forgot to consider what they *should* do.[45]

Twenty-five hundred years earlier, the prophet Jeremiah offered the same counsel. Before we act we should stop and ask where the good way is and then walk in it. Just because we *can* do something doesn't mean we *should* do it.

If you heed this advice, you will find rest for your soul. If you don't, you just might get eaten by the dinosaurs in your life.

"I FOCUS ON GOD AND HIS PRIORITIES FOR MY LIFE."

DAY 226

TOTAL SURRENDER

L<small>ORD</small>, I know that people's lives are not their own; it is not for them to direct their steps.

JEREMIAH 10:23

My e-mail stopped working today, so I called an IT specialist. He said if I brought him my computer, he would fix it. Giving it up gave me an uneasy feeling, but I had tried to fix the problem myself and now I needed an expert. Then he added, "You should also bring me your phone and your iPad. I need to make sure they are synced."

Now that uneasy feeling became a knot in my stomach as I realized he wanted me to totally surrender all of my technology. But I knew if I held back one piece of equipment, it would mean I would not be operating at full capacity.

Most of us have a part that we hold back from God, who is the expert at making sure our lives are truly "synced." Totally surrendering your life to his purposes is difficult, but holding back even one part of yourself keeps you from living up to your full potential.

When you completely turn over every area of your life to God, he can do remarkable things in you. What area is the hardest for you to surrender? Ask God today to take over that part of your life and see what happens.

> "I DEDICATE MY LIFE TO GOD'S PURPOSES."

BIBLICAL COMMUNITY

Though one may be overpowered, two can defend themselves. A cord of three strands is not quickly broken.

ECCLESIASTES 4:12

God's Word clearly teaches that people are not meant to live separate and isolated. A visit to the Genesis 2 garden indicates that, in the beginning, Adam and Eve experienced the divine ideal of a rich, life-giving relationship with one another as well as with God himself.

But their rejection of God's vision for life together—their choice to live according to their rules, not his—resulted in their being escorted from the garden and out of community with the holy God. The divine ideal that Adam and Eve experienced in the garden had been shattered. And the rest of humanity has suffered the consequences.

But by the power of God's Spirit, resident within each person who names Jesus as their Savior and Lord, we can come together in community. If we invite God into that community and welcome his presence among us, we become a "cord of three strands" that is not easily broken.

Jesus' death on the cross and his resurrection enable us, his people, to know life-giving community and communion with him and with one another.

"I FELLOWSHIP WITH CHRISTIANS TO ACCOMPLISH GOD'S PURPOSES IN MY LIFE, IN THE LIVES OF OTHERS, AND IN THE WORLD."

SPIRITUAL GIFTS

I remind you to fan into flame the gift of God, which is in you through the laying on of my hands. For the Spirit God gave us does not make us timid, but gives us power, love and self-discipline.

2 TIMOTHY 1:6–7

Here Paul wrote to encourage Timothy, who had become timid in using the gift God deposited in him because some of the older believers were giving him a hard time due to his youth. Paul reminded Timothy to "fan into flame" the gift God had given him. What does "fan into flame" mean? Well-known pastor and author Max Lucado put it this way: "Do most, what you do best."

Have you backed down because of your youth? Or maybe it isn't your youth, but instead you've been made to feel too old. Maybe you feel your contribution is insignificant, or someone has made you feel insecure about exercising your gift. Perhaps you have convinced yourself that what you have to offer is paltry. Maybe you have yet to discover what your gift is.

Don't listen to those negative voices. Take Paul's encouragement to heart! Find the spark of the gift God has placed in you, and begin to fan it through self-discipline and loving others. Do most, what you do best!

> **"I KNOW MY SPIRITUAL GIFTS AND USE THEM TO FULFILL GOD'S PURPOSES."**

OFFERING MY TIME

"My time is not yet here."

JOHN 7:6

It was Nick's dream job. It was crazy how he'd learned about the open position, how the interviews fell into place, and how he'd felt connections with people from the organization. Yet something about it didn't feel right. Nick prayed, asked his Bible study group to pray, and met with his pastor to discuss it. The position seemed like a fit and there weren't any red flags . . . but in the end Nick just didn't think it was God's plan for him. He turned down the offer and trusted God would provide the right job at the right time. Sometime later he learned the company was being investigated for fraud.

Jesus lived according to God's timetable, and no one else's. Not even his own. This fact made Jesus rather enigmatic. Sometimes opportunities seemed ideal for him to gain the kind of attention every revolutionary needs to further his cause. But Jesus lived out his priorities according to the timing of God the Father. Jesus kept God as his focus in everything he did, including the timing of his work.

Keep God as your focus and wait on his timing. If everything seems great but you have a sense it's not, seek prayer and counsel from others and just wait.

"I OFFER MY TIME TO FULFILL GOD'S PURPOSES."

DAY 230

GIVING MY RESOURCES

No one claimed that any of their possessions was their own, but they shared everything they had.

ACTS 4:32

Here are a few life lessons from Robert Fulghum's fun and insightful book *All I Really Need to Know I Learned in Kindergarten*:

- Share everything.
- Play fair.
- Don't take things that aren't yours.
- Say you're sorry when you hurt somebody.
- When you go out in the world, it is best to hold hands and stick together.[46]

Perhaps some of us could use a refresher course—or else a heart changed by the Holy Spirit. Sharing, for instance, doesn't come naturally. It's an acquired skill. In the early church, however, sharing came supernaturally: "God's grace was so powerfully at work in them all that there were no needy persons among them" (vv. 33–34).

You don't need to go back to kindergarten; just go back to your belief in stewardship: "I believe everything I am and everything I own belong to God." What and with whom does God want you to share today?

> **"I GIVE MY RESOURCES TO FULFILL GOD'S PURPOSES."**

SHARING MY FAITH

Our gospel came to you not simply with words but also with power, with the Holy Spirit and deep conviction. You know how we lived among you for your sake.

1 THESSALONIANS 1:5

Reflect for a moment on your buying experiences with salespeople. You have probably been sold cars, insurance, and appliances of different sorts. When buying these different kinds of goods, you have encountered different types of sellers. Some vendors seemed sincerely interested in you and your needs. Some peddlers, however, seemed more concerned about what was in it for them, and you sensed that you were just a means to their end. One sort of seller was there for your sake and the other for their interests.

We must be careful not to try to share, or *sell*, the gospel to make us feel better about ourselves by putting another notch on our gospel-belts. People can smell a sales pitch a mile away.

Paul shared the good news of Christ for the sake of others. He spoke not just with his words but with his life. For Paul, sharing his faith meant investing his life in others by the power of the Holy Spirit.

May we all share the gospel as Paul did, with our whole lives. Remember, people will know if we are giving them just a sales pitch.

> **"I SHARE MY FAITH WITH OTHERS TO FULFILL GOD'S PURPOSES."**

WORSHIP

"The greatest among you will be your servant. For those who exalt themselves will be humbled, and those who humble themselves will be exalted."

MATTHEW 23:11–12

We have a much easier time respecting and following leaders who have done what they want us to do. Consider the swim coach who does every stroke of both the early morning and afterschool workouts with his team, the cross country coach who runs the daily three miles with her athletes, and the spiritual leader who humbly serves his people as he calls them to humbly serve one another.

Jesus didn't hesitate to point out the hypocrisy of religious leaders in his day: "You hypocrites! . . . On the outside you appear to people as righteous but on the inside you are full of . . . wickedness" (Matthew 23:27–28).

Jesus is a leader who commands respect. He modeled for us everything he wanted us to do. He showed us how to go to our heavenly Father for direction, how to serve each other humbly, and how to unconditionally love and accept others.

Check your ego. Do your best to remove hypocrisy from your life so you can worship and serve Jesus, and lead others with integrity to worship him as well.

> **"I WORSHIP GOD FOR WHO HE IS AND WHAT HE HAS DONE FOR ME."**

PRAYER

I pray that out of his glorious riches he may strengthen you with power through his Spirit in your inner being, so that Christ may dwell in your hearts through faith. And I pray that you, being rooted and established in love, may have power . . . to grasp how wide and long and high and deep is the love of Christ, and to know this love that surpasses knowledge—that you may be filled to the measure of all the fullness of God.

EPHESIANS 3:16–19

Have you ever prayed wondering if what you are asking for is God's will? Sometimes we question if we are wasting our time and breath, and we give up praying. These thoughts can stalk the halls of our hearts. But what if we knew with sunrise certainty that what we are praying is God's will and that God will answer our prayers? That would be a prayer game-changer, wouldn't it?

All Scripture is inspired by God, which means that so is Paul's prayer. His prayer is included in Scripture to help us pray. Read Paul's prayer again, but this time pray his prayer for your life. Imagine your prayer is answered by God, knowing you have just prayed God's will for your life. Now pray the same for others and watch what God does.

> **"I PRAY TO GOD TO KNOW HIM, TO FIND DIRECTION FOR MY LIFE, AND TO LAY MY REQUESTS BEFORE HIM."**

BIBLE STUDY

The law of the LORD is perfect, refreshing the soul. The statutes of the LORD are trustworthy, making wise the simple. . . . They are more precious than gold, than much pure gold; they are sweeter than honey . . . from the honeycomb.

PSALM 19:7, 10

Psalm 19:7–14 celebrates the multifaceted blessing of God's Word. The author of this psalm seems to know God's Word intimately. He relied on Scripture to refresh him, to help him in a crisis, and to provide him with understanding in confusing times. He rejoiced in the trustworthiness he found in God's instructions.

God's Word offers us all these blessings and more. No wonder the psalmist joyfully proclaimed that God has provided us with his laws, statutes, precepts, and commands. God's Word indeed is "more precious than gold" and "sweeter than honey . . . from the honeycomb."

What warnings found in Scripture have been a blessing of guidance and protection to you? What faults of yours has Scripture helped you recognize and remove? What statements of reassurance of God's forgiveness and love have given you hope and comfort? The more you become intimately acquainted with God's Word, the more blessings you will be able to celebrate as the psalmist did.

> "I STUDY THE BIBLE TO KNOW
> GOD AND HIS TRUTH AND TO FIND
> DIRECTION FOR MY DAILY LIFE."

SINGLE-MINDEDNESS

"Do not worry about your life, what you will eat or drink; or about your body, what you will wear. . . . Can any one of you by worrying add a single hour to your life?"

MATTHEW 6:25, 27

Maybe you've heard a physical trainer say, "Use it or lose it!" Our trust muscle is no different. If you don't use it, don't expect it to get strong or stay strong.

Life offers plenty of opportunities to exercise our trust. As Jesus promised, "In this world you will have trouble" (John 16:33). A lack of life's basic necessities can cause us to lose focus. The international economy impacts the local economy . . . which impacts the job market . . . which can impact your job . . . which impacts how well-stocked your pantry is—yet Jesus tells us not to worry about what we will eat.

We find reasons to worry about our children, our aging parents, news headlines, medical tests, paying our bills, and even where our next meal is coming from. The list continues, but every item falls under the truth Jesus taught: seek first his kingdom, and all these things will be given to you.

Chase after things you think you need, and you won't have God's blessing or the things you truly need. Focus on God's priorities, and he will satisfy all your needs.

> **"I FOCUS ON GOD AND HIS PRIORITIES FOR MY LIFE."**

TOTAL SURRENDER

Now if we died with Christ, we believe that we will also live with him.

ROMANS 6:8

John Huss spoke out against the pope's selling of indulgences. He fought against the Catholic Church's teaching about the Eucharist. He argued that the Bible—not the pope, not any man—was the final authority for the church. And he was martyred—burned at the stake— on July 6, 1415. He had been given several occasions to recant, including one last time at the stake. He again refused and instead prayed, "Lord Jesus, it is for thee that I patiently endure this cruel death. I pray thee to have mercy on my enemies." He was heard reciting psalms as the flames engulfed him.[47]

The apostle Paul was imprisoned, flogged, beaten, stoned, ship-wrecked, hungry, thirsty, cold, naked, and "in danger from rivers, in danger from bandits, in danger from my fellow Jews, in danger from Gentiles; in danger in the city, in danger in the country, in danger at sea; and in danger from false believers" (2 Corinthians 11:26). Paul chose to lose himself—lose his life as a respected Pharisee—and risk his life in wholehearted service to his resurrected Lord.

John Huss and the apostle Paul knew exactly what they believed and why. Huss and Paul made sacrifices and even suffered in service of their Lord. They totally surrendered their lives for God's purposes. Have you?

"I DEDICATE MY LIFE TO GOD'S PURPOSES."

PRAYER

If you will save Israel by my hand as you have promised—look, I will place a wool fleece on the threshing floor. If there is dew only on the fleece and all the ground is dry, then I will know that you will save Israel by my hand, as you said.

JUDGES 6:36–37

Gideon experienced PTSD—that is, Pre-Trauma Self-Doubt. He prayed, *Lord, how can I save Israel? My clan is the weakest in Manasseh, and I am the least in my family.* His faith in God was strong, but he lacked faith in himself. Gideon required more courage and strength than he could muster on his own. So he prayed. He had a conference with God asking for a sign, perhaps hoping to convince God he wasn't right for the job.

God answered Gideon clearly, not once, but twice, infusing Gideon with courage. Then God whittled Gideon's army down to three hundred men to ensure everyone knew that the strength for this victory came from the Lord.

Are you facing a battle in your life? Has PTSD set in? Go to God in prayer. See if he will fill you with courage. And remember, he may not want to use your strength for this victory; he might use your weakness to display his might.

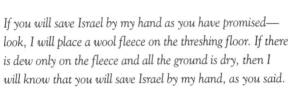

"I PRAY TO GOD TO KNOW HIM, TO FIND DIRECTION FOR MY LIFE, AND TO LAY MY REQUESTS BEFORE HIM."

BIBLICAL COMMUNITY

The wall was completed . . . in fifty-two days. . . . This
work had been done with the help of our God.

NEHEMIAH 6:15–16

The word *community* brings to mind friends and neighbors, support and encouragement, even prayer and godly counsel. Biblical community also means everyone working together, using their gifts, resources, and time to accomplish tasks important to God.

While serving as cupbearer to King Artaxerxes of Persia, Nehemiah learned that "the wall of Jerusalem [was] broken down, and its gates [had] been burned with fire" (Nehemiah 1:3). He responded with weeping, mourning, fasting, and praying. In obedience to the Lord's call, Nehemiah returned to spearhead the rebuilding of the wall around the city and protect his people from the bullying of surrounding nations. Everyone in the community, including children, was called to help with this massive project. The wall in Jerusalem—which was fifteen feet thick[48] and, according to the historian Josephus, approximately 4.5 miles long[49]—was built in just fifty-two days because the biblical community worked together to make it happen.

What task is God calling your church community to accomplish? Join in. Working together under his blessing, it can be done.

> "I FELLOWSHIP WITH CHRISTIANS TO ACCOMPLISH GOD'S PURPOSES IN MY LIFE, IN THE LIVES OF OTHERS, AND IN THE WORLD."

SPIRITUAL GIFTS

Each of you should use whatever gift you have received to serve others, as faithful stewards of God's grace in its various forms.

1 PETER 4:10

An episode of the television series *Touched by an Angel* showed the angel Monica unsatisfied with her gift of speaking truth into people's lives. Monica wanted to be able to sing like other angels with heavenly voices, but Monica couldn't carry a tune.

In a series of interviews, highly successful professional golfers were asked whose swing they would want to have if they could have anyone's. No one chose their own.

Do these scenarios sound familiar? Many of us compare ourselves to others, wishing we had the gifts they have, as if the ones we were given are somehow less necessary or even inferior. Why can't we be satisfied with and rejoice in our own gifts? God is probably asking us the same question.

What if your special gift from God is not primarily for you but for others? What if your life is meant to be God's gift to others? What if God, the Giver of gifts, has given you your own special gifts for others to enjoy? Rejoice in the Giver, rejoice in your gifts, and use them for his glory. Someone will be thankful.

> **"I KNOW MY SPIRITUAL GIFTS AND USE THEM TO FULFILL GOD'S PURPOSES."**

BIBLE STUDY

"A farmer went out to sow his seed. . . . The seed falling on good soil refers to someone who hears the word and understands it. This is the one who produces a crop."

MATTHEW 13:3, 23

What does a plant need to grow? Air, water, and sun are all necessary, but a plant can have all of these and still not thrive if the soil is not fertile.

What do followers of Jesus need to grow? We need to guard against the evil one who would snatch the truth before it fully takes root in our hearts. And rather than fluffy humanistic philosophy, we need solid biblical teaching so our faith doesn't wither when trouble comes.

A heart prepared to receive God's Word is good soil. We need to distance ourselves from "the worries of this life and the deceitfulness of wealth" that may strangle our faith (v. 22). The fruit that mature believers produce honors him and attracts others who want to know what makes us different—what makes us peaceful and even joyful in a painful and sorrow-filled world.

Before you read God's Word, take a minute to clear your mind and open your heart to what his words are saying. It will help you successfully grow into a devoted Christ follower and point others to him as well.

> **"I STUDY THE BIBLE TO KNOW GOD AND HIS TRUTH AND TO FIND DIRECTION FOR MY DAILY LIFE."**

OFFERING MY TIME

"Lord, when did we see you hungry and feed you, or thirsty and give you something to drink?"

MATTHEW 25:37

Her face looked vaguely familiar, though she couldn't remember the woman's name, but Laura was used to that. Her husband had been in ministry for twenty-three years, and they'd gotten to know a lot of people.

Fortunately, the woman introduced herself before she began her story. "You probably don't remember, but I haven't forgotten—and I'll never forget—when you took time to listen when I needed to talk. You managed to find a quiet corner for us, and as I talked about my recently broken engagement and broken heart, you listened. You held me. But most of all, Laura, you cried with me. Your tears made me feel so loved and so heard. For those precious minutes, you were Jesus with flesh and bones to me."

We don't always know when God is using us to touch a heart, encourage someone, or sow a seed that will bear the fruit later, but those moments matter. As the king in Jesus' story—representing God—said, "Whatever you did for one of the least of these brothers and sisters of mine, you did for me" (v. 40).

What you do as his hands and feet in this world—what you do to serve people in practical ways—our Lord will not forget.

"I OFFER MY TIME TO FULFILL GOD'S PURPOSES."

GIVING MY RESOURCES

Whoever sows sparingly will also reap sparingly, and whoever sows generously will also reap generously.

2 CORINTHIANS 9:6

Bankers who understand compound interest know that sowing generously can definitely mean reaping generously. Although twenty-somethings may be reluctant to follow it, this advice is sound: live on 80 percent of your salary; put 20 percent straight into retirement—starting now. (Many believers put 10 percent in savings and give 10 percent to their home church.)

If a twenty-year-old making an average salary saved 20 percent each year for forty-five years, they could, with the help of annual compound interest, end up with almost a million dollars!

Young people who sow generously and consistently like this will see the discipline pay off. Compound interest can look like a miracle, but compound interest is nothing compared to the way God blesses what we give to his kingdom work. He stretches his people's dollars, hours, and talents so that more is accomplished—more people are fed and more clothes are gathered for the homeless—than seemed possible.

Be encouraged to save wisely but, more importantly, remember that miracles happen when you give generously of your money, time, and talents in support of service that is close to God's heart.

"I GIVE MY RESOURCES TO FULFILL GOD'S PURPOSES."

SPIRITUAL GIFTS

The eye cannot say to the hand, "I don't need you!" And the head cannot say to the feet, "I don't need you!" On the contrary, those parts of the body that seem to be weaker are indispensable.

1 CORINTHIANS 12:21–22

The legendary World War II commander General George Patton delivered a speech to the US Third Army on June 5, 1944. Patton told his men, "An Army is a team. It lives, sleeps, eats, and fights as a team. Every single man in this Army plays a vital role. Don't ever think your job is unimportant. Every department, every unit is important. The Quartermaster is needed to bring up food and clothes. The man on K. P. has a job to do. Every man is a vital link in the great chain. Every man serves the whole. Without team effort the fight would be lost."[50]

We all have a role to play in the body of Christ, and every role is essential. Some speak, some pray, some cook, some hold babies, some teach children, some organize, some administer, some lead—we all have a part to play.

Do you know your role in the body of Christ, and are you living it for the good of the whole? You are indispensable!

> **"I KNOW MY SPIRITUAL GIFTS AND USE THEM TO FULFILL GOD'S PURPOSES."**

PART 3: BE

Who Am I Becoming?

THE TEN KEYS OF "BE"

Love

Joy

Peace

Self-Control

Hope

Patience

Kindness/Goodness

Faithfulness

Gentleness

Humility

LEARNING TO BE LIKE JESUS

"Remain in me, as I also remain in you. No branch can bear fruit by itself; it must remain in the vine. Neither can you bear fruit unless you remain in me."

JOHN 15:4

An Australian winemaker named David Anderson had an unusual bumper crop in 1994. So many grapes, in fact, he was unable to harvest three rows of his vineyard. A friend wandering by David's vineyard three weeks after harvest noticed the overripe grapes and asked David about them. David had forgotten all about those grapes that remained on the vine.

He halfheartedly harvested them but produced the vintage separately from the other wine, then gave most of it away, certain it was not very good. To his surprise, however, here's how people described it: "A wine of power, concentration, structure and balance." It now sells for $290 a bottle.[51]

Jesus told us he is the vine, and we are the branches (v. 5). The longer we remain on the vine, the richer, more full-bodied fruit we produce. Ultimately, those around us experience the powerful and balanced life of a mature believer.

As you concentrate on the beliefs and make the practices your daily habits, you will be able to give a taste of Jesus away to others. They will pick up a hint of joy, a touch of patience, a full-bodied peace.

The longer you remain in Jesus, the more you will be like him. The fruit you produce will be very good!

LOVE

This is love: not that we loved God, but that he loved us and sent his Son as an atoning sacrifice for our sins. Dear friends, since God so loved us, we also ought to love one another.

1 JOHN 4:10–11

Parental love is likely the purest expression of love within the human race. Parents spend their lives depositing their love into their children. The children will never remember the caressing of their cheeks as babies, but the parents know it contributes to the overall physical, spiritual, emotional, and relational health of the children.

The greatest joy of parents is seeing their children all grown up and living a life of love—blessing their own children, their spouse, and their neighbors. When the children decide to live a life of love, the parents know their love has been received and made complete.

This is how it is for God, your Father. He has been pouring his love into you all your life, even when you were too young to remember it. When you grow up and choose to live a life of love, you give evidence that God's love has been born in you and has been made complete in you.

Do you want to give evidence that God's love is in you? Go love someone else.

> **"I AM COMMITTED TO LOVING GOD AND LOVING OTHERS."**

> *"I have told you this so that my joy may be in you and that your joy may be complete."*
>
> JOHN 15:11

"Nona, do you smile *all* the time?" These were my granddaughter's words to my shocked ears.

"I do when you're with me."

The truth is, finding joy in spite of my circumstances is one of my biggest struggles. If I'm not careful, even the smallest frustration can rob me of my joy. Apparently, my granddaughter has not yet seen this side of me.

Jesus told his disciples that there is a brand of joy that is complete joy—the kind he experienced even when he knew the cross was just around the corner. Now that's a circumstance I have never faced. This kind of joy is available to you and me as well, if we stay close to him.

My granddaughter isn't always with me, but Jesus is. If I stay close to him, I can experience joy in spite of any circumstance that comes my way.

Every time you choose to smile genuinely even though your circumstances are less than joyful, you give evidence that the same joy Jesus experienced, in spite of the cross, is in you.

"DESPITE MY CIRCUMSTANCES, I FEEL INNER CONTENTMENT AND UNDERSTAND MY PURPOSE IN LIFE."

PEACE

Do not be anxious about anything, but in every situation, by prayer and petition, with thanksgiving, present your requests to God.

PHILIPPIANS 4:6

Philippians 4:6–7 is on many people's "My Favorite Bible Verses" list—and for good reason.

The passage addresses real issues: "Do not be anxious" acknowledges that there is much in life that can prompt anxiety and worry.

It's practical: it tells us what to do when we are tempted to feel anxious. The plan? Pray for anything and everything, and pray with thanksgiving. We may not be thankful *for* the circumstances, but that is not the command. We can always be thankful *despite* the circumstances—thankful to be a child of our good, gracious, perfect heavenly Father.

Philippians 4:7 contains a promise too: "The peace of God, which transcends all understanding, will guard your hearts and your minds in Christ Jesus." Peace comes when we lift our gaze off sources of anxiety and fix our eyes on our almighty, all-loving, all-wise God. Paul had experienced that peace amid persecution, wrongful imprisonment, and a shipwreck. In every difficult situation, Paul presented his requests to God. When you do likewise, you will find peace in God through prayer.

> "I AM FREE FROM ANXIETY BECAUSE I HAVE FOUND PEACE WITH GOD, PEACE WITH OTHERS, AND PEACE WITH MYSELF."

SELF-CONTROL

*The grace of God . . . teaches us to say "No" to
ungodliness and worldly passions, and to live self-
controlled, upright and godly lives in this present age.*

TITUS 2:11–12

There's a conversation I had with renowned pollster George Gallup Jr. that I will never forget. We were working on the assessment tool built around the key ideas found in this devotional and discussing the virtue of self-control. I was pontificating on how Christians needed to pull themselves up by their spiritual bootstraps and stop doing ungodly things. George said, "You're not an alcoholic, are you?" I answered no.

"Well, I am, and so was my father. When I took my first drink, it affected me differently than most people. I couldn't stop. Even as a Christian, I tried and tried, and I couldn't lick it. Then one day I heard Jesus whisper, 'George, if you never figure this out, it is okay. I already died for this.' And I haven't taken a drink in thirty years."

It was because of this conversation that we added the words "through Christ" to the key idea below. The law of "have to" only makes us want to do the things we shouldn't do even more. But grace, when embraced in our soul, gives us the power to say no to those things that harm us and others. Jesus offers you the same grace to overcome your greatest temptations. Hear him whisper this offer to your soul.

**"I HAVE THE POWER THROUGH
CHRIST TO CONTROL MYSELF."**

DAY 249

HOPE

We have this hope as an anchor for the soul, firm and secure. It enters the inner sanctuary behind the curtain, where our forerunner, Jesus, has entered on our behalf.

HEBREWS 6:19–20

The first-century symbol of Christianity was an anchor, not a cross. Pictured on the epitaphs of first-, second-, and third-century believers, it symbolized the hope they had in the life beyond because of Christ. If you look closely, however, you will notice a large portion of an anchor is made up of a cross. Strangely enough, while ships have changed dramatically since that time, the anchor used today has pretty much remained unchanged from ancient times.

The writer of Hebrews tells us, "Jesus Christ is the same yesterday and today and forever" (13:8). Much like the anchor.

Life changes from day to day, and turmoil and tempests come with no warning, but Jesus Christ never changes. You can count on him to hold you steady no matter what the storms of life throw at your boat. He will hold you secure until the billows have calmed and the skies have cleared.

The cross has always been the anchor of hope for those who believe. When tempests in life shake your boat, put your hope in the eternal life offered through our anchor, Jesus Christ.

> **"I CAN COPE WITH THE HARDSHIPS OF LIFE BECAUSE OF THE HOPE I HAVE IN JESUS CHRIST."**

PATIENCE

Whoever is patient has great understanding, but one who is quick-tempered displays folly.

PROVERBS 14:29

When you think of the virtue of patience, think of a thermometer. When you are in a situation that pushes your buttons and frustrates you, put a spiritual thermometer under your tongue and monitor how quickly you are burning up with anger.

Developing a resistance and immunity to the bacteria of frustration involves ingesting daily doses of God's patience toward you. Aren't you glad that God cuts you some slack and loves you in spite of your foibles and failures? In spite of your missteps and mistakes? As a growing follower of Christ, you long to be like him and offer that same patience to others.

The vision? The next time you are in that same frustrating situation, place the spiritual thermometer under your tongue again and see if it doesn't take a bit longer for your temperature to rise. If that is indeed the case, you will have tangible evidence that you are growing in the virtue of patience.

> "I AM SLOW TO ANGER AND ENDURE PATIENTLY UNDER THE UNAVOIDABLE PRESSURES OF LIFE."

KINDNESS/GOODNESS

Make sure that nobody pays back wrong for wrong, but always strive to do what is good for each other and for everyone else.

1 THESSALONIANS 5:15

Words matter, particularly in the Greek language of the New Testament. The Greek word Paul used for "wrong" in the verse above is *kaka*. Now, that is a perfect choice—"Make sure that nobody pays back *kaka* for *kaka*." What an awful way to live.

When Paul countered with a word translated "good," he could have used the Greek word *kalos*. It refers to outer beauty. When you gaze at a sunset, you might say, "That is so *kalos*." If you give a *kalos* response to someone, you might offer a kind or courteous word on the outside while you are steaming with anger on the inside. But instead of using *kalos*, Paul used *agathos*, which refers to an outward act toward others that is first generated from an inner moral sense of what is right and best for that person. This inward sense rests in our hearts, where the key beliefs of Christianity and Christ himself reside. Regardless of what people offer us, we offer Jesus back to them.

The next time someone dishes you up a little *kaka*, don't repay them with *kaka* or even some nice *kalos*. Go deep into your heart and pull out a serving of *agathos*.

> **"I CHOOSE TO BE KIND AND GOOD IN MY RELATIONSHIPS WITH OTHERS."**

FAITHFULNESS

Let love and faithfulness never leave you; bind them around your neck, write them on the tablet of your heart. Then you will win favor and a good name in the sight of God and man.

PROVERBS 3:3–4

The other day at a coffee shop, a young lady sitting at a nearby table called out my name. Knowing I didn't recognize her, she introduced herself as Duane Whitfield's granddaughter. The first words out of my mouth were, "Anybody connected with Duane Whitfield is a friend of mine." Why did I say this? Because Duane has established a good name with me and simply won my favor. For years this man has been an advocate for me. He has never turned down any of my requests and has actively sought to encourage me and stand up for me. He has been a faithful friend.

I can't speak for God, but I'd guess that Duane has established a good name with him because he faithfully relies on God's presence. Through Duane's good name, people like me who have been blessed by him extend favor to his offspring. What a wonderful gift to give to your children.

Everyone has a name, but not everyone has established a good name. In God's strength, shoot for a good name.

> "I HAVE ESTABLISHED A GOOD NAME
> WITH GOD AND OTHERS BASED ON MY
> LOYALTY TO THOSE RELATIONSHIPS."

DAY 253

GENTLENESS

Let your gentleness be evident to all. The Lord is near.

PHILIPPIANS 4:5

When you study the virtue of gentleness throughout the Bible, it carries three practical ideas:

- Thoughtfulness—Think before you speak.
- Consideration—Put yourself in other people's shoes and give them room to make mistakes.
- Calmness—Don't raise your voice or tense up your facial muscles.

Because we belong to Christ, these qualities should be evident to everyone who comes in contact with us. But why does Paul throw in the next sentence? "The Lord is near." This can mean one of two things. One, the Lord's return to earth is near. When Christ returns we don't want to be found as harsh, arrogant, uptight, and loud. Two, it could simply mean that the Lord's presence is near us right now. He is watching everything we are doing all the time.

Bottom line: in all of your encounters with people, imagine Jesus in the room with you, because he is in you and he might actually show up face-to-face in front of you today. Act accordingly.

> **"I AM THOUGHTFUL, CONSIDERATE, AND CALM IN MY DEALINGS WITH OTHERS."**

Do nothing out of selfish ambition or vain conceit. Rather, in humility value others above yourselves, not looking to your own interests but each of you to the interests of others.

PHILIPPIANS 2:3–4

We all know that the person who has a strong self-esteem and feeds their ego through self-promotion, often at the expense of others, is not the poster child for biblical humility. However, biblical humility also isn't demonstrated through the person who has a low self-esteem, acts humble and shy, and lacks confidence, allowing people to walk all over them. That's humiliation.

Truly humble people have strong self-esteem stemming from a knowledge of who they are in Christ. A firm grasp of your eternal position as a child of God gives you confidence that you have nothing to lose. Knowing that your position is not up for grabs affords you the opportunity to put the needs of others above your own.

In Philippians 2:8 Paul cites Jesus as the poster child for humility: "being found in appearance as a man, he humbled himself by becoming obedient to death." Jesus, with a strong sense of who he was, put your needs above his own and suffered so that you could gain a relationship with God. If you want to be like Jesus, take on his brand of humility.

"I CHOOSE TO ESTEEM OTHERS ABOVE MYSELF."

DAY 255

LOVE

"I have made you known to them, and will continue to make you known in order that the love you have for me may be in them and that I myself may be in them."

JOHN 17:26

"God is love" (1 John 4:8, 16). God's love is abundant and over-flowing, no matter our response. God's love is for our eternal well-being. God's love is not diminished by our worst faults or increased by our best efforts. We who live in a "you get what you earn" world cannot fathom a being such as God, who gives us what we don't deserve—his unconditional love.

Being told to love as God loves is like telling a man-eating lion to act like a man-loving golden retriever. Impossible! It's not in the nature of the lion to do so. But what if the nature of the golden retriever was put into the big cat? That changes everything, doesn't it? This is the hope of the New Covenant in Christ.

The Law commands me to have selfless love for my fellow man and *for* God above.

My love-barren heart cries out, *Futility! Selfless love is not in me.*

Christ's new command bids me to have selfless love for my fellow man *from* God above.

My love-rich heart rejoices free, for Love himself lives in me.

> **"I AM COMMITTED TO LOVING GOD AND LOVING OTHERS."**

JOY

You make known to me the path of life; you will fill me with joy in your presence.

PSALM 16:11

Our little beagle dog, Lady, was amazing. During her eighteen years, every time I walked into the house, she came running, barking, and wagging her whole rear end. Whether I was returning from a thirty-minute jog, a whole day of work, or a two-day trip, Lady was always happy to see me when I came home. She would run and jump over the furniture and flip around, so excited to see me. She wouldn't stop until I put down whatever was in my arms and petted her.

If I worked at home, Lady was always nearby, keeping me company, curled up next to my desk for hours. If I made a move to get up, she picked up her head as if to say, "What are we going to do now?" She found great joy and contentment in being near me.

May we be as excited to greet our heavenly Father each day. May we be aware of his movement in our lives and be ready to move with him. May we be aware of God's presence and find great contentment in it.

Lord, teach me to know joy in your presence, whatever the circumstances of my life.

> **"DESPITE MY CIRCUMSTANCES, I FEEL INNER CONTENTMENT AND UNDERSTAND MY PURPOSE IN LIFE."**

PEACE

Let the peace of Christ rule in your hearts. . . . And be thankful.

COLOSSIANS 3:15

know there has to be a Starbucks close by," I told Randy. "There's always a green sign within sight—until you need it! But no worries, I have a trusty phone app that'll help us find one."

In just a few moments our desire for a "coffee of the day" and a refreshing Frappuccino was satisfied.

And that's what businesses count on. Marketers understand that apps generate what's called a "virtuous circle." The more users Twitter has, the more willing a company is to invest in developing effective applications. And the more developers create good apps for Twitter, the more people use Twitter.[52]

Paul's words above point to a virtuous circle as well. The more gratitude you have in your heart, the more peace you'll feel; the more peace you feel, the more willingly and naturally you will do all you do in the name of Jesus. The more you do in the name of Jesus, the more peace of Christ and gratitude you'll have in your heart. Start on this virtuous cycle today!

> **"I AM FREE FROM ANXIETY BECAUSE I HAVE FOUND PEACE WITH GOD, PEACE WITH OTHERS, AND PEACE WITH MYSELF."**

SELF-CONTROL

Pursue righteousness, godliness, faith, love, endurance and gentleness. Fight the good fight of the faith.

1 TIMOTHY 6:11–12

Bed always feels the most comfortable just as the alarm goes off, but there is much value in beginning the day with God and his Word. Sitting by the window with a cup of coffee, reading the Bible, and asking God to open your heart to the truth is a great way to start the day.

If you're like me, your brain is filled with schedules, projects, worries, and people you love, and it can be hard to focus. But memorizing Scripture enables us to recall God's principles during difficult situations. The Lord can bring to mind a verse exactly when we need it.

Our days are busy and demanding. Writing down things to remember is important, and journaling answers to prayers helps you remember God's faithfulness. It gives testimony to his involvement in your days. Looking through a prayer journal can build your faith and help you persevere through a present trial.

Reading God's Word. Memorizing Scripture. Keeping a journal. Making time for prayer. Worshipping. Attending a small group. These are some good ways to pursue righteousness, godliness, faith, love, endurance, and gentleness, which will all lead to self-control and "[fighting] the good fight of the faith." How do you pursue godly self-control?

> **"I HAVE THE POWER THROUGH CHRIST TO CONTROL MYSELF."**

DAY 259

HOPE

Those who hope in the LORD will renew their strength. . . .
They will run and not grow weary, they will walk and not
be faint.

ISAIAH 40:31

The absence of peace in the Middle East . . . droughts, earthquakes, hurricanes . . . terrorism and war, hunger and disease . . . Much in the headlines can bring on hopelessness.

The relentlessness of parenting, pinching pennies, and paying bills . . . the ongoing house projects . . . and people who want three meals a day *and* clean clothes! . . . Much at home can bring on weariness.

But our faithful God's promises—of his presence and power, guidance and protection, provision and redemption, deliverance and transformation—speak to the big situations on our planet as well as to the details of our day. Knowing God's promises is where hope for daily living starts. When we truly believe them for ourselves, God's grace renews our strength to keep getting out of bed in the morning and to continue putting one foot in front of the other.

Claim God's promises as though they were made to you directly. They can change your plodding into a confident walk and your heavy-hearted downward glance into an upward gaze of hope.

> **"I CAN COPE WITH THE HARDSHIPS OF LIFE**
> **BECAUSE OF THE HOPE I HAVE IN JESUS CHRIST."**

PATIENCE

Endure hardship as discipline; God is treating you as his children. For what children are not disciplined by their father?

HEBREWS 12:7

'm still not quite clear how the baseball went through the plate-glass window. Maybe my brother and I underestimated our own strength, or it was just a poor decision to play catch so near our neighbor's house. What I do clearly remember is my dad's response.

Dad wasn't happy with us—and for good reason. This depression-raised, blue-collar worker never liked spending money, and this expense could have been avoided. His response was, "When you do something wrong, make it right." So we did. We apologized to our neighbor, cleaned up the glass, went to the store to buy a replacement window, and earned the money to pay Dad back. Not easy, but Dad's disciplinary process taught us an important lesson: when you do something wrong, accept responsibility for it and make it right—and try not to do it again.

When we make mistakes, and we all do, we can learn something from it. Loving fathers discipline children and give them lessons to carry with them into adulthood so future mistakes or poor choices can be prevented. What lesson might your heavenly Father be teaching you from a current mistake or poor choice in your life?

"I AM SLOW TO ANGER AND ENDURE PATIENTLY UNDER THE UNAVOIDABLE PRESSURES OF LIFE."

KINDNESS/GOODNESS

Give thanks to the LORD for his unfailing love and his wonderful deeds for mankind, for he satisfies the thirsty and fills the hungry with good things.

PSALM 107:8–9

Macaroni and cheese? Mashed potatoes? Ice cream? Grilled cheese? Chocolate cake? What are your go-to comfort foods? The comfort that comes from certain foods is not just in your imagination. Science has shown that the significant amount of fat in most comfort foods impacts brain chemistry and, yes, lifts one's mood.

Now consider the connection between food and fellowship in the Bible and in the life of your church. The two often go hand-in-hand: Jesus' Last Supper with his disciples; preaching on the hill and serving the crowd fish and bread; Communion during Sunday worship; Wednesday night potluck fellowship suppers. It seems God loves to "[satisfy] the thirsty and [fill] the hungry with good things."

A meal with friends, a celebration dinner with family, a cup of coffee with a soulmate—these feed body and soul at the same time. Our good and kind God delights in giving us double blessings like that!

Share the kindness and goodness God has shown you with friends this week. Invite them over for a cup of coffee or even your favorite comfort food. You'll feed your body and soul.

> **"I CHOOSE TO BE KIND AND GOOD IN MY RELATIONSHIPS WITH OTHERS."**

FAITHFULNESS

Your love, LORD, reaches to the heavens, your faithfulness to the skies.

PSALM 36:5

How big is the sun? That question can be answered in multiple ways, all of them mind-boggling: The sun's circumference is 2,713,406 miles and its diameter is 864,938 miles. About 109 earths could be lined up across the face of the sun, and about 1.3 million earths could fit inside it.[53]

Even though the sun is the largest object in our solar system, it's only a medium-sized star in comparison to the hundreds of billions of stars in the Milky Way galaxy. So when David looked up at the vastness of the sky, he must have marveled at the great expanse of the universe God created. Those moments surely came to mind as he celebrated God's faithfulness reaching "to the skies."

Living in a world with as much uncertainty as ours, David found great comfort in the extent of God's devotion. God never forgets what he has promised.

Spend some time humbly thanking God for his great faithfulness. Our faithfulness may not reach "to the heavens," but perhaps it can reach to the spouse sitting next to you or the neighbor next door.

> **"I HAVE ESTABLISHED A GOOD NAME WITH GOD AND OTHERS BASED ON MY LOYALTY TO THOSE RELATIONSHIPS."**

GENTLENESS

Shimei was . . . cursing as he went and throwing stones at him and showering him with dirt.

2 SAMUEL 16:13

She was in the first row of the "colored" section in the middle of the bus. The white section was full, and not every white man had a place to sit. Despite the bus driver's request that she give up her seat, Rosa Parks remained seated. She was arrested, given a thirty-minute hearing, found guilty, fined $10, and assessed a $4 court fee.

In the 1960s, African Americans were assaulted with withering looks, second-class treatment, limited opportunities, and harsh words. Sometimes there were nightsticks, tear gas, and bloodshed. A student of the words of Gandhi and a disciple of Jesus, Martin Luther King Jr. was not going to retaliate. He explained that the law of "an eye for an eye" leads to blindness for all. Hardly a doormat and advocating action in the form of civil disobedience, King led African Americans through the civil rights movement with wisdom and gentleness.

The same God who enabled King David to lead, and gave him the wisdom and self-control not to retaliate when Shimei insulted him and threw things at him, can enable you to be gentle and restrained, but still firm and righteous, with the Shimeis in your life.

> **"I AM THOUGHTFUL, CONSIDERATE, AND CALM IN MY DEALINGS WITH OTHERS."**

HUMILITY

*In your relationships with one another, have the same
mindset as Christ Jesus: Who, being in very nature God,
did not consider equality with God something to be used
to his own advantage; rather, he made himself nothing by
taking the very nature of a servant.*

PHILIPPIANS 2:5–7

Humility is the hardest virtue to obtain. As soon as you think you
have it—guess what? You've lost it again. All the other virtues are
building blocks that bring you closer to the humble mind-set of Jesus.

Poet Alfred Tennyson called humility "the highest virtue; the
mother of all the virtues." Yet attempting to "grasp" humility by trying
harder to be humble is almost as frustrating as trying to add inches to
your stature.

Jesus, the perfect example of humility, never worked hard at
becoming humble. He simply surrendered who he was—an equal
with God—and focused on others. His motivation was his love for us.
Perhaps humility only comes as we surrender ourselves and fixate on
gaining all the other virtues for the sake of those around us.

While you will never be able to add inches to your height, you
can build your stature in humility. May you share the same mind-set as
Jesus by focusing on your love for those around you.

"I CHOOSE TO ESTEEM OTHERS ABOVE MYSELF."

LOVE

What does the LORD your God ask of you but to fear the LORD your God, to walk in obedience to him, to love him, to serve the LORD your God with all your heart and with all your soul?

DEUTERONOMY 10:12

Spoiler alert! If you haven't read O. Henry's short story "The Gift of the Magi," find it online and then come back!

As Christmas approaches, Jim and Della don't have much money for bills, much less gifts. Jim has a gold pocket watch that was once his dad's, Della has long, beautiful hair, and they both have an idea! Della cuts her hair and sells it so she can buy Jim a chain for his watch. Jim sells his watch in order to purchase some nice combs for his wife's lovely hair.

Both Jim and Della gave up their most prized possession for each other. What a precious picture of one human being's sacrificial love for another!

The cross is the ultimate picture of Jesus' profound, sacrificial, and life-giving love for us sinful human beings. Think back over your life. What sacrifices have you made to show God your great love for him?

What opportunity do you have this week to show your heavenly Father that you love him? Put that love into action and ask God to teach you how to better love him with all your heart, soul, and strength.

> **"I AM COMMITTED TO LOVING GOD AND LOVING OTHERS."**

I have learned the secret of being content in any and every situation.

PHILIPPIANS 4:12

P aul shared his secrets to being content in letters he wrote while in prison. He tells us we can experience joy in *all* life situations.

Discouraging past? Paul persecuted Christians before he met Jesus. Your past couldn't be as hard to overcome as his! He names himself the chief of sinners (1 Timothy 1:15).

People pulling you down? Ever thought others may feel that way about you? Paul reminds us we were all sinners until Jesus gave us life (Colossians 2:13).

"Doing without" a lot of things? Paul could identify. But even when he enjoyed seasons of plenty, they were not the source of his joy; his relationship with Jesus was. Don't find joy *in* your stuff; rather add your stuff to the joy you have in Christ.

Circumstances can change anyone's mood quickly. Paul said to endure with patience and joyfully give thanks to "the Father, who has qualified you to share in the inheritance of his . . . kingdom" (Colossians 1:12). Get your eyes off your circumstances and remember God's promise.

Sometime this week read Paul's words on joy and discover his secret.

> **"DESPITE MY CIRCUMSTANCES, I FEEL INNER CONTENTMENT AND UNDERSTAND MY PURPOSE IN LIFE."**

PEACE

He poured out his life unto death, and was numbered with the transgressors. For he bore the sin of many, and made intercession for the transgressors.

ISAIAH 53:12

Like many people in history, the Incas of South America turned to religion in an attempt to control the uncontrollable in their world. They would trade something of value—food, cloth, animals—for peace from the weather and other natural phenomena. They even resorted to human sacrifice.[54] Analysis of Incan child mummies indicates the regular consumption of coca leaves (from which cocaine is made) and alcohol, which probably made them more compliant as their death approached.[55] No mention is made of whether parents sacrificed their children or if children were taken from their homes.[56]

What a contrast with Jesus' sacrifice! The Inca children were forced into the sacrifice and likely torn away from their homes and parents; Jesus came from his heavenly home, willingly leaving his Father, freely offering himself as a peace offering. Pleasing the different Inca gods meant ongoing sacrifices; Jesus died once, for all.

Because of Jesus' choice to bear your sins and die for you, you can know peace with God.

> **"I AM FREE FROM ANXIETY BECAUSE I HAVE FOUND PEACE WITH GOD, PEACE WITH OTHERS, AND PEACE WITH MYSELF."**

SELF-CONTROL

[Delilah] prodded [Samson] day after day until he was sick to death of it. So he told her everything.

JUDGES 16:16–17

Jessica told her therapist, "I never saw it. I couldn't see how broken my marriage was until I found him with my stepsister."

"Sometimes our eyes keep from us the things our hearts don't want to see," the therapist responded.

Reflecting back, Jessica, who was a therapist herself, recognized all the signs that had been hidden in plain sight: her husband coming home late, keeping his phone close, deleting his texts. "How could I not have seen what was always in front of me?" Jessica asked.[57]

Jessica is not alone. Our eyes can keep us from seeing what our hearts don't want to acknowledge when we let fear or pride blind us. That was apparently the case for Samson, who couldn't see Delilah's manipulation for what it was and lost his hair, his eyes, and eventually his life. He let lust get the better of him, instead of having the self-control he needed to see the truth in front of him.

Ask the Lord to give you self-control to open your eyes to things you need to see, in your own life or in the lives of others.

> **"I HAVE THE POWER THROUGH CHRIST TO CONTROL MYSELF."**

DAY 269

HOPE

Oh, that I might have my request . . . that God would be willing to crush me, to let loose his hand and cut off my life!

JOB 6:8–9

A Vietnam vet who struggles with PTSD (post-traumatic stress disorder), multiple sclerosis, blindness, hallucinations, forced inactivity, and loneliness, Larry Browning is something of a modern-day Job. Yet if you knew him, it would be hard to imagine Job's words above being Larry's.

Is he ever angry at God? "No," Larry said, "I get discouraged, but I look back on my life, and I see all that God has done for me. I'm just thankful that he was faithful when I was faithless. He's blessed me so much. . . . I try to be more thankful than upset."

How do you stay faithful when your all-powerful, all-loving God chooses not to heal you? "I stay faithful because . . . all the years that I was walking in the world, God never forsook me. He never gave up on me even though I was in open rebellion against him. Knowing . . . he's promised that one day I'm going to be made whole—it's pretty easy for me to recognize the faithfulness of God. God is always faithful."[58]

Ask God to help you see beyond your pain to his faithfulness.

"I CAN COPE WITH THE HARDSHIPS OF LIFE BECAUSE OF THE HOPE I HAVE IN JESUS CHRIST."

PATIENCE

You, Lord, are a compassionate and gracious God, slow to anger, abounding in love and faithfulness.

PSALM 86:15

Winston Churchill was known for his quick temper. In one particular instance, Lady Astor triggered his ire. She had expressed her desire to become the first female member of the British Parliament, and Churchill was leading the charge in opposition to her election. After a long and angry debate, a frustrated Lady Astor told Churchill that should she be married to him, she would poison his tea. Equally angry, Churchill responded that if she were his wife, he'd drink it!

Anger doesn't always accomplish much, if anything. In the case of Lady Astor and Mr. Churchill, their anger may have made you chuckle, but it did nothing to resolve the situation.

In many cases a hair-trigger reaction of anger can make a given situation much worse. God does not have a hair-trigger temper. Just the opposite, in fact. God is slow to anger. Instead of immediately sending the punishment our sin deserves, God shows us mercy and love: he is long-suffering and slow to anger in hopes that we will recognize our sin and repent.

Join with the psalmist in gratefully praising God for his compassion, grace, love, faithfulness . . . and patience.

> "I AM SLOW TO ANGER AND ENDURE PATIENTLY UNDER THE UNAVOIDABLE PRESSURES OF LIFE."

KINDNESS/GOODNESS

[Rahab] had taken [the two spies] up to the roof and hidden them under the stalks of flax she had laid out on the roof.

JOSHUA 2:6

While Wesley Autrey and his daughters were waiting for a subway train, he saw a man fall onto the tracks. Cameron Hollopeter had had a seizure, started convulsing, and tumbled off the platform as the speeding train rounded the corner.

Autrey jumped down, covered Hollopeter with his body, and pushed them both between the train tracks. The subway operator couldn't stop in time, and all five cars of the train rolled over both men, just a few inches from Autrey's head. Onlookers' screams of terror became shouts of joy and amazement when the train stopped and Autrey called out that he and Hollopeter were okay.[59]

Without hesitating, Autrey protected Hollopeter and saved the man's life. Rahab was faced with a similar choice. She risked her life to protect the enemy soldiers, showing them life-saving kindness. And when Joshua and his men brought down the walls of Jericho, they returned that kindness by sparing Rahab and her family.

What acts of kindness has your faith in God prompted—or is God perhaps prompting now?

"I CHOOSE TO BE KIND AND GOOD IN MY RELATIONSHIPS WITH OTHERS."

FAITHFULNESS

*Because of the LORD'S great love we are not
consumed, for his compassions never fail.*

LAMENTATIONS 3:22

Robertson McQuilkin was president of Columbia Bible College and Seminary when his wife was diagnosed with Alzheimer's. He offers a powerful example of a husband's faithful love for his wife:

> [For years I struggled] with the question of what should be sacrificed: ministry or caring for Muriel. . . . To put God first means that all other responsibilities he gives are first, too. Sorting out responsibilities that seem to conflict, however, is tricky business. . . .
>
> When the time came, the decision . . . took no great calculation. It was a matter of integrity. Had I not promised, forty-two years before, "in sickness and in health . . . till death do us part"? This was no grim duty to which I stoically resigned, however. It was only fair. She had, after all, cared for me for almost four decades with marvelous devotion; now it was my turn. And such a partner she was! If I took care of her for forty years, I would never be out of her debt.[60]

God calls us to stay faithful in our relationships!

"I HAVE ESTABLISHED A GOOD NAME WITH GOD AND OTHERS BASED ON MY LOYALTY TO THOSE RELATIONSHIPS."

DAY 273

GENTLENESS

May you be blessed for your good judgment and for keeping me from bloodshed this day and from avenging myself with my own hands.

1 SAMUEL 25:33

Would you think gentle words could spare someone's life? Abigail, the wife of Nabal, decided to try it.

The mighty warrior David was running low on supplies. He sent some of his soldiers to Nabal, a wealthy man in the area, to ask for assistance. The request was flatly refused. Nabal was "surly and mean" (v. 3), unwilling to part with any of his provisions to help David.

When David's men went back with Nabal's response, David became enraged and said to his men, "Each of you strap on your sword!" (v. 13). He strapped his on, too, and they went after Nabal with a vengeance. However, one of Nabal's servants told Abigail what had transpired, and she acted quickly in an attempt to save her husband.

She took loaves of bread, two skins of wine, five dressed sheep, roasted grain, raisin cakes, and pressed figs and took off to meet David before he got to Nabal (v. 18). The verse above is David's thankful words to Abigail for saving him from killing Nabal.

Never discount what gentle words can accomplish. The life you save might be your spouse's or even your own.

> **"I AM THOUGHTFUL, CONSIDERATE, AND CALM IN MY DEALINGS WITH OTHERS."**

HUMILITY

> *In order to keep me from becoming conceited, I was given a thorn in my flesh . . . to torment me. . . . [The Lord] said to me, "My grace is sufficient for you, for my power is made perfect in weakness." Therefore I will boast all the more gladly about my weaknesses, so that Christ's power may rest on me.*

2 CORINTHIANS 12:7, 9

I am not the proficient public speaker my husband is. Getting up in front of people makes my heart race with nervousness. As I strap on the microphone, I just know the pounding of my heart will overpower my voice. As the event draws near, I find myself asking, "Why did I agree to this?"

But each time my nervousness falls away after the first few sentences. Is it possible my anxiousness gives God an opportunity to show his power? My weakness in this area forces me to be aware that I don't have the power necessary to accomplish anything myself and compels me to give God the glory for anything that is accomplished. My pounding heart reminds me I need God, and that *he's* got this!

We all have thorns in our flesh where God's might and power can shine through. When challenges to your weakness come, embrace them. Wait with heartfelt anticipation to see what your powerful God can do through you.

"I CHOOSE TO ESTEEM OTHERS ABOVE MYSELF."

LOVE

These three remain: faith, hope and love. But the greatest of these is love.

1 CORINTHIANS 13:13

Have you ever committed to reading through the Bible in a year? Many have. Some journal as they read; others read and let Scripture wash over them. Some listen to the Bible through apps on their phone. Everyone has a different strategy.

If you do read the entire Bible, what are the major elements you will find? You will see how God created man and came down to walk with him in the garden. God wanted be in a relationship with us, but we chose a different path and ruined that relationship. You will notice how God's heart is broken when we turn away in rebellion, and you will see God's endless pursuit to be back in relationship with us, even to the point of sacrificing his only Son to die for us. Then you will see at the end, in Revelation, that one day God will come down and live among us, his children, again in a new garden—the new kingdom.

However, the major theme that runs throughout all sixty-six of the books that comprise God's Word—and your primary takeaway from reading the Bible—is that God loves you.

Lord, enable me to accept your love and to share it with other people for their good.

> "I AM COMMITTED TO LOVING
> GOD AND LOVING OTHERS."

JOY

*We want each of you to show this same diligence to the
very end, so that what you hope for may be fully realized.*

HEBREWS 6:11

I have known several friends who have trained to run a half-marathon. They knew the training would be demanding. They also knew the large amount of running would test not just their bodies but also their faith and perseverance. But they choose to do it anyway. There's something about conquering the mental aspect of the physical demands that attracts them. As they train they become aware of improvement along the way. Every one of them has told me it isn't all joy, but it's definitely joyful when your work pays off and you cross that finish line.

The trials of physical pain can pale in comparison to the trials of life's emotional pain, yet we can learn from half-marathoners. We know life is hard—Jesus promised that—and it will test not just our mental, physical, and emotional stamina, but also our faith in God and in his process of strengthening our trust in him. We can choose to consider the training time pure joy. We can be absolutely confident that the training will pay off, and we can trust that there will be all kinds of blessings at the end of the race.

> **"DESPITE MY CIRCUMSTANCES, I FEEL INNER CONTENTMENT AND UNDERSTAND MY PURPOSE IN LIFE."**

PEACE

"The LORD turn his face toward you and give you peace."

NUMBERS 6:26

Remember any dates that started out promising, but your date droned on and on about his promotion, his new car, his fancy apartment . . . and oh, had he mentioned his new car?

Just when you thought he was going to ask about you, he said, "Well, enough about me, let's talk about you . . . What do you think about me?"

Dating seems to be all about impressing the other person. It's exhausting.

"We are our favorite topic of conversation," author Leslie Hughes observes. "This deep-seated obsession to be central is boasting. In direct opposition to boasting is a broken and contrite heart . . . that acknowledges that it can do nothing and bring nothing to God."[61]

There's nothing you can do to earn God's love. Only a surrendered heart can be reconciled with him. Peace with God comes as we stop trying to impress him and others. Rest in the peace your amazingly gracious God offers.

> **"I AM FREE FROM ANXIETY BECAUSE I HAVE FOUND PEACE WITH GOD, PEACE WITH OTHERS, AND PEACE WITH MYSELF."**

SELF-CONTROL

Joseph was well-built and handsome, and after a while his master's wife took notice of Joseph and said, "Come to bed with me!" But he refused.

GENESIS 39:6–8

When Nancy Reagan became first lady, she spearheaded the effort to solve the drug problem in America. It was in Oakland, California, that she unwittingly found the name for her campaign. Mrs. Reagan was visiting with some schoolchildren when a young girl raised her hand. "What do you do if somebody offers you drugs?" she asked.

Mrs. Reagan said, "Well, you just say no!" The phrase caught on.

Psychologists will explain why saying no isn't always simple and why people need to be armed with more than a single word. But with that straightforward statement, Mrs. Reagan gave young people across the country permission to say no, and a starting point for resisting.

Joseph just said no to his boss's wife—several times. Joseph knew what was right. He undoubtedly prayed and asked God to give him the strength to act on what he knew. Joseph must also have been aware of the possible consequences of saying no, but he trusted his life to the Lord.

In what situation do you need to be saying no? Rely on the Holy Spirit to provide you with the strength and self-control to do exactly that.

"I HAVE THE POWER THROUGH CHRIST TO CONTROL MYSELF."

HOPE

"Of what value is an idol carved by a craftsman? . . . For the one who makes it trusts in his own creation; he makes idols that cannot speak. . . . Can [wood or lifeless stone] give guidance? . . . There is no breath in it."

HABAKKUK 2:18–19

D o not arouse the wrath of the great and powerful Oz. I said come back tomorrow." The voice boomed as Toto grabbed a corner of the curtain and pulled it open. "I am the great and powerful . . ."

At that moment, the great and powerful Oz saw Dorothy, the Scarecrow, the Tin Man, and the Cowardly Lion—and the four of them saw a normal man speaking into a microphone as he controlled the smoke machine.

" . . . Wizard of Oz," he ended meekly.[62]

Just as Toto helped Dorothy and her friends recognize the Wizard for what he was, we need the Holy Spirit to help us recognize our idols for what they are. Are we putting our hope in income, prestige, house, family, cars, degrees, appearance? These things appear great and powerful, but "of what value is an idol carved by a craftsman" in light of eternity?

What idol do you need to pull the curtain away from and acknowledge "there is no breath in it"?

"I CAN COPE WITH THE HARDSHIPS OF LIFE BECAUSE OF THE HOPE I HAVE IN JESUS CHRIST."

PATIENCE

"How long will these people treat me with contempt? How long will they refuse to believe in me?"

NUMBERS 14:11

Kids: "Why can't I buy lunch at school every day? I got to last year." "I don't want to share a bathroom with my sister."

Mom: "Because we are trying to save money." "You have your own bedroom. I think you'll survive."

Israelites: "If only we had meat to eat! We remember the fish we ate in Egypt at no cost—also the cucumbers, melons, leeks, onions and garlic" (Numbers 11:4–5).

God: "But you were slaves who had to gather your own straw for the bricks you were forced to make—and Pharaoh gave you impossible quotas to fill!"

Complaining kids reveal their sense of entitlement. Whining Israelites showed their ingratitude, greed, and selective memory. It's not a pretty picture . . . but we've all been there! The pressures of life fuel impatience, and impatience can prompt complaining.

What pressures are making you impatient? Are there ways you are whining to God like a self-centered child, or ignoring his goodness like the Israelites? Turn to God in honesty and humility. He can help with both the excessive pressures and your limited patience!

"I AM SLOW TO ANGER AND ENDURE PATIENTLY UNDER THE UNAVOIDABLE PRESSURES OF LIFE."

KINDNESS/GOODNESS

David asked, "Is there anyone still left of the house of Saul to whom I can show kindness for Jonathan's sake?"

2 SAMUEL 9:1

It was 1941 in war-torn Poland. Zofia Banya didn't have any money, but shopkeeper Israel Rubinek told her she could take what she needed to care for her family and repay him later. Two years afterward, when Nazis were sending Jews like Rubinek to concentration camps, Banya took Rubinek and his wife into her home—for two and a half years. On several occasions soldiers came to search for concealed Jews. One night soldiers slept in Banya's living room, inches away from where the Rubineks were hiding in a crawl space.[63]

Rubinek's kindness begat Banya's kindness. The same occurred in the lives of David and Jonathan. Traditionally the new king would wipe out the previous king's family, but Jonathan, the rightful heir to the throne, loved David, who was God's choice for the position. Surrendering his claim, Jonathan protected David from his father's wrath. His kindness led to David's desire to return kindness to Jonathan's family, specifically to his son, Mephibosheth. David brought Mephibosheth to his table to eat and sent servants to work his land.

Think about an especially meaningful act of kindness you received. Have you responded?

"I CHOOSE TO BE KIND AND GOOD IN MY RELATIONSHIPS WITH OTHERS."

FAITHFULNESS

An elder must be blameless, faithful to his wife.

TITUS 1:6

I met Rozanne at church when I was fifteen years old. We started "going out," but we didn't actually *go* anywhere. I didn't have a driver's license. We mostly sat together in church. It is the only season of my life when I wanted the preacher to drone on and on.

When I was twenty years old, I asked Rozanne to marry me, and we set the date for July 18, 1981.

As the day approached, I got cold feet. My fear had nothing to do with my fiancé. She was absolutely breathtaking and amazing. I doubted my ability to make a promise at the age of twenty to one person and keep it for a lifetime. I questioned my capacity to be faithful. We canceled the wedding a month out.

I went back to college for my junior year and was so lonely without Rozanne. I somehow got her and her parents to agree to a new date—December 19, 1981.

What about my question of faithfulness? God whispered to me, "Stay close to me, lean into me, and I will help you." Well, that was over thirty years ago, and we have both remained faithful to each other. The secret of our success? God!

> **"I HAVE ESTABLISHED A GOOD NAME WITH GOD AND OTHERS BASED ON MY LOYALTY TO THOSE RELATIONSHIPS."**

GENTLENESS

"Take my yoke upon you and learn from me, for I am gentle and humble in heart, and you will find rest for your souls."

MATTHEW 11:29

What's your name?" the high school teacher hosting after-school detention asks every student who walks in. "What did you do to end up spending this afternoon with me? Who sent you? Please thank that teacher because now I have a chance to meet you, encourage you, and talk to you. Are you involved in clubs, band, sports, student government, drama? You don't have to be in trouble to come visit me. I'm always here to offer you encouragement."

The teacher's gentle approach with these students is impactful. His words of encouragement may be the first some of these young people have ever heard. Because he takes the time to make suggestions about different paths they could take, they may realize they have options.

This teacher—a believer who regards the public school campus as the mission field to which God has called him—offers students a new perspective on school and themselves, the possibility of a different path, and encouragement whenever they need it.

Jesus does this for us, his weary and burdened people, offering us his peace, guidance, and support. Thank Jesus for the way he loves you, and extend Christlike gentleness to others.

> **"I AM THOUGHTFUL, CONSIDERATE, AND CALM IN MY DEALINGS WITH OTHERS."**

HUMILITY

"Your Father who sees what is done in secret, will reward you."

MATTHEW 6:18

Comedian Brian Regan describes sharing a story at a party about having two wisdom teeth pulled and a gentleman interrupting him, saying he had all four of his pulled. Then another interjects that his were impacted and he stayed swollen for days. In the middle of his spiel, Brian asked why people feel the need to boast about everything and try to one-up each other!

Great question! Jesus admonishes us to keep what we do a secret in Matthew 6. He tells us to give, not letting the left hand know what the right hand is doing, and to pray in our room.

Dallas Willard wrote, "One of the greatest fallacies of Christian faith, and actually one of the greatest acts of unbelief, is the thought that spiritual acts and virtues need to be advertised to be known. . . . Secrecy, rightly practiced, enables one to place the public relations department entirely in the hands of God. . . . We allow God to decide when deeds will be known and when light will be noticed." Dallas goes on to suggest that as we practice the discipline of secrecy, we develop love and humility, and begin to desire others' good above our own.[64]

Next time you're at a party, if someone shares about their Florida vacation, keep quiet about your trip to Hawaii!

"I CHOOSE TO ESTEEM OTHERS ABOVE MYSELF."

DAY 285

LOVE

"This is to my Father's glory, that you bear much fruit, showing yourselves to be my disciples."

JOHN 15:8

Some farmers have particular practices that cooperate with nature so that their land bears abundant fruit. For instance, they will avoid growing a single family of crops on the same plot of land year after year in order to protect vegetables from pests and diseases. They also will give land plots every fourth year off from cash crop production. During that year they replenish the land's soil by growing cover crops and tilling them under, and boost its fertility and control pests by letting hens graze on it.

What can we do to cooperate with the Holy Spirit so that we bear the abundant and life-giving fruit of a loving life? We can wear the armor of God to protect our souls from pests and diseases (Ephesians 6). We can keep the soil of our hearts rich and healthy by reading God's Word regularly. And we can spend time with fellow believers who enrich our lives, help us stand strong against temptation, and keep us walking the narrow path.

Like farmers working in cooperation with nature, you can take steps to cooperate with the Holy Spirit so that he bears fruit in your life.

> **"I AM COMMITTED TO LOVING GOD AND LOVING OTHERS."**

JOY

Though the olive crop fails and the fields produce no food . . . yet I will rejoice in the LORD, I will be joyful in God my Savior.

HABAKKUK 3:17–18

Claire wasn't expected to live very long. She was born with a rare disease called epidermolysis bullosa, which requires regular protective bandaging of her entire body to prevent blistering. Now sixteen, Claire is doing well, and so—by God's grace—is her older sister, who was diagnosed with a different life-shortening disease four years ago.

Now meet their amazing mom. For more than twenty years, Cindy has closed her e-mails with "Choosing joy." The first time I read that, I was taken aback. *Can that be possible? With all that she is dealing with, Lord, is she really choosing joy?* Close on the heels of that thought came, *She absolutely does! That woman totally lives joy!* Her sense of fun, her knack for getting people engaged with one another, the laughter she adds to any gathering, the readiness with which she shares her love of Jesus—Cindy chooses and lives joy! And her joy is contagious!

Lord, I want to choose joy even when crops fail and the fields produce no food.

"DESPITE MY CIRCUMSTANCES, I FEEL INNER CONTENTMENT AND UNDERSTAND MY PURPOSE IN LIFE."

PEACE

The LORD is my shepherd, I lack nothing.

PSALM 23:1

Just reading Psalm 23 brings my stress level down a few notches. I picture myself being led by my Shepherd to serene waters and resting quietly in the green pastures, a gentle breeze blowing as I enjoy the sunshine on my face. Just imagining this makes my soul more peaceful.

The most stress-free people I have ever seen are Bedouin shepherds who roam the outskirts of the Holy Land. The Israeli government became fascinated with these people because most live to be more than a hundred years old, thirty years longer than most people groups. A study uncovered only one difference in their lifestyle—no stress.[65]

The Bedouin secret? Work hard during the day, but when dusk comes, waste away the evening with family and friends around a fire, sharing dinner and stories. Doctors agree that our fast-paced, overcommitted lifestyle causes stress that makes us sick and can kill us thirty years before God intended.[66]

Want peace? Abandon your work at 6:00 p.m., and sit down; breathe deeply; read this psalm. Call a friend to share dinner with you and don't resume working until tomorrow. Follow your Shepherd. He longs to lead you beside still waters and replenish your soul.

> **"I AM FREE FROM ANXIETY BECAUSE I HAVE FOUND PEACE WITH GOD, PEACE WITH OTHERS, AND PEACE WITH MYSELF."**

SELF-CONTROL

> *"While [his son] was still a long way off, his father saw him and was filled with compassion for him; he ran to his son, threw his arms around him and kissed him."*

LUKE 15:20

You've heard it said, "Parenting isn't for wimps."

It's not easy to let kids experience the natural consequences of their choices in the name of tough love. Sometimes as a good parent you have to let a forgetful daughter take a zero when her homework is left at home *again*, or let her be a little hungry if she has *again* forgotten her lunch. Sometimes you have to take away a favorite item (the gaming system, the phone, the car) if she persistently breaks the rules you've established. And sometimes you simply have to trust that the Lord will watch over your son as he takes his inheritance and squanders it in wild living.

These actions require a parent to have self-control, be consistent, and stand by and let the consequences do their teaching and character building rather than intervene. But you can do it with the Lord's help! Then, like the prodigal's father, be ready to love the repentant child.

P. S. The prodigal's return is a wonderful moment *not* to be self-controlled! Run to him!

"I HAVE THE POWER THROUGH CHRIST TO CONTROL MYSELF."

DAY 289

HOPE

He predestined us for adoption to sonship through Jesus Christ, in accordance with his pleasure and will.

EPHESIANS 1:5

The following words—spoken to fellow adoptees—were from a man excited and grateful to have been part of a family God had chosen just for him:

> I refuse to believe my family was random or some sort of accident. I believe that adoption, and my family's adoption, was part of God's plan. I believe that when people don't see adoption in that way that it minimizes who God is and dismisses His power, eventually leaving us with a sense of hopelessness and the feeling that we are victims. We are not. Regardless of how you came into this world, adoption is God's plan for your life. The Bible says you are a child of destiny! You are not an accident! You are a divine project, not an abandoned project. A victor, not a victim.[67]

Now think for a moment about the amazing truth that God the Father has chosen you and adopted you as his child. There is no more solid reason to have hope for today and tomorrow. You are a child of the King! Almighty God has adopted you!

> **"I CAN COPE WITH THE HARDSHIPS OF LIFE BECAUSE OF THE HOPE I HAVE IN JESUS CHRIST."**

PATIENCE

The Lord is not slow in keeping his promise . . . Instead he is patient . . . not wanting anyone to perish, but everyone to come to repentance.

2 PETER 3:9

There's nothing the heart of a Christian parent desires more than to know our children have trusted God and are walking in the truth. When our yearning isn't satisfied, it leads to many tears and long hours on our knees, begging God to bring that child back to him.

I have a dear friend whose college-age daughter said she no longer accepted the faith they had raised her with. My friend prayed boldly, telling God she didn't want to live in the new kingdom without her girl! If she could have, she would have made the decision to accept Christ as Savior for her daughter, but God requires everyone to make the salvation decision personally.

It requires a lot of patience when prayers for our prodigal children aren't answered quickly. Sometimes it takes years and even decades before they return.

Realizing that God loves your child even more than you do and desires all to repent before it's too late can bring you hope and give you the patience you need to keep on praying for them. Realizing your child has to choose his own faith can help direct your prayers.

"I AM SLOW TO ANGER AND ENDURE PATIENTLY UNDER THE UNAVOIDABLE PRESSURES OF LIFE."

KINDNESS/GOODNESS

How priceless is your unfailing love, O God! People take refuge in the shadow of your wings.

PSALM 36:7

The words *unfailing love* above are just one word in the Hebrew language: *hesed*. Other translations use the word *lovingkindness* to capture this rich word. Surprisingly, the Hebrew word for *stork*—yes, the bird known for bringing babies—has the same root word. As we study the behavior of the stork, we understand why. The stork is the only bird that shows devotion to its family throughout its life, reminiscent of an unfailing covenant love.

Ostriches, on the other hand, are known for carelessly stepping on their eggs or abandoning their unhatched young, leaving them as prey for predators. Storks are loyal to each other until the end. The young even return to care for their aging parents. Job captures this contrast in Job 39:13: "The wings of the ostrich flap joyfully, though they cannot compare with the wings and feathers of the stork." The huge wings of the ostrich flap joyfully for their own benefit while the wings of the stork provide safety, warmth, and refuge for the sake of those in their care.

What a beautiful picture of God's lovingkindness toward us. His love is unfailing and his wings cover you. May you be like God and the stork for the sake of others in your life.

> **"I CHOOSE TO BE KIND AND GOOD IN MY RELATIONSHIPS WITH OTHERS."**

FAITHFULNESS

*Know therefore that the LORD your God is God; he
is the faithful God, keeping his covenant of love to a
thousand generations of those who love him and keep his
commandments.*

DEUTERONOMY 7:9

We don't know what kind of training Mary, Jesus' mother, had,
but the Magnificat—her song of praise at the announcement
that she would be the Messiah's mother found in Luke 1:46–55—shows
that she knew the Hebrew Scriptures well. In her song of thanksgiving
and praise, she proclaimed much about God's character, actions, and
faithfulness. And she trusted that he would be faithful in this chapter
of her life.

Even in the face of public humiliation, Mary had the courage to
say, "I am the Lord's servant. . . . May your word to me be fulfilled"
(Luke 1:38).

Memorizing scripture about God's faithfulness and recalling how
God has been faithful in your own life can bring you courage, as it did
Mary, to face whatever challenge may come your way.

God, keep me faithful to you as you have been faithful to me.

> "I HAVE ESTABLISHED A GOOD NAME
> WITH GOD AND OTHERS BASED ON MY
> LOYALTY TO THOSE RELATIONSHIPS."

DAY 293

GENTLENESS

A gentle answer turns away wrath, but a harsh word stirs up anger.

PROVERBS 15:1

Ask a group of scientists what the strongest materials known to man are, and you might be surprised to find spider silk listed among them. Scientists have discovered silk has five times more strength per weight than steel. How? It bends using the trampoline effect. Sometimes instead of being sturdy or inflexible, what's needed is the kind of strength that will yield, bend, and stretch, like a trampoline. As bugs fly into a silk web, it withstands the weight of the bug, and also its speed by yielding so the bug can't break through it. Steel threads of the same width would simply snap under the velocity and weight.

The military is experimenting with adding silk to the lining of soldiers helmets to add further protection when bullets or shrapnel hit. This silk lining would help absorb the impact and soften injuries.

Jesus wants us to be gentle as silk when shrapnel of disagreement flies. He's calling us to stand firm on truth, but exercise strength by yielding to hear the other side of the story, absorbing the impact of hurtful words without returning them, and bending a bit, allowing room for others to disagree with us. If we don't, we just might crack!

> "I AM THOUGHTFUL, CONSIDERATE, AND CALM IN MY DEALINGS WITH OTHERS."

HUMILITY

Being found in appearance as a man, he humbled himself
by becoming obedient to death—even death on a cross!

PHILIPPIANS 2:8

I n his tender letter to the church at Philippi, the apostle Paul called his fellow believers to practice humility and pointed to Jesus as the supreme example of one who had a humble heart.

In today's culture, humility too often suggests weakness, being a doormat, not being willing or able to stand up for oneself, and even lacking self-esteem. Simply and biblically put, though, humility is choosing to esteem others above oneself. We are only able to do that when we draw from an internal sense of "God-esteem" and rest in being the person he made us to be.

When we have received God's unconditional love and embraced our inherent worth as his children, we can more freely serve each other. When we are confident that God values us, we can more easily choose to focus on other people's needs, and we won't experience the need to tear someone else down to make ourselves look better.

As C. S. Lewis put it in *Mere Christianity*, "The essence of gospel-humility is not thinking more of myself or thinking less of myself, it is thinking of myself less."[68]

"I CHOOSE TO ESTEEM OTHERS ABOVE MYSELF."

DAY 295

LOVE

Love one another, for love comes from God. Everyone who loves has been born of God and knows God.

1 JOHN 4:7

In the summer of 2012, the gay community was outraged when Dan Cathy, president and CEO of Chick-fil-A, refused to support gay marriage. While the controversy raged, Cathy privately introduced himself to Shane Windmeyer, an openly gay man and gay activist, wanting to hear the gay community's concerns. Windmeyer said this about the conversation in *The Huffington Post*:

> Dan expressed a sincere interest in my life, wanting to get to know me on a personal level . . . where I grew up, my faith, my family, even my husband, Tommy. In return, I learned about his wife and kids and gained an appreciation for his devout belief in Jesus Christ. . . . Dan expressed regret and genuine sadness when he heard of people being treated unkindly in the name of Chick-fil-A—but he offered no apologies for his genuine beliefs about marriage.[69]

Cathy initiated a friendship with a man who had criticized him and called for a boycott of his business. Which "enemy" in your life will you reach out to in love this week?

"I AM COMMITTED TO LOVING GOD AND LOVING OTHERS."

JOY

"Now is your time of grief, but I will see you again and
you will rejoice, and no one will take away your joy."

JOHN 16:22

Yikes! I recognized that pain. Even though it had only been three years since baby number one, I was surprised by how much the contractions hurt! It was definitely time to take big sister to a friend's house and me to the hospital. When a contraction came, I grabbed my stomach and started breathing hard to get through it. The contraction would pass, I'd relax, and all too soon I was at it again.

Soon we were at the hospital. The nurses admitted me and pointed to the room across the hall. Each contraction became worse and worse until finally the time to push arrived, and after another thirty minutes, we had a baby boy!

Fast-forward two years and four months, and I had a third; then two years and five months later, I had a fourth!

Jesus was absolutely right: "A woman giving birth to a child has pain . . . ; but when her baby is born she forgets the anguish because of her joy that a child is born" (John 16:21). Jesus knew that pain at his crucifixion would be eclipsed by joy in his resurrection. Whatever your current pain, keep your eyes on that empty tomb!

> **"DESPITE MY CIRCUMSTANCES, I**
> **FEEL INNER CONTENTMENT AND**
> **UNDERSTAND MY PURPOSE IN LIFE."**

PEACE

"Look at the birds of the air; they do not sow or reap or store away in barns, and yet your heavenly Father feeds them. Are you not much more valuable than they?"

MATTHEW 6:26

When you hear the word *worry*, what comes to mind? A specific situation? A particular person in your life? Do you get a certain empty feeling in the pit of your stomach or notice your heartrate increasing?

Worry is the chief robber of peace in our lives. Worry keeps us from restful sleep at night, and it keeps us on edge during the day. But Jesus, our Prince of Peace, emphasized the immense capacity of God the Father to love and care for his people. Completely capable of providing sufficiently, abundantly, often in ways far greater than we could ask or imagine, the Almighty doesn't want the worries of this life to overtake us.

Do the birds, Jesus asked, worry about where their next meal will come from? Do the "flowers of the field" worry about their appearance or how they are adorned (v. 28)? No!

May the birds and flowers you see in the course of a day remind you of your heavenly Father's ability to provide for you.

"I AM FREE FROM ANXIETY BECAUSE I HAVE FOUND PEACE WITH GOD, PEACE WITH OTHERS, AND PEACE WITH MYSELF."

SELF-CONTROL

*Since an overseer manages God's household, he must be
blameless—not overbearing, not quick-tempered, not given
to drunkenness, not violent, not pursuing dishonest gain.*

TITUS 1:7

When we think of the virtue of self-control, we almost always think of exercising control over the temptations of addictions and habits—alcohol, drugs, sex, overeating, laziness . . . the list goes on. We seldom think of having self-control from being "controlling."

Wielding power over people and controlling them can be as addictive as any drug. The greatest temptation comes to the person who has authority over another's life. There is a fine line between using that authority for the other person's good and using that authority to feed an addiction to control.

In the passage above, Paul challenged overseers of the church, the elders, not to be overbearing, either in their home or at the church. Right there with controlling their intake of alcohol and their output of anger is the charge not to be overbearing or over-controlling.

So, with the power of Christ within us, let us show self-control in being controlling.

> **"I HAVE THE POWER THROUGH
> CHRIST TO CONTROL MYSELF."**

DAY 299

HOPE

If only for this life we have hope in Christ, we are of all people most to be pitied. But Christ has indeed been raised from the dead.

1 CORINTHIANS 15:19–20

A story is told of a New York police officer who saw a man standing on a bridge apparently contemplating suicide. The officer went to him and said, "Let me make a deal with you. Give me ten minutes to tell you why I think life is worth living, then you take ten minutes and tell me why you think life is *not* worth living. If I'm unable to convince you, I'll let you jump." Twenty minutes later they joined hands and jumped into the water.

People cannot live without hope.

Maybe the greatest thing about the Christian life is our hope. The resurrection of Jesus from the dead proclaims that he is God and will fulfill his promise to raise us from the dead. Guaranteed! Paul said if Jesus didn't rise from the dead, we would be in the same position as the rest of the world: without hope.

The next time you stand on the bridge of despair, give Jesus ten minutes to tell you why life is worth living. Not only will you not jump, you will walk away from that bridge with an extra bounce in your step.

> **"I CAN COPE WITH THE HARDSHIPS OF LIFE BECAUSE OF THE HOPE I HAVE IN JESUS CHRIST."**

PATIENCE

The LORD delivered you into my hands today, but I would not lay a hand on the LORD'S anointed.

1 SAMUEL 26:23

Scott and Matt were at the front of the pack in the triathlon. Matt was making good time on his bike and felt good about his lead going into the run.

Scott wasn't far behind. What a great finish for the two friends— first and second place!

But then, as he ran, Scott lunged forward and bumped Matt, causing him to stumble and fall behind. Scott took the lead, and claimed first place for himself.

Ignoring the rules of sport, Scott had taken matters into his own hands.

David could have done something similar when he found himself in a cave with a sleeping King Saul, who had been trying to kill him. David could have killed Saul right then and there as an act of defense or revenge, but he didn't. He showed respect for the king, whom the Lord had anointed, as well as a patient willingness to trust God's timing for his own ascension to the throne.

What opportunity do you have right now to choose between waiting patiently on God and taking matters into your own hands?

> "I AM SLOW TO ANGER AND ENDURE PATIENTLY UNDER THE UNAVOIDABLE PRESSURES OF LIFE."

DAY 301

KINDNESS/GOODNESS

"When you give a banquet, invite the poor, the crippled, the lame, the blind, and you will be blessed."

LUKE 14:13–14

The barista at the local coffee shop was surprised to receive the invitation. The homeless woman was even more surprised. The high school student already in trouble with the law got an invitation. So did the jobless man, the girl on her way to becoming a prostitute, the known drug dealer at the local college, and the neighborhood gardener who didn't have a green card.

The invitation was to a banquet at the home of a highly respected member of the community who usually hobnobbed with society people. That social circle was a tight-knit group, regularly exchanging hosting duties and never expanding the guest list. Until today . . .

Today's host would never be repaid by those coming to his home for dinner, but that didn't seem to bother him at all. He was happy to open his home and extend hospitality. Kindness is like that. Kindness delights in the act of making others happy. Kindness doesn't act only if it's expected to be reciprocated.

How do you decide to whom you are kind? Does Jesus' parable in Luke 14 give you something to think about?

> **"I CHOOSE TO BE KIND AND GOOD IN MY RELATIONSHIPS WITH OTHERS."**

FAITHFULNESS

His mercy extends to those who fear him, from generation to generation. He has performed mighty deeds.

LUKE 1:50–51

P sychologists say that the best predictor of future behavior is past behavior, as long as certain conditions like these are met:

- Habitual behaviors are more predictive than infrequent ones.
- Predictions work best over short time intervals.
- The person must remain essentially unchanged.
- The person must be fairly consistent in his or her behaviors.[70]

Now try applying this principle to your heavenly Father:

- God is always and habitually faithful (Deuteronomy 7:9).
- He is faithful in the short term . . . and in the long term (Lamentations 3:22–23).
- He remains essentially unchanged (Hebrews 13:8).
- He is absolutely consistent in his behaviors (James 1:17).

Great is God's faithfulness—now and always!

> **"I HAVE ESTABLISHED A GOOD NAME WITH GOD AND OTHERS BASED ON MY LOYALTY TO THOSE RELATIONSHIPS."**

DAY 303

GENTLENESS

We dealt with each of you as a father deals with his own
children, encouraging, comforting and urging you to live
lives worthy of God.

1 THESSALONIANS 2:11–12

Max Lucado still remembers the game. Dropping that fly ball was his second error of the game, and it allowed the winning run to score. Max didn't even go back to the dugout. He climbed over the left-field fence and was halfway home when his dad found him.

> We didn't speak, we didn't have to, and we both knew the world had come to an end. When we got home I went straight to my room, and Dad went straight to the kitchen. Presently, he appeared . . . with milk and cookies. He took a seat on the bed, and we broke bread together. Somewhere in the dunking of the cookies I began to realize that my life and my dad's love would go on. In the economy of male adolescence, if you love the guy who drops the ball, then you really love him.[71]

Max was blessed to have a gentle and strong dad who gave him a taste of his heavenly Father's unconditional, unfailing love. Who in your life could use a taste of God's gentle, strong, and unconditional love?

"I AM THOUGHTFUL, CONSIDERATE, AND CALM IN MY DEALINGS WITH OTHERS."

HUMILITY

When Haman entered, the king asked him, "What should be done for the man the king delights to honor?" Now Haman thought to himself, "Who is there that the king would rather honor than me?"

ESTHER 6:6

Have you ever responded to someone waving at you by waving back, and then realized they were acknowledging the person behind you? I have. I scratched my head to save face. Assuming something is for you and finding out it's not is embarrassing. There are times, however, when "assuming" could be described as arrogant.

Few people in the Bible were more assuming than Haman. Never considering there might be others the king wished to honor, his conversation with King Xerxes clarified how self-absorbed he was. Imagine the corners of his egotistical smile quickly turning downward as the king explained it was Haman's archenemy, Mordecai, who would be honored, and that Haman was to execute the plan.

Later Haman bragged about receiving Queen Esther's invitation to a private dinner with her and the king. Again he assumed he would be honored. This proved to be his last and fatal assumption.

Have you ever made an assumption because you let arrogance get the better of you? Take time to assess a situation before making assumptions, and remember God blesses the humble, not the proud.

"I CHOOSE TO ESTEEM OTHERS ABOVE MYSELF."

DAY 305

LOVE

As we have opportunity, let us do good to all people,
especially those who belong to the family of believers.

GALATIANS 6:10

We were on our way home, but our flight was severely delayed because of weather, and we missed our connecting flight. Running as soon as our feet hit the jetway, we headed to get on the next flight's standby list. Approaching the gate, we saw the line of people with the same goal was already forty deep. Our spirits dropped.

The lady before us became standby number 40; we assumed we would be 41 and 42. Much to our delight, we became numbers 6 and 7. We are frequent flyers on this particular airline; members have privileges. We got on the next flight!

When others saw us board, it probably ignited in them a desire to become frequent flyers too. Jesus had the same thing in mind here. He called those who follow him to love everyone, but to especially treat members of the body of believers well. So much so that anyone observing a community of believers would want to be a part of it.

When we rally around members of the body who are hurting or in need, we show a watching world that we take Jesus' command to love one another seriously.

Membership has its privileges.

> "I AM COMMITTED TO LOVING
> GOD AND LOVING OTHERS."

JOY

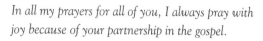

In all my prayers for all of you, I always pray with joy because of your partnership in the gospel.

PHILIPPIANS 1:4–5

I t is a joy to prepare a big meal for family and friends. Whether it's for dinner at dusk or celebrating a birthday or gathering for a holiday, cooking a feast for the people I love is satisfying and fun. But even better than doing that on my own is when I have extra helpers in my kitchen.

When a partner grabs a spoon to stir the gravy or a knife to slice the bread as I drain the pasta or put the finishing touches on the dessert, it's truly a joyful time. We laugh and talk. Our souls are being fed.

I have no trouble understanding Paul's joy when he thinks of and prays for those Philippians who were associates in the gospel with him. Partnering with another person—or with several other people—who love Jesus adds joy to any activity. Worshipping on Sunday morning, washing cars to raise money for camp, cleaning up around the community, serving at the homeless shelter—joy comes in partnering for God with his people.

What will you do this week to partner with someone to serve? You'll be blessed with joy!

> "DESPITE MY CIRCUMSTANCES, I
> FEEL INNER CONTENTMENT AND
> UNDERSTAND MY PURPOSE IN LIFE."

PEACE

The wisdom that comes from heaven is first of all pure;
then peace-loving. . . . Peacemakers who sow in peace
reap a harvest of righteousness.

JAMES 3:17–18

A young soldier had been assigned duty in Hiroshima, after the massive destruction of the atom bomb. Walking down a street one evening, he heard a chorus of beautiful singing in a nearby building. Curious, he investigated. He found American soldiers and Japanese civilians joyfully singing songs of praise and worship to Jesus.

The young man was astonished by the scene before him. He left wondering what power could bring unity to such bitter enemies. This agnostic young soldier had just had his first encounter with Jesus. It was not long after that he came to know the Prince of Peace, Jesus, who brought peace to his own troubled heart.

The young man knew he had found his life's calling as one who would proclaim the wisdom that comes from heaven, wisdom that is pure and peace-loving. For many years he sowed words of peace as a minister witnessing a great harvest of righteousness.

Strive to reveal the Prince of Peace in all that you are, all that you say, and all that you do. And then rejoice in the harvest.

"I AM FREE FROM ANXIETY BECAUSE I HAVE
FOUND PEACE WITH GOD, PEACE WITH
OTHERS, AND PEACE WITH MYSELF."

SELF-CONTROL

You are not your own; you were bought at a price. Therefore honor God with your bodies.

1 CORINTHIANS 6:19–20

We know we are to honor God by taking care of our bodies, but dieting and exercise can test self-control to the breaking point! Ask God to give you strength, and consider these wise words:

- Your willpower, like a muscle, will get stronger the more you use it.
- Be aware that a long, hard day at work can weaken your willpower to do what is good and right and healthy.
- Restore your supply of willpower (which is depleted by stress) with some "me time." Take a walk; listen to music.
- Growing in self-control in one area of life often leads to positive changes in other areas.
- Get some support! It's a lot easier to stick to a plan if you have someone holding you accountable.

The Spirit-fed fruit of self-control enables you to honor God not only with your body but with your entire life as well. Don't be afraid to ask for his help!

"I HAVE THE POWER THROUGH CHRIST TO CONTROL MYSELF."

HOPE

Command those who are rich in this present world not to be arrogant nor to put their hope in wealth.

1 TIMOTHY 6:17

I don't remember how old I was when I first heard about King Midas, but I still remember his story.

Midas, already a very wealthy man, was given the opportunity to have any wish come true. Midas asked that everything he touch turn to gold. When the granter of the wish told him to think this through, Midas insisted—and his wish was granted.

It was fine when a table, chair, door, and bathtub turned to gold at his touch, but fear started to rise as a grape, a slice of bread, a glass of water, and his beloved daughter turned to gold.

At Midas's request and to his great relief, the granter of the wish reversed the king's power—and changed the king's character. The once-greedy king became generous with his wealth, kind to others, and grateful for what he had rather than wanting more.

Having wealth is fine, but when you find your security in it, place your hope in it, or depend on it to make you happy, you are in danger of contracting Midas syndrome. Jesus is the only place to put your hope. He will transcend this world and carry you on to eternity.

> **"I CAN COPE WITH THE HARDSHIPS OF LIFE BECAUSE OF THE HOPE I HAVE IN JESUS CHRIST."**

PATIENCE

"Shall we accept good from God, and not trouble?" In all this, Job did not sin in what he said.

JOB 2:10

I knew a lot of married people and attended a good number of bridal showers and weddings before I got married, but somehow I missed any honest discussions about how hard marriage is. I'd also done a good amount of babysitting and been to many baby showers, but somehow I missed the straightforward talk about how tough parenting is.

While marriage and parenting bring great blessings, we get committed to both before we realize the full extent of the challenges, the demands, the "trouble." Yet we must—as Job did—accept with grace the trouble along with the blessings of these commitments. Realizing they are marathons and not sprints helps. Get your stride and focus on the long term, the big picture—not the moment. C. S. Lewis said, "To love at all is to be vulnerable. Love anything, and your heart will certainly be wrung and possibly broken."[72] Marriage brings the companionship of your best friend . . . and disillusionment of unmet expectations. Parenting brings amazing insight into God's love for us . . . and exhaustion, helplessness, and heartbreak beyond description.

Like Job, humbly receive the trouble as well as the blessings God gives.

"I AM SLOW TO ANGER AND ENDURE PATIENTLY UNDER THE UNAVOIDABLE PRESSURES OF LIFE."

KINDNESS/GOODNESS

Have him back forever—no longer as a slave, but . . . as a dear brother.

PHILEMON 1:15–16

The 2014 movie *Unbroken* told the story of Louie Zamperini, a World War II soldier who survived forty-seven days adrift at sea after a plane crash and endured two terrible years with sadistic captors, especially Mutsuhiro Watanabe, also known as "The Bird."

No movie can tell every aspect of a person's life, and at least two powerful scenes were missing from this film. Zamperini gave his life to Christ in 1949 and became freed from internal agonies, and free to extend forgiveness to "The Bird." The second omitted scene happened in 1998. Zamperini went to Japan, hoping to meet with Watanabe, but "The Bird" refused. Even still, this only-by-God's-grace act of kindness is a picture of Zamperini's healing, redemption, and courage. He went to Watanabe in a spirit of Christlike kindness and grace.

In the Bible, Onesimus, a slave who had run away, returned to his master, Philemon, and Paul encouraged Philemon to forgive Onesimus and to exhibit the same kind of mercy Zamperini showed his captor.

To whom might God be calling you to extend the kindness and grace of forgiveness?

> **"I CHOOSE TO BE KIND AND GOOD IN MY RELATIONSHIPS WITH OTHERS."**

FAITHFULNESS

"Whoever can be trusted with very little can also be trusted with much."

LUKE 16:10

George was on duty at the front desk one night when an older man and his wife entered the hotel and asked for a room. "I'm sorry, sir, the hotel is completely full." But it was late, and George knew that because of a local event, they would not be able to find a room anywhere in the city. Realizing the couple would have nowhere to sleep except their car, George offered them his room. They reluctantly accepted his generous offer.

Seven years later, the gentleman came back and found George Boldt, the kind hotel clerk. He told George he should be the manager of the best hotel in the world, which he, William Waldorf Astor, had built in New York. George's faithfulness to go above and beyond executing his front-desk duties at a small hotel led to managing one of the largest, most beautiful hotels in the country, the Waldorf-Astoria.

God is looking for more Georges in this life, to oversee much more in his new kingdom! What has God given you to manage? Manage whatever God has given you today in a trustworthy manner and who knows what surprises he might bring.

> **"I HAVE ESTABLISHED A GOOD NAME WITH GOD AND OTHERS BASED ON MY LOYALTY TO THOSE RELATIONSHIPS."**

DAY 313

GENTLENESS

What do you prefer? Shall I come to you with a rod of discipline, or shall I come in love and with a gentle spirit?

1 CORINTHIANS 4:21

Paul had the authority as an apostle to lead and guide the church in truth. The Corinthian church struggled greatly, and Paul had to confront them. He gave them a choice: "Shall I come to you with a rod of discipline" or "in love and with a gentle spirit?"

In Paul's day, the word *gentleness* was linked to the medical world and carried the idea of a "mild medication." We might say a gentle person is someone who is "easy on your stomach." This is the perfect word picture, isn't it? Think of a churning stomach, that almost nauseous feeling you get when you know you're going to encounter a prideful person who, while they may be right much of the time, often dispenses a dose of medicine that is too rough on your digestive system.

This takes being a "pill" to a whole new level. God wants us to speak the truth, but he wants us to do so with a gentle spirit. So, as you speak with people today—your friends, your coworkers, your spouse, or your children—concentrate on dispensing the truth in a way that doesn't upset their stomachs.

> "I AM THOUGHTFUL, CONSIDERATE, AND CALM IN MY DEALINGS WITH OTHERS."

HUMILITY

The time came for the baby to be born, and she gave birth to her firstborn, a son. She wrapped him in cloths and placed him in a manger, because there was no guest room available for them.

LUKE 2:6–7

Fireworks mark the birth of an heir to the throne. The swankiest hospital room is prepared for the celebrity's delivery. Pictures are taken. Articles are written. The world stands up and takes notice.

Jesus' arrival was hardly the focus of paparazzi. No one was anxiously awaiting the birth with Mary and Joseph except cattle and goats. No one even gave up a room at the inn when her time to deliver came. No designer nursery had been prepared. There was no traditional fanfare accompanying the arrival of this king.

The God of the universe entered this world through the womb of a young woman. A baby born in a stable is our supreme example of humility. If there ever was a baby born that should have been publicly celebrated and noticed, it was God's Son, yet he didn't require any of that.

As you begin to understand the amazing surrender of his nobility to come to earth and become your Savior, strive to follow his example. Live humbly and sacrifice for others the way he sacrificed himself for you.

"I CHOOSE TO ESTEEM OTHERS ABOVE MYSELF."

DAY 315

LOVE

Jonathan made a covenant with David because he loved [David] as himself.

1 SAMUEL 18:3

In November 2013, the Oxford University Press proclaimed *selfie* the word of the year and defined it this way: "a photograph that one has taken of oneself, typically one taken with a smartphone or webcam and uploaded to a social media website."

The word-use metrics indicated a jump in usage from 2012 to 2013 of 17,000 percent. Perhaps that should come as no surprise. *Selfie* has been proclaimed a concept of the current age, one which is fueled by technology.[73] It's a fitting result of an era when young adults are dubbed "The Me Generation."

Clearly, Jonathan's love for David was of a different generation. There was nothing self-focused about Jonathon's friendship with David. After David killed Goliath with only a slingshot, Jonathan recognized God's hand on David. Not only did Jonathan graciously step aside as the rightful heir to the throne so David could rule but he also went on to protect David from his jealous and insecure father, King Saul (see 1 Samuel 19:1–7).

If you are blessed with a Jonathan-like friend, let that person know you appreciate their love. Then make sure you are a Jonathan to someone else.

> **"I AM COMMITTED TO LOVING GOD AND LOVING OTHERS."**

JOY

For his anger lasts only a moment, but his favor lasts a lifetime; weeping may stay for the night, but rejoicing comes in the morning.

PSALM 30:5

Does life seem tough right now, and you can't see the sun for the clouds? Nothing can rob a person of joy like going through a season of life when it feels as though the darkness or trials will never end. We begin to focus on living one day at a time, one hour at a time, or perhaps one breath at a time just to get through it.

King David invites you to view dark seasons in the context of your entire life, much the way we look at the rainy season of spring. When a rainy day stretches into a week or two, or even a month, how long it seems. However, compared to the length of the beautiful summer it precedes, it's short-lived.

When the darkness of a stormy season overtakes you, and all you can do is take one breath at a time through your tears, depend on the One who gives you that very breath. His love is forever.

The clouds will disperse, and the joy you will experience as you appreciate seeing the sun again after the long, dark, rainy season will be beyond anything you can imagine.

> "DESPITE MY CIRCUMSTANCES, I FEEL INNER CONTENTMENT AND UNDERSTAND MY PURPOSE IN LIFE."

PEACE

"Though the mountains be shaken and the hills be removed, yet my unfailing love for you will not be shaken nor my covenant of peace be removed," says the LORD.

ISAIAH 54:10

The story is told of a gentleman on a search for the perfect painting depicting peace. Unable to find it, he announced a contest for artists to create a work of art that represented peace. Submissions began pouring in, and each was concealed behind a cloth.

Unveiling day drew a crowd. Each masterpiece was uncovered until only two remained. A judge revealed the first. "A mirror-smooth lake reflected lacy, green birches under the soft blush of the evening sky. Along the grassy shore a flock of sheep grazed undisturbed." Surely the winner!

Then the cloth from the last masterpiece was removed. The crowd gasped. "A tumultuous waterfall cascaded down a rocky precipice. . . . Storm-grey clouds threatened to explode with lightning, wind and rain. . . . A spindly tree clung to the rocks at the edge of the falls. . . . A little bird had built a nest in the elbow of [one of its branches]. Content and undisturbed in her stormy surroundings, she rested on her eggs. . . . She manifested peace that transcends all earthly turmoil."[74]

This is the peace Jesus offers you.

> **"I AM FREE FROM ANXIETY BECAUSE I HAVE FOUND PEACE WITH GOD, PEACE WITH OTHERS, AND PEACE WITH MYSELF."**

SELF-CONTROL

The fruit of the Spirit is love, joy, peace, forbearance, kindness, goodness, faithfulness, gentleness and self-control.

GALATIANS 5:22–23

Try this simple exercise with this verse.

First, read through the list of the fruit of the Spirit while inserting "Jesus is" before each one. "Jesus is love" . . . "Jesus is joy" . . . "Jesus is peace." After each virtue, pause and think about evidence of that trait in Jesus' life. You'll discover he was perfect in all of these.

Then slowly read through the list again, one fruit at a time, but now place your name before each fruit. "Randy is love" . . . "Randy is joy" . . . "Randy is peace." After each statement pause and ask yourself, *Would people who know me say I'm loving? Would others describe me as joyful? Would anyone say I'm peaceful?* Ask God to open your eyes to the areas where you need to grow. These are the "fruits" your Christian life should produce, and when you have these characteristics, others who know you notice and benefit from them.

As much as we want to, we can't be perfect at all these things—at least not in our own power. But if we allow him, the Holy Spirit can slowly transform us to be more like Jesus!

Choose one fruit of the Spirit and ask him to help it grow in your life.

"I HAVE THE POWER THROUGH CHRIST TO CONTROL MYSELF."

DAY 319

HOPE

*Woe to those who . . . do not look to the Holy One of
Israel, or seek help from the LORD.*

ISAIAH 31:1

I wanna help!"

Keith took a deep breath. "Okay, Dylan. Let's get a painting shirt
on you!"

After his dad's brief "how-to" on fence painting, he held his hand
for a few strokes until Dylan announced, "I wanna do it myself!"

Keith took a second deep breath. *What's the worst that could happen?* Dylan took his first solo stroke. *So far, so good . . .* until the third
stroke. It happened so quickly. Dylan knocked into the paint can, and
suddenly paint was everywhere.

Just like Dylan, we often want to work with God on whatever he's
doing in our lives, our families, our churches, our neighborhoods. But
then once we get an idea of his plan, we want to do it ourselves, and
inevitably we make a mess!

Woe to us who don't look—or don't look long enough—to the
Lord for help. The results can be far worse than spilled paint when we
try to do things our way instead of trusting in God.

What are you trying to do on your own instead of putting your
trust and hope in your God? Be patient, and let him hold your hand.

> **"I CAN COPE WITH THE HARDSHIPS OF LIFE
> BECAUSE OF THE HOPE I HAVE IN JESUS CHRIST."**

PATIENCE

> "The LORD gave and the LORD has taken away; may the name of the LORD be praised." In all this, Job did not sin by charging God with wrongdoing.

JOB 1:21–22

B eth was twenty-eight years old. She had two small daughters, a godly husband . . . and cancer. Her doctor said it was terminal.

Her pastor asked her, "Are you angry with God?" Without hesitating, she replied, "No! Angry with my heavenly Father? He knows best!" She thought that was the right answer. But in her heart, she really was angry, unhappy, and resentful.[75]

Beth didn't need to hide her anguish and heartache. Job didn't. He was honest with God about his grief. Upon hearing that all his children were dead, Job tore his robe and shaved his head. He "did not sin by charging God with wrongdoing," but neither did he pretend he wasn't heartbroken.

God already knows your heart. He knows the pain and agony; he knows the questioning and the rage. Be respectful when you cry out to him and share your pain: he is God. But also be honest: after all, he is your heavenly Father.

> **"I AM SLOW TO ANGER AND ENDURE PATIENTLY UNDER THE UNAVOIDABLE PRESSURES OF LIFE."**

DAY 321

KINDNESS/GOODNESS

*"If you love those who love you . . . if you do good to
those who are good to you, what credit is that to you?"*

LUKE 6:32–33

Twenty-one-year-old Charles Brown was flying his first combat mission. Half of the B-17 crew had been wounded and his tail gunner had been killed, his blood frozen in icicles on the machine guns.

Looking out the cockpit, Brown froze. "My God, this is a nightmare," his copilot said as they looked at the gray German Messerschmitt fighter hovering just three feet away from the tip of the wing.

"He's going to destroy us," Brown uttered. But when he and his copilot looked at the fighter pilot, the strangest thing happened. The German didn't pull the trigger. Instead, he nodded at Brown and flew away. [76]

Losing one's humanity has been cited as being worse than death itself. Soldiers in battles since the beginning of time have exhibited acts of mercy, recognizing the common humanity among those with whom they were fighting.

Who is the Spirit nudging you to love and do good to? When the Spirit puts on your heart to be kind to someone who is hard to be kind to, he will enable you to do exactly that. Try it and see.

> **"I CHOOSE TO BE KIND AND GOOD IN
> MY RELATIONSHIPS WITH OTHERS."**

FAITHFULNESS

Now it is required that those who have been given a trust must prove faithful.

1 CORINTHIANS 4:2

Since his first revival in Los Angeles in 1949, Billy Graham has preached the gospel of Jesus Christ to as many as 215 million people in more than 185 countries, and there is no way to know how many people around the world first heard about Jesus' saving grace through Graham's radio and TV messages, his books, and now his websites.

In recognition of his preaching as well as the integrity with which Graham lives and ministers, the Gallup organization named him "One of the Ten Most Admired Men in the World" an amazing fifty-one times. His list of awards is long and impressive, but Graham undoubtedly cares only about hearing the Lord say, "Well done, good and faithful servant." Clearly Graham proved himself faithful to the role God called him to.

How faithful are you to the example Christ has commanded you to be? How committed are you to living a life faithful to God and to those whom he has called you to love?

> "I HAVE ESTABLISHED A GOOD NAME WITH GOD AND OTHERS BASED ON MY LOYALTY TO THOSE RELATIONSHIPS."

GENTLENESS

Jesus asked [Peter] the third time, "Do you love me?" [Peter] said, "Lord, you know all things; you know that I love you."

JOHN 21:17

My friend often tailgates. When I told her not to follow so closely, she angrily said to stop my backseat driving. Not one minute later, we plowed into the car in front of us. While my sister was pregnant, her friends encouraged her to sign up her baby for preschool. She didn't, and now she's on three waiting lists. A spot will be open for him about the time he gets his driver's license. A publishing company demanded that Google stop linking to their content. Later, after having lost revenue because of this decision, they desperately wanted Google to *re-link* them.

It would be incredibly tempting in these scenarios to say, "I told you so." Jesus could have said those words to Peter as well. He had warned Peter that he would deny he knew Jesus, but Peter did not believe him. Jesus could have admonished his disciple. He chose love instead. "Do you love me?" With those words, Jesus restored Peter's relationship with him.

Your gentle words can bring healing, hope, and a taste of God's gentleness and love rather than his judgment. Choose gentleness over "I told you so."

> **"I AM THOUGHTFUL, CONSIDERATE, AND CALM IN MY DEALINGS WITH OTHERS."**

HUMILITY

> *I, Nebuchadnezzar, praise and exalt and glorify the King of heaven, because everything he does is right and all his ways are just.*

DANIEL 4:37

Often the good things we do and the successes we achieve can cause us to be arrogant. Our egos many times keep us from surrendering our lives completely to God. We all have egos, and we all need to keep them in check. Before we leave this life, we are required to humble ourselves before God and ask him to forgive us. If we can't, he just might get our attention because he loves us.

Just ask Nebuchadnezzar. Warned by God to keep his ego in check, one day the king remarked to himself on the rooftop of the palace, "Is not this the great Babylon I have built as the royal residence, by my mighty power and for the glory of my majesty?" (v. 30). He just couldn't get over himself, so before a watching kingdom, God punished his arrogance by causing him to eat grass for seven years. Those same subjects watched as his sanity returned and he declared his humility before God. God loved him enough to get his attention.

Our continual prayer should be for God to remove any arrogance from our lives. Remember, if we don't, he loves us enough to get our attention.

"I CHOOSE TO ESTEEM OTHERS ABOVE MYSELF."

DAY 325

LOVE

Follow God's example, therefore, as dearly loved children and walk in the way of love, just as Christ loved us and gave himself up for us as a fragrant offering and sacrifice to God.

EPHESIANS 5:1–2

Follow God's example? Seriously?

To imitate God is to be like God—not to *be* God, mind you, but to be *like* God. But what is God like? What qualities does he possess that we are supposed to study and mirror?

God's words to us in this passage, through the apostle Paul's pen, shine light on the nature of God and his Son. He tells us we are to live lives of love, just as Jesus loved us and—catch this next word—*gave* himself up for us as a fragrant offering and sacrifice to God.

What is God like? God is a *giver*. God *gave* his one and only Son for your eternal need. The Son *gave* himself to the Father for your eternal well-being. God gives because God loves—to love is to give. Will you follow the example of God and his Son? Will you be a *giver*, offering yourself to God for the sake of others and live as his dearly loved child? You will be a sweet-smelling offering to your heavenly Father, and as others peer into the mirror of your life, they will see Jesus.

> **"I AM COMMITTED TO LOVING GOD AND LOVING OTHERS."**

Rejoice inasmuch as you participate in the sufferings of Christ. . . . If you are insulted because of the name of Christ, you are blessed.

1 PETER 4:13–14

Pastor and writer Dietrich Bonhoeffer boldly spoke against Hitler's persecution of the Jews. After working as a spy in an attempt to end Hitler's regime, Bonhoeffer was arrested, sent to concentration camps, and executed—during the last month of the war.[77] Consider his words to his brother-in-law in April 1943:

> There is not even an atom of reproach or bitterness in me about what has befallen. . . . Such things come from God and from him alone. . . . Before him there can only be subjection, perseverance, patience. . . . We have been able to enjoy so many good things together that it would be almost presumptuous were we not also ready to accept hardship quietly, bravely—and also really gratefully.[78]

Bonhoeffer suffered for his faith. Yet he received even life's hardships as coming from the hand of God, and he received them with gratitude and joy. May we adopt his philosophy and mirror his example.

"DESPITE MY CIRCUMSTANCES, I FEEL INNER CONTENTMENT AND UNDERSTAND MY PURPOSE IN LIFE."

PEACE

For to us a child is born, to us a son is given, and the government will be on his shoulders. And he will be called Wonderful Counselor, Mighty God, Everlasting Father, Prince of Peace.

ISAIAH 9:6

The news headlines rob us of peace. Relationships and finances weigh us down. We are concerned about our children. Life events can bring on anxiety, depression, and fear.

We desire a life of peace, but the peace we truly need is not about our external circumstances. First and foremost, we need peace with God. This peace can get us through our most dire situations. Yet we imperfect humans can't experience peace with our perfect God simply because we want it. Peace with God is made possible only through the Prince of Peace—Jesus Christ—whom Isaiah wrote about seven hundred years before his birth. He also wrote, "It was the LORD's will to crush him . . . [to make] his life an offering for sin" (Isaiah 53:10).

Peace costs. Peace between nations, between individuals, and between us sinners and God. It cost God his only Son's life. Jesus loved you enough to pay the horrendous cost so you could experience true peace that can get you through your most dreadful circumstances.

> "I AM FREE FROM ANXIETY BECAUSE I HAVE FOUND PEACE WITH GOD, PEACE WITH OTHERS, AND PEACE WITH MYSELF."

SELF-CONTROL

No temptation has overtaken you except what is common to mankind. . . . [God will] provide a way out so that you can endure it.

1 CORINTHIANS 10:13

Try not consuming that entire bag of M&M's in one sitting and you'll realize a stark reality: self-control is sometimes nearly impossible. Maybe you can refrain from gorging on the sweet stuff, but your friends know to stay out of your way if something salty is within reach! We all have areas where the urge to do something harmful can get the better of us.

Our sin nature will eventually wear us down if we don't have a plan in place. Thankfully, you, as a believer, have the presence and power of God within you. The Holy Spirit can enable you to live a life that isn't controlled by your inner desires and the corruption of the world.

Most of us overestimate our own ability to resist temptation and live a godly life. The first step is to avoid temptation at all costs, but if it sneaks up on you, remember you have the Holy Spirit inside you ready to assist. Ask him to help you walk away, and feel victorious when you do!

What an amazing promise! You have everything you need not only to resist things like chocolate and carbs but, more importantly, to live a godly life.

"I HAVE THE POWER THROUGH CHRIST TO CONTROL MYSELF."

DAY 329

HOPE

Why, my soul, are you downcast? . . . Put your hope in God, for I will yet praise him, my Savior and my God.

PSALM 42:11

Andy was a strong candidate for his dream school with his 4.2 GPA. He had varsity letters in tennis, was class president, and did community service. But where did God want him to go? Andy prayed and asked God to show him his will.

Andy will never forget the e-mail: "We regret to inform you . . ." He was crushed and angry. "Lord! I don't understand! Why didn't I get in? Well, you answered my prayer and made it very clear where I'm *not* going to school!"

Much in life can cause a soul to be downcast. Remembering that God's plans don't always align with ours is hard. When you're sad, follow the psalmist's example. He turned to God, the only source of real hope. Then, wisely wanting his thoughts to take precedence over his feelings, the psalmist chose to have his head remind his heart that one day he would again praise the Lord.

Proverbs 16:9 encourages us to remember, "In their hearts humans plan their course, but the LORD establishes their steps." Let your head remind your heart of that truth when you don't get what you want. Remember he's directing your steps.

> **"I CAN COPE WITH THE HARDSHIPS OF LIFE BECAUSE OF THE HOPE I HAVE IN JESUS CHRIST."**

PATIENCE

*Let perseverance finish its work so that you may be
mature and complete, not lacking anything.*

JAMES 1:4

The words *perseverance* and *patience* are cousins. They are similar and yet different. *Perseverance* comes from a compound word *hypo-mone* in the Greek language. *Hypo* means "under"; *meno* means "to remain." This virtue encourages us to learn how "to remain under" the unavoidable pressures of life because it is the right thing to do. Think of a super heavy pack strapped to your back.

There are situations outside of our control: an illness, a mate who goes through a dark season, a child born with a birth defect, an accident that takes the life of a friend. In these unavoidable situations, we might attempt to relieve our pressure by doing the wrong thing: abuse prescription drugs, get a divorce, seek revenge, give up. God encourages us instead "to remain under the pressure," to stay in the relationship, to forgive, to push through, to move forward.

While escape may seem like the *quickest* solution, God wants to offer the *best* solution. Through this process of staying put and remaining under the pressure, God makes us mature and complete people.

Carrying an unavoidable backpack today? Persevere in faith. God is producing in you a beautiful, finished product.

"I AM SLOW TO ANGER AND ENDURE PATIENTLY UNDER THE UNAVOIDABLE PRESSURES OF LIFE."

KINDNESS/GOODNESS

"You have heard that it was said, 'Love your neighbor and hate your enemy.' But I tell you, love your enemies and pray for those who persecute you."

MATTHEW 5:43–44

How tragic that Christians have become known more for what we are against than what we support. The world has come to identify us as a people with a long list of don'ts instead of a people who show kindness and goodness to everyone. We are also known for fighting and disagreeing among ourselves. It appears that those who want to come to Christ have to trip over us before they can get to know him.

Jesus teaches here that if you want to get someone's attention, do the unexpected.

The truth of the matter is, we all struggle with sin, but we tend to categorize sin from bad to worse to horrendous. To God, however, sin is sin and keeps us all from his presence.

The person who realizes the tremendous mercy our heavenly Father has shown, and truly understands how underserving we are of Jesus' love, is the one who can show the kind of response Jesus refers to.

Stop judging the person at the end of your pointing finger, and let mercy guide your heart to respond with kindness and goodness. You just may draw the kind of attention that will lead people to Jesus.

> **"I CHOOSE TO BE KIND AND GOOD IN MY RELATIONSHIPS WITH OTHERS."**

FAITHFULNESS

When [Potiphar] saw that the LORD was with [Joseph] and
that the LORD gave him success in everything he did, . . .
Potiphar put him in charge of his household.

GENESIS 39:3–4

When George Mueller became a pastor, he refused to let the small church pay him a salary. He instead trusted God to provide for him and his family; God did.

When God called him to start an orphanage, Mueller asked God to provide a building, staff, furniture, and money for feeding and clothing the children. God faithfully provided for every need of that orphanage, home to more than ten thousand children through the years. Whenever these children were ready to live on their own, George put a Bible in their right hand and a coin in their left. Then he explained that if they held on to what was in their right hand, God would be sure they had something in their left hand as well.

George Mueller completely depended on God to provide for his family and orphanage. Likewise, in his service to Potiphar, Joseph remained loyal to his faithful God and depended on him to keep him safe and provide for him. How can you be more like George and Joseph and be a witness of God's faithfulness?

> **"I HAVE ESTABLISHED A GOOD NAME**
> **WITH GOD AND OTHERS BASED ON MY**
> **LOYALTY TO THOSE RELATIONSHIPS."**

GENTLENESS

Get Mark and bring him with you, because he is helpful to me in my ministry.

2 TIMOTHY 4:11

On Paul's first missionary journey, around AD 50, he had a sharp disagreement with his partner, Barnabas. Barnabas wanted to go back through all the towns where they had preached the gospel, and he suggested they take Mark with them. Paul objected, sighting how Mark had deserted them on an earlier journey. Paul stood his ground and would not budge, and as a result, the partnership came to an end.

Fast-forward around eighteen years, and Paul is sitting in a prison cell in a Roman dungeon. He is only months away from being executed for his faith. The only person he requests to see before he dies is Mark.

What happened? It appears Paul experienced a little spiritual growth in the virtue of gentleness. The younger, hard-driving apostle seemed to have given little room for people to make mistakes. Now, the more mature Paul longs for Mark to be with him.

Do you struggle with being gentle and giving people room to make mistakes? In Christ you can grow to become more like him.

"I AM THOUGHTFUL, CONSIDERATE, AND CALM IN MY DEALINGS WITH OTHERS."

HUMILITY

"Blessed are the meek."

MATTHEW 5:5

I was collecting blood samples from patients. We did not have enough protective equipment to use [and] I developed the same symptoms," says Kiiza Isaac, a nurse from Uganda. "On November 19, 2007, I received laboratory confirmation: I had contracted Ebola. MSF came to Bundibugyo [in Uganda] and they ran a treatment center. Many patients were cared for. Thank God, I survived. After my recovery, I joined MSF."

Kiiza's decision is a picture of meekness. A recovered victim of the deadly Ebola, he joined the efforts of Médecins Sans Frontières (MSF—in English, Doctors Without Borders) and continued to work with Ebola sufferers.[79]

Meekness is often considered to be having strength under control, and can be pictured as a wild stallion that has been tamed. That stallion has the same strength and energy it had when it ran wild, but that strength and energy are now under control. In Kiiza's case, that strength and energy are manifest through his courage (he knows the risks), hard work (giving physical, emotional, and spiritual support to hurting people), and compassion (he knows the disease firsthand).

Tame the wild stallion in you, and serve others with courage, God-given strength, and compassion.

"I CHOOSE TO ESTEEM OTHERS ABOVE MYSELF."

DAY 335

LOVE

Now that you have purified yourselves by obeying the truth so that you have sincere love for each other, love one another deeply, from the heart.

1 PETER 1:22

Margery Williams wrote a classic children's book that chronicles the story of a stuffed velveteen rabbit and his quest to become real through the love of his owner. One day the rabbit asked the old Skin Horse, "What is *real?*"

The Skin Horse replied, "When a child loves you for a long, long time, not just to play with, but *really* loves you, then you become Real."

The young rabbit then asked, "Does it happen all at once?"

Skin Horse replied, "It doesn't happen all at once. You become. It takes a long time. That's why it doesn't happen often to people who break easily, or have sharp edges, or who have to be carefully kept. Generally, by the time you are Real, most of your hair has been loved off, and your eyes drop out and you get loose in the joints and very shabby. But these things don't matter at all, because once you are Real you can't be ugly, except to people who don't understand."

The old Skin Horse understands an important truth. Sometimes loving others will rub your hair off and you may become a little worn out, but it's truly what makes you Real in God's eyes!

"I AM COMMITTED TO LOVING GOD AND LOVING OTHERS."

Sing for joy to God our strength.

PSALM 81:1

One afternoon a young boy went out to ride his new bike as his father jogged alongside him. Nearing the end of their journey, the two faced a long, steep hill. When the boy saw the hill, he stopped and said, "I'll never make it. That hill is too long and too steep."

The boy's father replied, "You will never know the joy of reaching the top unless you try. So get on your bike and pedal as hard as you can."

The boy began going up the hill, pedaling as fast as he could, his dad by his side. Toward the top his bike began to slow down. Moments before he would have come to a stop and start sliding backward, the father put his hand on the back of the seat and provided enough power for the boy to reach the top of the hill. The son's face lit up with joy at his achievement. His father asked, "Son, that was amazing. How did you do it?" The boy replied, "It was really hard, and I thought I wasn't going to make it. I couldn't have done it without you, Daddy!"

No matter how long or steep the slope you're facing, just keep pedaling and find joy in your heavenly Father's strength. He's right beside you!

> "DESPITE MY CIRCUMSTANCES, I
> FEEL INNER CONTENTMENT AND
> UNDERSTAND MY PURPOSE IN LIFE."

DAY 337

PEACE

Abram said to Lot, "Let's not have any quarreling between you and me, or between your herders and mine, for we are close relatives."

GENESIS 13:8

First, the setting: Abram and Lot, their families, and their herds had moved from Egypt to the Negev and finally settled in Bethel.

Second, the cast: Lot was Abram's nephew, and both were wealthy.

Next, the conflict: "The land could not support them while they stayed together, for their possessions were so great that they were not able to stay together. And quarreling arose between Abram's herders and Lot's" (vv. 6–7).

Now, the resolution: Abram took the initiative to calm their dispute. Although Abram, as the elder, would normally have first pick of the land, he put peace in the family above his own wishes.

Choosing peace can definitely cost the one who makes that choice. It's a self-sacrificial, Christlike act—a step of faith that honors God and one that God will honor. Are you facing situations where you might be able to absorb the cost of peace? As hard as it is to give up what may be rightfully yours, God will honor your willingness to strive for peace "as far as it depends on you" (Romans 12:18).

> **"I AM FREE FROM ANXIETY BECAUSE I HAVE FOUND PEACE WITH GOD, PEACE WITH OTHERS, AND PEACE WITH MYSELF."**

SELF-CONTROL

The tongue also is a fire, a world of evil among the parts of the body. It corrupts the whole body, sets the whole course of one's life on fire, and is itself set on fire by hell.

JAMES 3:6

When you arrive at your doctor's office, what's one of the first things he checks? Your tongue. Its color and appearance indicate a wide range of medical conditions, from a simple cold or poor circulation to the beginning stages of cancer. As it turns out, the tongue is a great indicator of deeper problems within.

A Scottish proverb tells us, "When the heart is full, the tongue will speak." Jesus, the Great Physician, wants us to know unkind words spilled from a loose tongue signify a deeper problem—a form of "heart disease." Hearts filled with insecurities, anger, hatred, and bitterness spew out sarcasm and hurtful words.

The symptoms your tongue displays won't disappear until your doctor cures the deeper problem. Simply trying to control your tongue will be impossible until Jesus treats your deeper problem and does open-heart surgery to replace your fears and animosities with his eternal security, love, and peace.

What's your tongue indicating?

> **"I HAVE THE POWER THROUGH CHRIST TO CONTROL MYSELF."**

DAY 339

HOPE

Faith is confidence in what we hope for and assurance about what we do not see.

HEBREWS 11:1

Watching professional golf tournaments has changed for me, first of all because my neighbor, Jimmy Walker, is on the PGA Tour. I usually record the tournaments so I can watch later, and if I get too stressed about the conclusion (*Who won the playoff? Did Jimmy get a top-ten finish? Did he win?*), I can watch the ending first. If it's the outcome I want, then I can sit back and enjoy the competition. Knowing the end brings me confidence in what I hoped for!

A friend of ours reads mysteries that way. When the protagonist is in danger, a quick peek reassures her the protagonist wins.

When we who trust Jesus as Savior become stressed about life, we also can turn to the back of the Bible to remind us our hero wins. The New Earth comes down from heaven and "there will be no more death or mourning or crying or pain" (Revelation 21:4).

Looking at the sure promise of the future can give us hope for the present.

If you feel yourself losing hope, don't hesitate to peek at the end and remind yourself Jesus is coming to save the day!

"I CAN COPE WITH THE HARDSHIPS OF LIFE BECAUSE OF THE HOPE I HAVE IN JESUS CHRIST."

PATIENCE

*I remain confident of this: I will see the goodness of the
LORD in the land of the living. Wait for the LORD; be
strong and take heart and wait for the LORD.*

PSALM 27:13–14

I n Psalm 27, David was under enormous pressure. His circumstances
were desperate, his enemies closing in. David's very life was threatened
and his future was uncertain. Have you ever been there, feeling the pressure of time and circumstances backing you into a corner? Read this
powerful psalm. Then reflect on how David ended his meditations in the
verses above. David would *wait* for the Lord, confident that he would see
the goodness of the Lord in the land of the living.

When time is running out, when your back is against the wall,
when there is nowhere to go, when all promise of hope seems to have
disappeared, this is the very time to take heart and wait patiently for
the Lord. Instead, we tend to become anxious and impulsive and take
matters into our own hands.

Follow David's example. When pressures mount, when you are
anxious and tempted to act impulsively—stop, take heart, and wait
patiently for the Lord. After all, isn't the goodness of the Lord worth
waiting for?

**"I AM SLOW TO ANGER AND ENDURE PATIENTLY
UNDER THE UNAVOIDABLE PRESSURES OF LIFE."**

DAY 341

KINDNESS/GOODNESS

*"Why do you look at the speck of sawdust in your
brother's eye and pay no attention to the plank in your
own eye?"*

LUKE 6:41

Criticism and judgment of other people's character and behavior
come all too easily to us sinful, insecure, hurting human beings.
Our sinful nature and wounded hearts might explain why we judge,
but there is another factor commonly in play: we often exhibit the very
same attitude or behavior that we are criticizing.

The truth is that the traits we find most irritating in other people
tend to be traits we share with them. But we don't always realize the
struggle in our own lives. This truth—however uncomfortable it
makes us—can help us, by God's grace, become less judgmental and
significantly kinder to people who annoy us. The plank in our own eye
should keep us from being overly concerned about the speck of sawdust
in our brother's eye.

Ask the Lord God to show you the traits in yourself that fuel your
ready criticism of others. Yield those traits to God and his transforming
power so that you can be quicker to extend kindness rather than criticism. The truth is, if you are occupied with getting that big plank out of
your eye, you won't have time to fixate on the speck in someone else's.

> **"I CHOOSE TO BE KIND AND GOOD IN
> MY RELATIONSHIPS WITH OTHERS."**

FAITHFULNESS

> *The woman had taken the two men and hidden them. She said, "Yes, the men came to me, but . . . they left. I don't know which way they went.*

JOSHUA 2:4–5

We love *The Sound of Music!* One of our favorite scenes happens toward the end of the movie. The Von Trapps have sung their command performance, and now the family—loyal Austrians and opponents of Hitler—need to flee from the Nazis. Who will help them? Sister Berthe holds up a spark plug and some wires she'd pulled from the Nazis' car, and the Von Trapps flee to safety. God used Sister Berthe's disobedience to her country's government.

We also love the story of Rahab. Two spies were sent ahead to scope out Rahab's country before Israel attacked it. They were in danger of being found out. Who would help them? Rahab, a harlot, would keep them safe in her house. Joshua 2:4–5 reveals Rahab's lie to the king's soldiers who were sent to find the spies. God used Rahab's defiance of her government to save his spies and give his people possession of the promised land.

Faithfulness to your country is good and encouraged in Scripture—but it should never overstep faithfulness to God!

> **"I HAVE ESTABLISHED A GOOD NAME WITH GOD AND OTHERS BASED ON MY LOYALTY TO THOSE RELATIONSHIPS."**

GENTLENESS

As God's chosen people, holy and dearly loved, clothe yourselves with compassion, kindness, humility, gentleness and patience.

COLOSSIANS 3:12

I n early 2015, everyone was asking, "What color *is* that dress?" The battle raged. Were you in the blue with black lace camp? Or the white with gold lace group? Scientists tried to explain what was happening in the human eye and why not everyone saw the same color. It has something to do with how daylight changes the color of an object and how our brain interprets it. "What's happening here is your visual system is looking at this thing, and you're trying to discount the chromatic bias of the daylight axis," said Bevil Conway, a neuroscientist who studies color and vision. "So people either discount the blue side, in which case they end up seeing white and gold, or discount the gold side, in which case they end up with blue and black."[80] Got it?

If only the clothes that Christians put on in response to the command of Colossians 3:12 would prompt such attention and generate such discussion!

What will you do to be sure you're clothed with compassion, kindness, humility, and patience? Your gentleness and the way you love others may get people talking!

> **"I AM THOUGHTFUL, CONSIDERATE, AND CALM IN MY DEALINGS WITH OTHERS."**

HUMILITY

*When they measure themselves by themselves and
compare themselves with themselves, they are not wise.*

2 CORINTHIANS 10:12

We tend to compare ourselves with other people. "I can't believe she _____," or "I wish I could _____ like him." Go ahead; fill in the blanks.

When we compare ourselves with others, we either find it makes us feel better about ourselves, which leads to pride instead of humility, or it makes us feel inadequate, as though we don't measure up, which leads to humiliation.

Paul warns us that comparing ourselves with others is not wise. He later says that if we are going to boast, we should boast in only the Lord, "for it is not the one who commends himself who is approved, but the one whom the Lord commends" (v. 18).

Our self-worth, along with our boasting, needs to be rooted in the unconditional love and acceptance of our heavenly Father and the immense sacrifice Jesus gave when he humbled himself to die on the cross for our sins—pride included. When we do this, we no longer need to use people to make us feel worthwhile, or become intimidated by them. We become free to love and appreciate others.

Now you can fill in these blanks: "Did you notice how well she _____?" or "He is so good at _____."

"I CHOOSE TO ESTEEM OTHERS ABOVE MYSELF."

DAY 345

LOVE

Love does no harm to a neighbor. Therefore love is the fulfillment of the law.

ROMANS 13:10

Sometimes doing one thing correctly makes other things fall easily into place. For example, while swimming, turn your head to your shoulder—and no farther—to breathe. This will keep your body level in the water and allow more efficient movement. Or, if you ever need to stand on only one leg, keep your eyes fixed on an unmoving object at a distance in front of you. It will help you to stand steady and balanced.

More important than these examples is what happens when you work on obeying God's command to love your neighbor. When you do so, you'll find yourself also obeying God's commands not to covet, steal, murder, lie, or commit adultery. That's why Paul could argue that any and every command in God's Word is "summed up in this one command: 'Love your neighbor as yourself'" (v. 9).

Sometimes doing one thing helps other things fall into place. It's not hard to see why loving God and loving others are the key principles that can guide your life as a Christ follower.

> **"I AM COMMITTED TO LOVING GOD AND LOVING OTHERS."**

DAY 346

JOY

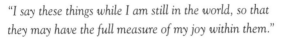

"I say these things while I am still in the world, so that they may have the full measure of my joy within them."

JOHN 17:13

Ever wondered what the whole of creation and the human experiment is all about? What's in it for God? Could it be the same thing he has in mind for us? Could it be joy? Could joy be God's reason for it all? Psalm 149:4 assures us God delights in his people. Yes, it's joy!

We were created to live in union and communion with God, bringing joy to God's heart. Our Creator made us to enjoy him, and he delights in us. He created us to enjoy each other and everything he created.

This was God's intent, but something dreadful happened. The apostle Paul summed it up this way in Romans 3:23: "For all have sinned and fall short of the glory of God." Apart from God, we find intermittent, fleeting joy, but fall far short of experiencing the joy-filled lives God intended.

When man sinned, man lost God. When man lost God, man lost his joy. Jesus made it possible to get God back in man, and with God's return comes the full measure of his joy. Why? For the pure joy of it!

Your God delights in you! Re"joy"ce in that!

> **"DESPITE MY CIRCUMSTANCES, I FEEL INNER CONTENTMENT AND UNDERSTAND MY PURPOSE IN LIFE."**

353

PEACE

"Peace I leave with you; my peace I give you. I do not give to you as the world gives. Do not let your hearts be troubled and do not be afraid."

JOHN 14:27

Peace. Such a simple word, yet it eludes most of us much of the time.

It was time for Jesus to say good-bye to his disciples, and his parting gift to them (and to us) was peace. But not the peace they had known in the world; this would be a peace far greater. He wanted them to have the same kind of peace he was experiencing in the wake of his pending crucifixion.

If we want to know Jesus' brand of peace, it would be wise to understand what brought Jesus peace. First of all, Jesus was sure of who he was, God's son. Nothing to prove. Second, he treated people with love and respect, right down to the most detested outcast. He loved unconditionally. Nothing to lose. Perhaps most importantly, Jesus didn't care what others thought about him. He didn't conform to the world's standards. Only what God thought mattered. Nothing to hide.

Want peace? Live more like Jesus, so when it's time for you to say good-bye, you can do it with nothing to prove, nothing to lose, and nothing to hide.

> **"I AM FREE FROM ANXIETY BECAUSE I HAVE FOUND PEACE WITH GOD, PEACE WITH OTHERS, AND PEACE WITH MYSELF."**

SELF-CONTROL

Therefore confess your sins to each other and pray for each other so that you may be healed.

JAMES 5:16

Alcoholics Anonymous began with sponsorship. When Bill W., only a few months sober, was stricken with a powerful urge to drink, this thought came to him: 'You need another alcoholic to talk to. You need another alcoholic just as much as he needs you!' He found Dr. Bob, who had been trying desperately and unsuccessfully to stop drinking, and out of their common need A.A. was born."[81]

This is what James is espousing in our passage above. When we develop a mutual community of confession, accountability, and prayer, we experience healing. Bottom line: *self-control* requires *other-patrol*.

We understand our children's need for community guidance, but as adults we often rid ourselves of the invasive, style-cramping burden of accountability. James warns us that this is a colossal mistake.

Want to avoid waking up one day to the painful consequences of a bad habit? Form a mutual community of accountability around you now. Already overtaken with a behavior you know will one day result in bad news? It is never too late to do what you've needed to do all along: get with other people who know they are susceptible to stumbling and share your desire to live a healthy and productive life.

> **"I HAVE THE POWER THROUGH CHRIST TO CONTROL MYSELF."**

DAY 349

HOPE

*I eagerly expect and hope that I will in no way be
ashamed, but will have sufficient courage so that now as
always Christ will be exalted in my body, whether by life
or by death. For to me, to live is Christ.*

PHILIPPIANS 1:20–21

Hoping is hard! Hoping and expecting are risky business because they make us feel like we are setting ourselves up for future disappointment. Here's the equation we often apply to our lives:

$E - R = D$. *Expectations minus Reality equals Disappointment.*

Whether it's a vacation, a child, a marriage, or a job, what we expect minus what happens equals our level of disappointment, discouragement, and even despair. Consequently, we might hope for less to avoid disappointment. A teacher once told her always negative student, "Keep on expecting the worst. You'll never be disappointed!"

What we expect in life matters. If we have hope in our circumstances rather than Christ, we are setting ourselves up for a huge letdown. Paul's hopeful expectation was that Christ would be exalted (literally, displayed as great) in his life no matter what happened. For Paul, his life was an extension of Christ's life. And Christ never disappoints.

Put your hope in Christ, where you will find courage to go wherever God is calling you. You won't be disappointed!

> **"I CAN COPE WITH THE HARDSHIPS OF LIFE
> BECAUSE OF THE HOPE I HAVE IN JESUS CHRIST."**

PATIENCE

The one who has knowledge uses words with restraint, and whoever has understanding is even-tempered.

PROVERBS 17:27

Which of these thoughts have you had?

I wish she could forget what I said, but there's no delete key in a human brain.

I can't believe I said that! I'd give anything to have a do-over on that conversation!

I got angry and said things I didn't mean.

All of us have probably thought these things! And that means we can appreciate the wisdom in Scripture's instruction to "be quick to listen, slow to speak and slow to become angry" (James 1:19). Moving from appreciating its value to actually living it, though, requires a good amount of patience—and a good reduction of self-centeredness—on our part. Most of us would rather talk than listen; we too easily speak and *then* think, and we aren't perfectly able to control our temper.

It's good that we can call on the Lord for his help. It's good that one gift of the Holy Spirit is patience and another is self-control. *We need you, Lord! Help us, Holy Spirit!*

Greek philosopher Epictetus may have a point: two ears and one mouth suggest that we should listen twice as much as we talk!

"I AM SLOW TO ANGER AND ENDURE PATIENTLY UNDER THE UNAVOIDABLE PRESSURES OF LIFE."

DAY 351

KINDNESS/GOODNESS

"I have set you an example that you should do as I have done for you."

JOHN 13:15

Here's a question for the ladies: Did you dance with your daddy when you were little?

With your father securely holding your hands, you carefully put your little feet—one at a time—onto your daddy's much bigger shoes. As he moved around the room, you moved with him. When he spun, you spun. When he slid, you slid. He set the pace and chose the direction; you just had fun, enjoying the laughter you two shared during the dance.

At that point in your life, it was easy to follow your dancing father's footsteps: you simply stood on his feet. Now, when you want to follow Jesus' example—and God commands that—you'll find it easier to do if you rely on the power of his Spirit and remember the dance steps of faith he's taught you as you've read his Word.

Life becomes a much more beautiful dance when we choose to follow in Christ's footsteps of kindness, goodness, and love for others. Maybe you are someone people look up to and try to emulate. As they follow the footsteps of your acts of kindness, you may dance them to Jesus.

> **"I CHOOSE TO BE KIND AND GOOD IN MY RELATIONSHIPS WITH OTHERS."**

FAITHFULNESS

Many claim to have unfailing love, but a faithful person who can find?

PROVERBS 20:6

It was a "good day" when Willie Nelson bought Trigger in 1969. What is Trigger? His beloved guitar. It is now distressed with memories of their journey etched in its wood and a huge hole where his hand has repeatedly strummed over the years. Willie can afford a new guitar, yet this is the *only* guitar he will use. Willie's band members agree that they are all expendable; Trigger is the only nonnegotiable. "When Trigger is done, we will all be done." Willie tells the story of coming home one day to find his house engulfed in flames. Without hesitation Willie ran in to save—you guessed it—Trigger.

Both Willie and Trigger are getting "pretty old," according to Willie, and they share a few scars, but as they age together, their relationship has created a rich, beautiful tone.

Willie says he doesn't know who will last longer, the man or the guitar. They both show the wear and tear of life, but they'll keep going until there's nothing left.

Who is your faithful Trigger? A mate? A friend? More importantly, are you a faithful Trigger for someone else?

> **"I HAVE ESTABLISHED A GOOD NAME WITH GOD AND OTHERS BASED ON MY LOYALTY TO THOSE RELATIONSHIPS."**

DAY 353

GENTLENESS

Opponents must be gently instructed, in the hope that God will grant them repentance leading them to a knowledge of the truth.

2 TIMOTHY 2:25

N o one can change my mind about getting an abortion! Not my friends in the waiting room and definitely not you."

The worker at the crisis pregnancy center told Gina that it was not her intention to force her to keep her baby. The worker got to know Gina—her life objectives, her relationship with the baby's father—and talked with Gina about the options of parenting and adoption so she could make a well-informed decision. With this opportunity to think about pregnancy from different perspectives, Gina was nevertheless determined to abort . . . until she had an ultrasound. "That's my baby!" she cried. Gina carried the pregnancy to term and kept her child.[82]

It was the loving social worker's gentle words and the clear picture of her baby peacefully moving in her womb that changed Gina's mind. It may sound paradoxical, but gentleness can be a strong force for change.

When has gentleness been a force for change in your life? In what current relationship might your gentle approach be just the thing to move someone to follow God?

> **"I AM THOUGHTFUL, CONSIDERATE, AND CALM IN MY DEALINGS WITH OTHERS."**

HUMILITY

Clothe yourselves with humility toward one another.

1 PETER 5:5

Humility is not a trait the world values or even understands. Serving someone? Putting someone's needs before your own? Doing something out of kindness and expecting nothing in return?

The world demands you look after number one: yourself. But Jesus, the one who deserves our undivided praise and adoration, calls us to put others first and to look for ways to serve, just as he did. Such actions reflect the servant heart of Jesus himself. Humility serves without concern about appearance or reputation and regardless of the action's impact on status or career.

The ability to choose to esteem others above oneself must be rooted in a solid internal foundation of God's unconditional love and eternal promises. Individuals who are willing and able to choose to clothe themselves with Jesus-like humility have undoubtedly embraced their inherent worth as God's children.

Are you confident enough in your relationship with God to be able to serve others without worry of how it will make you appear to onlookers? Can you lift a brother or sister up and not be concerned how it will affect your own status or career?

May your confidence in God's love for you and your position as a child of God enable you to truly love others by serving them.

"I CHOOSE TO ESTEEM OTHERS ABOVE MYSELF."

LOVE

[David and Jonathan] kissed each other and wept
together—but David wept the most.

1 SAMUEL 20:41

A pit bull loved being with his puppies and had no trouble expanding the circle to include a Siamese cat and a group of chicks who, strangely enough, were quite fond of one another.

A lioness had been separated from her pride. She had no cubs of her own, so she adopted a baby antelope. The predator babied her prey, walking with it, sleeping with it, and never eating it!

A 230-pound ape used sign language to tell her teacher that she wanted a cat for her birthday. Stuffed cats didn't work. When the ape got a kitten from an abandoned litter, she was maternal, affectionate, and gentle.[83]

Jonathan was the rightful heir to his father's throne, but he had seen God's hand on David's life and never doubted that the throne of Israel should be his friend's. Their love for God and for one another mattered more than politics.

What odd or at least unexpected friendship might God be calling you to initiate? Ask him; he'll guide you. Then step out in faith. You will be a blessing to each other and a witness of God's unexpected, extraordinary love.

> **"I AM COMMITTED TO LOVING**
> **GOD AND LOVING OTHERS."**

JOY

We . . . glory in our sufferings, because we know that suffering produces perseverance.

ROMANS 5:3

One afternoon a mother and her two daughters rode their bicycles to a distant park. Their route carried them up and down one steep hill after another. At one point during their ride, the mother asked her two daughters, "Hey, girls, what part do you like best, going uphill or downhill?" The older daughter said, "That's a silly question. Of course I like going downhill better." The younger daughter answered, "I like the uphill part best." The mother, surprised by her daughter's response, asked why she liked going uphill more. The girl answered, "It's so much fun to reach the top after working so hard to get there, and going uphill makes me stronger."

Sometimes we coast in life, enjoying the ride. Other times we pedal with all we've got just to keep going uphill. May you find joy in both experiences, remembering the exhilarating feeling you will have when you reach the top! Enjoy the ride, and even more, enjoy the One who is with you on the ride of your life.

> "DESPITE MY CIRCUMSTANCES, I FEEL INNER CONTENTMENT AND UNDERSTAND MY PURPOSE IN LIFE."

PEACE

"I tell you that anyone who is angry with a brother or sister will be subject to judgment."

MATTHEW 5:22

In Jesus' day people found his teaching both radical and amazing. He taught that doing good on the Sabbath was not wrong (Luke 6:8–10). He instructed his followers to serve one another humbly (John 13:12–17). He pointed out faults in the religious establishment (Matthew 23:13–36). Whatever the topic, Jesus taught with authority (Matthew 7:29).

In the collection of his teachings called the Sermon on the Mount, Jesus encouraged his listeners to make living peacefully with one another a priority, even above acts of worship. He said, "If you are offering your gift at the altar and there remember that your brother or sister has something against you, leave your gift there in front of the altar. First go and be reconciled to them; then come and offer your gift" (vv. 23–24). God clearly teaches throughout Scripture that he values relationship and the condition of the heart over sacrifice.

If you are not at peace with others, Jesus urges you to pursue reconciliation first before you worship. Is there someone in your life you need to call, e-mail, or sit down with? Worshipping God is a continual act for believers, so the sooner you get this done, the better!

> **"I AM FREE FROM ANXIETY BECAUSE I HAVE FOUND PEACE WITH GOD, PEACE WITH OTHERS, AND PEACE WITH MYSELF."**

PATIENCE

Live a life worthy of the Lord . . . being strengthened with all power according to his glorious might so that you may have great endurance and patience.

COLOSSIANS 1:10–11

Waiting is difficult, isn't it? Why? Because waiting requires patience. We can run out of patience waiting for our Internet to connect because it's ten seconds too slow. We quickly run out of patience with others and even God because they are not complying with what we want in the moment. In our fast-paced, "I want what I want now" modern age of technology, our patience is becoming increasingly thin.

Life is a long journey with God and each other. It's not perfect, and neither are we. We will need patience and endurance to get through. Our patient God promises both through his power that indwells us who believe. God is patient with us when we blow it. Remembering he's a God of second chances helps us slow down enough to be patient with others.

Have you ever tried to rush life, rush God, or rush others? How did that work out? If you impatiently run through life, there is no telling all the blessings and lessons you will miss.

Take God up on his offer of patient endurance. He promises you will get there on time, and enjoy the journey along the way.

> "I AM SLOW TO ANGER AND ENDURE PATIENTLY UNDER THE UNAVOIDABLE PRESSURES OF LIFE."

KINDNESS/GOODNESS

You are my Lord; apart from you I have no good thing.

PSALM 16:2

In sidewalk surveys asking, "If you had one wish, what would you ask for?" the replies predictably fell into two categories—wealth and fame.[84] No one asked for goodness. This is strange, since most of the suffering we experience in life is at the hands of other people pursuing wealth and fame but without goodness.

Perhaps our greatest human need is for goodness. As Jesus said, "No one is good—except God alone" (Mark 10:18). David was called a man after God's own heart because he knew that pursuing a heart like God's was his greatest need. He had wealth, fame, and power, but he knew without God's goodness, his unbridled human rule would cause his subjects suffering.

David confessed his need for God's goodness. We need to do the same, and then pursue a heart like our good God's. When you do, you can be sure "that he who began a good work in you will carry it on to completion until the day of Christ Jesus" (Philippians 1:6).

Would those you have authority over say you exercise it with goodness like David?

> **"I CHOOSE TO BE KIND AND GOOD IN MY RELATIONSHIPS WITH OTHERS."**

FAITHFULNESS

Where you go I will go, and where you stay I will stay.
Your people will be my people and your God my God.

RUTH 1:16

Jim and Philip were best friends, and they did everything together. They joined the marines together and were stationed in Germany together. One day too much gunfire raged, so the commanding officer ordered a retreat. As the soldiers ran to safety, Jim panicked. *Where's Philip?* Defying the officer's orders, Jim went to find Philip.

Soon the officer saw Jim stumbling back, carrying the lifeless body of his friend. Relieved and angry, the officer said, "I knew your friend was already dead! You could have been killed!"

Jim said, "He was alive when I got to him, and his last words were 'I knew you'd come back.'" Philip knew he had a loyal friend in Jim.[85]

Such faithfulness and loyalty can cost as we give sacrificially to others and make decisions on principle rather than practicality. Leaving behind her family and all that was familiar in Moab, Ruth stayed with Naomi, returning with her to the town of Bethlehem. Ruth's faithfulness to Naomi brought her a future that included a place in the lineage of Jesus—she was King David's great-grandmother.

How can you choose faithfulness to a friend today?

> **"I HAVE ESTABLISHED A GOOD NAME WITH GOD AND OTHERS BASED ON MY LOYALTY TO THOSE RELATIONSHIPS."**

DAY 361

JOY

*If only we had died by the LORD's hand in Egypt!
There we sat around pots of meat and ate all the food we
wanted, but you have brought us out into this desert to
starve this entire assembly to death.*

EXODUS 16:3

Imagine joy-filled excitement rising as Moses told the children of Israel they were finally leaving Egypt behind to embark on a journey to a new and beautiful home. Yet not a month and a half later, they were disgruntled and complaining in the desert. They wondered if staying in Egypt would have been better. Anticipation of their new home was gone, along with their joy. They were stuck in the day-to-day mess of the desert.

Much like the children of Israel, we are on a journey to a beautiful, permanent home. Our journey, however, is through a broken world, filled with potholes that cause us to get stuck, painful sights that distract our eyes from the main road, and wrong turns and detours that cause us to lose the vision of our end destination: eternity with Jesus. It's easy to get sidetracked by the day-to-day mess of this life.

When you find yourself disgruntled and complaining, refocus your anticipation on the permanent home Jesus is preparing for you. No matter what circumstances the journey brings, it is only temporary!

> "DESPITE MY CIRCUMSTANCES, I
> FEEL INNER CONTENTMENT AND
> UNDERSTAND MY PURPOSE IN LIFE."

PEACE

Make up your mind not to put any stumbling block or obstacle in the way of a brother or sister. . . . Make every effort to do what leads to peace and to mutual edification.

ROMANS 14:13, 19

The Greek word for "edification" is *oikodomé*. It literally means "to build, specifically a house." The Bible teaches that our bodies are God's temple or dwelling place (1 Corinthians 6:19), so if we make every effort to edify a brother or sister in Christ, you could say we are building them up to become a suitable house for God.

Do you know someone who battles alcohol addiction? Or someone who is on a diet, trying not to overeat? While the Bible gives us permission both to eat and to drink alcohol in moderation, our decisions affect others. The action we take could either exacerbate their battle with temptation or give them a boost toward their goals.

Sometimes we aren't aware of things we do that create a "stumbling block or obstacle" in the faith walk of a fellow believer. But God will bless you if you ask him to make your heart sensitive to those around you who are struggling. He can direct your heart to make merciful choices that will lead to peace in your heart and in your relationships.

> "I AM FREE FROM ANXIETY BECAUSE I HAVE FOUND PEACE WITH GOD, PEACE WITH OTHERS, AND PEACE WITH MYSELF."

DAY 363

FAITHFULNESS

Today in the town of David a Savior has been born to
you; he is the Messiah, the Lord.

LUKE 2:11

my dad and my mom are separated i barely see my dad but sometimes he
will call me and promise he will take me somewhere or get me that gift i
wanted or something like that but more and more lately my dad has been
breaking promises and i can't help but cry he has broken so many and i
am tired of crying but i always do . . . i don't want to cry over him any-
more . . . help me stop crying over him.[86]

The pain in that twelve-year-old's prayer is unmistakable. Broken
promises have shaken his trust in his dad. Broken promises make the
world a less predictable, less secure place. In sharp contrast, unbroken
promises enable children to learn to trust and feel secure.

Our heavenly Father always keeps his promises. Two thousand and
thirty years after God made the promise to Abraham that his descendants would bless all people, Jesus was born from the tribe of Judah, the
family of David, in Bethlehem. Promise fulfilled.

Be an example of your faithful God. Keep your word just as God
always keeps his.

> **"I HAVE ESTABLISHED A GOOD NAME**
> **WITH GOD AND OTHERS BASED ON MY**
> **LOYALTY TO THOSE RELATIONSHIPS."**

GENTLENESS

Remind the people . . . to be peaceable and considerate, and always to be gentle toward everyone.

TITUS 3:1–2

The origin of the English word *gentleness* may surprise you. It did me. Embedded in *gentleness* is the root word *gens*. This same derivation is in the words *Genesis* (the book of "beginnings"), *genealogy*, *genetics*, *genes*, and *generations*. The notion is that gentleness develops "from the beginning" and is passed down. We would say a gentleman is one who is from a good family, is wellborn, or was raised from birth to be gentle.

Studies show that a child's brain is 95 percent developed during the period from birth to five years of age, and 85 percent of their personality and social skills are established during that same time frame.[87] So this means we have only a short window to teach our children how to be gentle. Who will they learn gentleness from? Their mom and dad, their aunts and uncles, and their grandparents. Our discipline of them must be firm, but without punitive words or harsh actions. Boundaries must be established but with gentleness and grace.

If you have a vision to raise your children to become gentle adults, begin by letting them see and experience your gentleness. What a great opportunity and a grand responsibility to make our children great!

"I AM THOUGHTFUL, CONSIDERATE, AND CALM IN MY DEALINGS WITH OTHERS."

HUMILITY

"Now that I, your Lord and Teacher, have washed your feet, you also should wash one another's feet."

JOHN 13:14

The "I" in this scene is Jesus. The divine One, who had entered the world in utter humility and was now nearing the end of his time on earth, offered an unforgettable example of humility for us to imitate.

A bit of history makes this scene even more remarkable. In Jesus' day, people walked everywhere on the dusty roads of Israel, so feet were filthy. Washing those dusty and dirty feet was a task assigned to slaves, who tended to the feet of guests before the meal began.

Apparently on this day no one had been assigned the foot-washing task—and none among the Twelve felt compelled to take on the responsibility, most likely because they thought themselves above such a service.

But their beloved Rabbi, the Son of God, the Holy One himself, rose and lovingly cleaned their feet. And when he finished, he said, "You should do as I have done for you" (v. 15).

Serve as Jesus served, regarding no act of service as beneath you and seeing every task as an opportunity to honor God.

"I CHOOSE TO ESTEEM OTHERS ABOVE MYSELF."

THE POWER OF "BELIEVE"

These men who have caused trouble all over the world have now come here.

ACTS 17:6

A sociologist embarked on a quest to answer this question: "How did the marginal Jesus movement become the dominant force in the Western world within just a few centuries?" By his estimates, the number of Christians grew to 33,882,008 believers by AD 350. After researching he concluded, "I believe that it was the religion's particular doctrines that permitted Christianity to be among the most sweeping and successful revitalization movements in history. And it was the way these doctrines took on actual flesh, the way they directed organizational actions and individual behavior that led to the rise of Christianity."[88]

In a nutshell, the early Christians *believed*.

The Thessalonians in Acts 17 saw the ministry of Christ as a worldwide movement of trouble. As Christianity did indeed spread beyond Thessalonica, it proved not to be a tribe of troublemakers but a movement of redemption, hope, and healing all over the world.

The same holds true for us today, not only in our own lives but also all over the world, if we will only *believe*!

> I PRAY THAT THE EYES OF YOUR HEART MAY BE ENLIGHTENED IN ORDER THAT YOU MAY KNOW . . . HIS INCOMPARABLY GREAT POWER FOR US WHO BELIEVE. —EPHESIANS 1:18–19

NOTES

1. Sarah Cairoli, "Statistics on Pollution in the Pacific Ocean," *Seattle Pi*, accessed May 25, 2015, http://education.seattlepi.com/statistics-pollution-pacific-ocean-6027.html.
2. "Faith Has a Limited Effect on Most People's Behavior," *Barna Group*, accessed July 14, 2015, https://www.barna.org/barna-update/article/5-barna-update/188-faith-has-a-limited-effect-on-most-peoples-behavior#.VWxevVxViko.
3. "How Many Adoptees Search?" *Adoption Statistics: Birth Family Search*, accessed July 14, 2015, http://statistics.adoption.com/information/adoption-statistics-birth-family-search.html.
4. J. C. Ryle, "Heirs of God," GraceGems.org, accessed June 13, 2015, http://www.gracegems.org/Ryle/heirs_of_god.htm.
5. Janelle P., "Iraq: Easter Being Celebrated Despite Dangerous Situation," *Open Doors USA*, accessed July 14, 2015, http://www.opendoorsusa.org/newsroom/tag-news-post/iraq-easter-being-celebrated-despite-dangerous-situation.
6. Janelle P., "Libyan Christians Plead for Prayer after Weekend Massacre," *Open Doors USA*, accessed July 14, 2015, www.opendoorsusa.org/newsroom/tag-news-post/libyan-christians-plead-for-prayer-after-weekend-massacre/.
7. Janelle P., "Yemen: Christians Reaching Out to Others, Despite Growing Crisis," *Open Doors USA*, accessed July 14, 2015, www.opendoorsusa.org/newsroom/tag-news-post/yemen-christians-reaching-out-to-others-despite-growing-crisis/.
8. Elizabeth Curran, "Compassion Means to Suffer With," EnochMagazine.com, accessed July 14, 2015, http://www.enochmagazine.com/articles/general/compassion-means-to-suffer-with.
9. "Why do people fear death?" Yahoo Answers, accessed March 12, 2015, https://in.answers.yahoo.com/question/index?qid=20130809181125AAwA1hA.

10. "Freedom from the Fear of Death (John 14:1-6 and Hebrews 2:14-15)," Bible.org, accessed July 14, 2015, https://bible.org/seriespage/freedom-fear-death-john-141-6-and-hebrews-214-15.

11. C. S. Lewis, *The Great Divorce* (New York: HarperOne, 2015), 138.

12. Stuart Walton, "The World of GK Chesterton, and what's wrong with it," *The Guardian*, accessed July 14, 2015, http://www.theguardian.com/books/booksblog/2010/jan/08/gk-chesterton-world-whats-wrong.

13. C. S. Lewis, *Mere Christianity* (New York: HarperOne, 2015), 135.

14. "Covenant," *Theopedia*, accessed June 15, 2015, http://www.theopedia.com/Covenant.

15. Matthew Henry, "Complete Commentary on Hebrews 4:1," StudyLight.org, accessed July 14, http://www.studylight.org/commentaries/mhm/view.cgi?book=heb&chapter=4.

16. "The Importance of Family Dinners VI." The National Center on Addiction and Substance Abuse at Columbia University, New York, NY, September 2010, accessed July 14, 2015, http://casafamilyday.org/familyday/files/media/The%20Importance%20of%20Family%20Dinners%20VI%202010%20-%20FINAL.pdf.

17. Dan Bernard, SermonIllustrations.com, accessed August 27, 2015, http://www.sermonillustratrations.com/a-z/c/church.htm.

18. "Church," Sermonillustrations.com, accessed June 15, 2015, http://www.sermonillustrations.com/a-z/c/church.htm.

19. Stephen Pressfield, *The Legend of Bagger Vance* (New York: Avon, 1995), 121.

20. Greg Laden, "How Many Cells Are There in the Human Body?" ScienceBlogs, accessed July 14, 2015, http://scienceblogs.com/gregladen/2011/11/28/how-many-cells-are-there-in-th/.

21. C. S. Lewis, *Mere Christianity* (New York: HarperOne, 2015), 135.

22. *Sympathy.* By permission. From *Merriam-Webster's Collegiate® Dictionary, 11th Edition* © 2015 by Merriam-Webster, Inc. (www.Merriam-Webster.com).

23. *Compassion.* By permission. From *Merriam-Webster's Collegiate® Dictionary, 11th Edition* © 2015 by Merriam-Webster, Inc. (www.Merriam-Webster.com).

24. Max Lucado, *A Love Worth Giving* (Nashville: Thomas Nelson, 2002), 39–40.

25. "Jim Elliot: No Fool," Christianity.com, accessed July 14, 2015, http://www.christianity.com/church/church-history/church-history-for-kids/jim-elliot-no-fool-11634862.html.

26. Susie Larson, *Your Sacred Yes* (Bloomington, MN: Bethany House, 2015).

27. Raymond Goldstone, "Well Known Expressions," BookBrowse.com, accessed July 14, 2015, https://www.bookbrowse.com/expressions/detail/index.cfm/expression_number/238/you-can-run-but-you-cant-hide?

28. "A Heart for Praise," *Our Daily Bread*, accessed July 14, 2015, http://www.sermonsearch.com/sermon-illustrations/4754/a-heart-for-praise/.

29. "A Lifestyle of Worship," TrulyWorship.com, accessed June 15, 2015, http://www.trulyworship.com/lifestyle_of_worship.html.

30. *Jealousy.* By permission. From *Merriam-Webster's Collegiate® Dictionary, 11th Edition* © 2015 by Merriam-Webster, Inc. (www.Merriam-Webster.com).

31. Meg Wagner, "SEE IT: Softball players carry opponent around to bases after she hits home run and her knee goes out," *New York Daily News*, accessed July 14, 2015, http://www.nydailynews.com/news/national/softball-players-injured-rival-home-plate-article-1.1772769.

32. "John Wooden Quotes," Wordpress, accessed June 17, 2015, https://smoothmat.wordpress.com/great-quotes/john-wooden-quotes/.

33. Lee Strobel, "Mismatched Marriage," ThrivingFamily.com, accessed July 14, 2015, http://www.thrivingfamily.com/Features/Magazine/2012/mismatched-marriage.aspx.

34. "Funniest Last Words of Famous People," memolition.com, accessed July 14, 2015, http://memolition.com/2013/10/16/funniest-last-words-of-famous-people-21-pictures/.

35. Barbara O'Dair, "Funny Last Words of 13 Notable People," *Reader's Digest*, accessed July 14, 2015, http://www.rd.com/slideshows/funny-last-words-notable-people/#slideshow=slide9.

36. "Funniest Last Words of Famous People," memolition.com, accessed July 14, 2015, http://memolition.com/2013/10/16/funniest-last-words-of-famous-people-21-pictures/.

37. "First ever photograph of light as both particle and wave," Phys.org, accessed July 14, 2015, http://phys.org/news/2015-03-particle.html.

38. E. Stanley Jones, *Liberating Ministry from the Success Syndrome* (Carol Stream: Tyndale House, 1988), 73.

39. William Nicholson, *Shadowlands* (New York: Samuel French, 1989), 81.

40. "Three Lessons We Can Learn from a 'Miracle'," Leadership Impact, accessed July 14, 2015, http://www.leadershipmpact.com/tag/miracle-on-ice/.

41. Sherry Taylor, "Q: The average man or woman will spend 3 days and 8 hours doing this over their lifetime?" literockz95.1, accessed July 14, 2015, http://literockz951.com/sherry-taylor/q-the-average-man-or-woman-will-spend-3-days-and-8-hours-doing-this-over-their-lifetime/.

42. *Entitlement.* By permission. From *Merriam-Webster's Collegiate® Dictionary, 11th Edition* © 2015 by Merriam-Webster, Inc. (www.Merriam-Webster.com).

43. "Guide to Quitting Smoking," American Cancer Society, accessed July 14, 2015, http://www.cancer.org/healthy/stayawayfromtobacco/guidetoquittingsmoking/guide-to-quitting-smoking-success-rates.

44. Joanna Stern, "Cellphone Users Check Phones 150x/Day and Other Fun Internet Facts," ABC News, accessed July 14, 2015, http://abcnews.go.com/blogs/technology/2013/05/cellphone-users-check-phones-150xday-and-other-internet-fun-facts/.

45. *Jurassic Park*, directed by Steven Spielberg (1993; Universal Pictures), film.

46. Robert Fulghum, *All I Really Need to Know I Learned in Kindergarten* (New York: Random House Children's Books, 2011).

47. "John Huss," ChristianHistory.net, accessed July 14, 2015, http://www.christianitytoday.com/ch/131christians/martyrs/huss.html?start=2.

48. Adam Pivec, "Nehemiah's Wall Discovered," *Biola Magazine*, accessed July 14, 2015, http://magazine.biola.edu/article/08-spring/nehemiahs-wall-discovered/.

49. "What Was the Length of the Jerusalem Walls Nehemiah Had to Rebuild?" Answers.com, accessed June 14, 2015, http://www.answers.com/Q/What_was_the_length_of_the_Jerusalem_walls_Nehemiah_had_to_rebuild.

50. Bill O'Reilly, *Killing Patton* (New York: Henry Holt and Company, 2014), 328–29.

51. "Wild Duck Creek Estate," Healthcote Wine Club, accessed July 14, 2015, http://www.heathcotewinehub.com.au/wineries/wild-duck-creek-estate/.

52. "Virtuous and Vicious Circle," IES Business Strategy, accessed May 19, 2015, https://strategicthinker.wordpress.com/vicious-cycle/.

53. Tim Sharp, "How Big Is the Sun?" Space.com, accessed July 14, 2015, http://www.space.com/17001-how-big-is-the-sun-size-of-the-sun.html.

54. Kim MacQuarrie, "Why the Incas Offered Up Child Sacrifices," *The Guardian*, accessed July 14, 2015, http://www.theguardian.com/science/2013/aug/04/why-incas-performed-human-sacrifice.

55. Joseph Castro, "Final Moments of Incan Child Mummies' Lives Revealed," Live Science, accessed July 14, 2015, http://www.livescience.com/38504-incan-child-mummies-lives-revealed.html.

56. John Townsend, *Dreary Dwellings and Frightful Families: A Painful History of Childhood* (Chicago: Heinemann-Raintree, 2006), 13.

57. Dana S. Iyer, "When We Can't See What's Right in Front of Us," *Psychology Today*, accessed July 14, 2015, https://www.psychologytoday.com/blog/life-liberty-and-the-pursuit-insight/201309/when-we-can-t-see-what-s-right-in-front-us.

58. Tom Nash, "Tell Me Your Story: A Modern-Day Job," Comfort Café, accessed June 18, 2015, http://www.comfort-cafe.net/?p=6144.

59. Beverly Jenkins, "10 Acts of Kindness That Saved a Life," Oddee.com, accessed July 14, 2015, http://www.oddee.com/item_98659.aspx.

60. Robertson McQuilkin, "Living by Vows," *Christianity Today*, accessed July 14, 2015, http://www.christianitytoday.com/ct/2004/februaryweb-only/2-9-11.0.html.

61. Leslie C. Hughes, *The Gospel for the Visual Learner: the Fork Illustration* (Bloomington: Trafford Publishing, 2007).

62. *The Wizard of Oz*, directed by Victor Fleming, et al., (1939; Metro-Goldwyn-Mayer), film.

63. Beverly Jenkins, "10 Acts of Kindness That Saved a Life," Oddee.com, accessed July 14, 2015, http://www.oddee.com/item_98659.aspx.

64. Dallas Willard, *The Spirit of the Disciplines* (New York: HarperCollins, 1988), 172–174.

65. Randy Frazee, "The Secret of the Bedouin Shepherd," *Real Simplicity* (Grand Rapids: Zondervan, 2011), 46.

66. Ibid., 47–48.

67. Mark Molzen, "Chosen with Purpose - Redefining Adoption & Identity," kickstarter.com, accessed July 14, 2015, https://www.kickstarter.com/projects /1580538814/chosen-with-purpose-redefining-adoption-and-identi.

68. C. S. Lewis, *Mere Christianity* (New York: HarperOne, 2015).

69. Shane Windmeyer, "Dan and Me: My Coming Out as a Friend of Dan Cathy and Chick-fil-A," Huffingtonpost.com, accessed July 12, 2015, http://www .huffingtonpost.com/shane-l-windmeyer/dan-cathy-chick-fil-a_b_2564379.html.

70. Karen Franklin, "'The Best Predictor of Future Behavior Is . . . Past Behavior.' Does the Popular Maxim Hold Water?" *Psychology Today*, accessed July 14, 2015, https://www.psychologytoday.com/blog/witness/201301/the-best-predictor -future-behavior-is-past-behavior.

71. Max Lucado, *You Changed My Life: Confident of Dad's Love* (Nashville: Thomas Nelson, 2010), 19–20.

72. C. S. Lewis, *The Four Loves* (New York: Harcourt, 1988), 121.

73. "Oxford Dictionaries Word of the Year: Selfie," blog.oxforddictionaries.com, accessed July 14, 2015, http://blog.oxforddictionaries.com/press-releases/oxford -dictionaries-word-of-the-year-2013/.

74. "His Peace," Crossroad, accessed June 18, 2015, http://www.crossroad.to/Bible _studies/Wardrobe/4-Peace.htm.

75. Alexander C. DeJong, "Being Honest with God," *Leadership Journal*, accessed July 14, 2015, http://www.christianitytoday.com/le/1981/fall/81l4117.html.

76. John Blake, "Two enemies discover a 'higher call' in battle," CNN.com, accessed July 14, 2015, http://www.cnn.com/2013/03/09/living/higher-call -military-chivalry/.

77. Tejvan Pettinger, "Dietrich Bonhoeffer Biography," Biographyonline.net, accessed July 14, 2015, http://www.biographyonline.net/spiritual/dietrich-bonhoeffer.html.

78. Robin Phillips, "Gratitude, Joy in the Midst of Suffering," *The Christian Worldview Journal*, The Chuck Colson Center for Christian Worldview, accessed July 14, 2015, http://www.breakpoint.org/the-center/columns/changepoint/16437 -gratitude-joy-in-the-midst-of-suffering.

79. "Ebola," Medecins Sans Frontieres (MSF), accessed May 17, 2015, http://www .doctorswithoutborders.org/our-work/medical-issues/ebola.

80. Adam Rogers, "The Science of Why No One Agrees on the Color of This Dress," Wired.com, accessed July 14, 2015, http://www.wired.com/2015/02 /science-one-agrees-color-dress/.

81. "Questions and Answers on Sponsorship," A. A. General Service Conference, accessed July 14, 2015, http://www.aa.org/assets/en_US/p-15_Q&AonSpon.pdf.

82. Sarah Terzo, "78% of Pregnant Women Seeing an Ultrasound Reject Abortions," LifeNews.com, accessed July 14, 2015, http://www.lifenews.com/2013/02/07/78-of -pregnant-women-seeing-an-ultrasound-reject-abortions/.

83. Jennifer Holland, *Unlikely Friendships: 47 Remarkable Stories from the Animal Kingdom* (New York: Workman Publishing, 2011).

84. Sharon Jayson, "Gen Y's attitudes differ from parents'," Usatoday.com, accessed July 13, 2015, http://usatoday30.usatoday.com/news/nation/2007-01-09-views_x.htm.

85. "Wanted: A Loyal Friend," Pastortea.blogspot.com, accessed July 14, 2015, http://pastortea.blogspot.com/2010/11/wanted-loyal-friend.html.

86. Marie Hartwell-Walker, "I Cry Every Time My Dad Breaks a Promise," psychcentral.com, accessed July 14, 2015, http://psychcentral.com/ask-the -therapist/2011/02/03/i-cry-every-time-my-dad-breaks-a-promise/.

87. Mackenzie Ryan, "Most vital part of education takes place early: Child's first five years," StatesmanJournal.com, accessed July 14, 2015, http://www .statesmanjournal.com/article/20080928/NEWS/809280322/Most-vital-part -education-takes-place-early-Child-s-first-five-years.

88. Rodney Stark, *The Rise of Christianity* (New York: HarperCollins, 1996), 209–10.

SCRIPTURE INDEX

TOPICAL INDEX

BELIEVE

POWERED BY ZONDERVAN®

Dear Reader,

Notable researcher George Gallup Jr. summarized his findings on the state of American Christianity with this startling revelation: "Churches face no greater challenge...than overcoming biblical illiteracy, and the prospects for doing so are formidable because **the stark fact is, many Christians don't know what they believe or why."**

The problem is not that people lack a hunger for God's Word. Research tells us that the number one thing people want from their church is for it to help them understand the Bible, and that Bible engagement is the number one catalyst for spiritual growth. Nothing else comes close.

This is why I am passionate about *Believe*—a Bible engagement experience to anchor every member of your family in the key teachings of the Bible.

Grounded in Scripture, *Believe* is a spiritual growth experience for all ages, taking each person on a journey toward becoming more like Jesus in their beliefs, actions, and character. There is one edition for adults, one for students, and two versions for children. All four age-appropriate editions of *Believe* unpack the 10 key beliefs, 10 key practices, and 10 key virtues of a Christian, so that everyone in your family and your church can learn together to be more like Jesus.

When these timeless truths are understood, believed in the heart, and applied to our daily living, they will transform a life, a family, a church, a city, a nation, and even our world.

Imagine thousands of churches and hundreds of thousands of individuals all over the world who will finally be able to declare – **"I know what I believe and why, and in God's strength I will seek to live it out all the days of my life."** It could change the world. It has in the past; it could happen again.

In Him,

Randy Frazee
General Editor, *Believe*

LIVING THE STORY OF THE BIBLE TO BECOME LIKE JESUS

Teach your whole family how to live the story of the Bible!

- **Adults** – Unlocks the 10 key beliefs, 10 key practices, and 10 key virtues that help people live the story of the Bible. Curriculum DVD and Study Guide also available.
- *Think, Act, Be Like Jesus* – A companion to *Believe*, this fresh resource by pastor Randy Frazee will help readers develop a personal vision for spiritual growth and a simple plan for getting started on the *Believe* journey.
- **Students** – This edition contains the same Scriptures as the adult edition, but with transitions and fun features to engage teens and students. Curriculum DVD also available.
- **Children** – With a Kids' Edition for ages 8-12, a Storybook for ages 4-8, and three levels of curriculum for preschool, early elementary, and later elementary, children of all ages will learn how to think, act, and be like Jesus.
- **Churches** – *Believe* is flexible, affordable, and easy to use with your church, in any ministry, from nursery to adult Sunday school, small groups to youth group…and even the whole church.
- **Spanish** – All *Believe* resources are also available in Spanish.

FOR ADULTS

9780310443834   9780310250173

FOR STUDENTS

9780310745617

FOR CHILDREN

9780310746010

9780310745907

9780310752226

FOR CHURCHES

Campaign Kit 9780310681717

BelieveTheStory.com

BELIEVE
POWERED BY ZONDERVAN